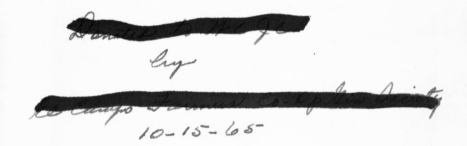

AMERICAN COOPERATIVES

In his notable book on *Principles of Political and Social Theory,* the eminent Oxford scholar, Sir Ernest Barker, surveys all the "isms" that have prevailed from Plato to Stalin, and concludes:

The conclusion to which we are led is not a conclusion in favor of that unhealthy individualism which means leaving individuals alone to shift for themselves by their own devices; nor again, on the other hand, is it a conclusion in favor of that perverted form of collectivism under which the State serves individuals so much that they have little or nothing to do for themselves, and thus lose much of their liberty in the very act of their own liberation.

It is rather a conclusion in favor of the maximum of voluntary self-help by groups of individuals, acting for themselves in the social area; thinking out for themselves in their own sphere of interest the requirements and conditions of their own development; and when they have thought such out for themselves, going on to achieve them by themselves, and by their own efforts, so far as in their own sphere they can. In one sense this may be called individualism, for it involves a belief in the value of spontaneous activity of individuals fully associated for the purpose of shifting for themselves, by their own devices in a scheme of voluntary self-help. In another sense, however, it may be called collectivism; for it involves a belief in the value of the concerted activity of collected groups, each knit together by a common interest of all the members in a common object and each seeking to achieve its object by means of common effort.

AMERICAN
COOPERATIVES

Where they come from
What they do
Where they are going

by Jerry Voorhis
Former United States Congressman and
Executive Director of The Cooperative League

HARPER & ROW, PUBLISHERS
New York, Evanston, and London

AMERICAN COOPERATIVES

Copyright © 1961 by Jerry Voorhis

Printed in the United States of America

All rights reserved.

K–N

Library of Congress catalog card number: 61–10239

CONTENTS

PREFACE

This is a book about cooperation. It is a book about the practical application of cooperation, or mutual aid, to the everyday affairs of people.

It is written to set forth some of the facts about a little-known segment of our American economy and our American life.

It is written because the author believes it can carry a message that is especially pertinent to the needs of our times.

The *Great Books* of man are those which gather into their pages the full spirit, philosophy, motivation, and idealism of a historical period. Homer's *Iliad* and *Odyssey* were the *Great Books* of ancient Greece. Dante's *Divine Comedy* was the *Great Book* of the Middle Ages. Paine's *Common Sense* characterized the American Revolutionary period. And so on.

The greatest of books, of course, like the Old and New Testaments, and the other writings upon which great religions have been founded, are timeless. We are not talking about them or their messages for every age and time.

What will be the *Great Books* of the mid-twentieth century in America? They will be books about kaleidoscopic technological change, more rapid change in the physical and scientific world than man ever before dreamed of—and what to do about it. They will be books about social and cultural lag, about the failure of social, political, and cultural progress to keep pace with "progress" in the physical sciences and in military weapons. They will be books about the strange paradox of societies requiring unquestioned conformity to outworn economic and political institutions at the same time that they feverishly fashion new weapons capable of blasting whole nations into bits.

They will be books about the struggle of the individual human being to keep his own ideals, faith, and beliefs alive in a time when rigid political and economic systems demand unswerving acquiescence and when gigantic organizations threaten to swallow the personalities of those who make them up. They will be books about the relentless pressure of events compelling unwilling societies to adjust their lives and mores to conditions so new that the past experience of man *seems* almost irrelevant.

It may be that among the *Great Books* of our time will be numbered *The Organization Man* by William H. Whyte, *The Affluent Society* by John Kenneth Galbraith, and *The Lonely Crowd* by David Riesman.

Whyte's book is described as an account of "the clash between the individual's beliefs which he is supposed to follow and the collective life he actually lives, and his search for a faith to bridge the gap."

Galbraith's book attempts to break out of our minds certain obsolete, and therefore dangerous, economic preconceptions which have been inherited from the past but which if employed to determine present action will lead certainly to disaster. Among these are the idea that at least two-thirds of mankind must always live in poverty if not on the very edge of privation; the idea that "production" consists only in the making of physical things, and that "employment" must overwhelmingly be found in such production; the idea that there is something sacred about a balanced national budget. Galbraith devotes the first third of his book to proving the almost irresistible holding power of old established ideas in our minds. He shows how subconsciously we return to such ideas again and again and twist the logic of our thinking by so doing.

But we shall never solve the so-called problem of farm "surpluses" until we overcome the notion that most people are somehow "supposed to be" at least a little bit hungry—just because in the past they indeed *had* to be. We shall not prevent mass technological unemployment if we persist in trying to consider "gainful employment" as limited to making of gadgets of one kind or another regardless of any real need for them. Employment in teaching, in educational work in its broadest aspects, in rebuilding and redeveloping cities, in solving problems of living together, in adding beauty to life on the land or in the town—all these have to be regarded as part of the employment pattern if indeed automobiles and television sets are to have a market at all.

But Riesman perhaps comes closest to holding before us a true mirror of ourselves as we now are trying to live. It is he who has symbolized in the very title of his book, *The Lonely Crowd,* the kind of tangled web of vines in which we now find ourselves—and the necessity for being able to see a sun and stars through the very thick foliage overhead. Riesman tells us that one hundred years ago the individual in American society directed his life—and *could* direct his life—largely according to his own inner beliefs and challenges. That was the age of the pioneer, the innovator, the giant who stood out from the crowd and led it into new paths. But today, in the age of revolutionary technological change, our social pattern has so congealed that most people have learned to fashion their lives so as to gain acceptance from the group to which they belong. Belonging to a group has become not only a sociological but a psychological necessity as well. The heroes of our time are those who see this, who cling to timeless ideals and *basic* faith, and who are able to translate these into what Riesman calls an "autonomous" life within groups. To such people goes the leadership of the groups and the ability to move them forward toward better days. After all, we do—and must—live close together in a crowded world.

Moreover, we seek to avoid individual decision making, says Riesman, and to be guided instead by the group ways. And more often than not the groups are concerned more with recreation than with vocation, having apparently given up any idea of decision making in their vocations. And why not, when it is so evident that farmers and other small independent economic agents who retain the power of individual decision are at tremendous economic disadvantage—apparently *because* of this very independence?

So decision making, the heartbeat of any democratic society, seems to be passing out of style. And out of reach of the average citizen, unless he does something to regain it.

He does *something,* of course.

He does "it" himself. He builds things. He moves to suburbs. He joins clubs. He buys boats. He works feverishly, exhaustingly, at accepted forms of "recreation." Sometimes, as we shall see, he carries this attempt at recapturing decision making into realms where *important* decisions are made. Sometimes he joins political organizations or economic mutual-aid organizations.

But mostly he retreats—lets "big people" make all the decisions that are big. Contents himself with little decisions.

The average citizen is losing his self-direction, and at a time when mankind must decide the most portentous questions that ever confronted any generation.

The first of these is:

Will freedom—government of the people, by the people, for the people—perish from the earth?

The second is:

Will mankind survive at all on this earth?

Can the right answer to these questions be given by this generation to the next one? Is there a way to make two autonomous self-directing people grow where only one grew before? Are there kinds of social and economic institutions which can bridge Whyte's gap between individual beliefs and the collective living which the times require? Are such institutions capable of redirecting the course of production and distribution so a glut of overpriced things can be replaced by a flow of goods and services geared to the satisfaction of real needs? Are there ways in which everyday economic activities can be so carried on that they condition people to assume responsibility, value ownership, and practice decision making?

If so, there is hope.

For by such institutions and in such ways we may yet develop enough truly free and autonomous people to give the leadership that is desperately necessary if the two great decisions of our time are to be rightly made.

There are several million people in the United States who know that such institutions do exist. They know this because they are active participants in these institutions. They are members—and owners—of cooperative enterprises of one kind or another.

They have not told their story or related their experiences effectively. Comparatively few Americans have a clear image of what cooperative businesses are, what they do, how they operate, or what taxes they pay.

Yet the *potential* contribution of these cooperatives to the solution of the most salient problems of our age is almost incalculable.

This book is written in the hope that it may contribute something to a better understanding of both the present—and possible future—role of cooperative enterprises and institutions in the life of our country.

AMERICAN COOPERATIVES

A WORLD IN CONFLICT

We live in a strange new world. We are confused and afraid. We do not know whether we are living in the twilight of the human race or in the dawn of a golden age of man.

We feel a need, deep and almost desperate, for the guidance and comfort of religion. Yet we wonder whether we can hope for this at the same time that we are mastering techniques for pulverizing God's universe.

Teen-age youths murder one another and fight gang wars in our city streets. And we say we wonder why. Yet to our shame we should not wonder, for we permit our press to blazon every act of violence across the pages in flaming script. And we permit the television screens to offer scarcely a program that does not feature violence in some form as its central theme. Worst of all, we forget that the generation that commits these crimes is one that has been told each day in all their lives that nuclear war could break upon them on any tomorrow night and bring an end to the civilization we feebly try to teach them to respect! We older ones have known periods when we were sure of peace and could look forward to future years of life with confidence. But our children and grandchildren have never known a time when total devastating war was not an imminent possibility. I once asked my youngest son and two of his junior high-school classmates what they would wish for if one wish of theirs could certainly be granted. They thought only a short time and then, in full agreement, declared that they would wish that they might be alive ten years from that day.

The good and ill are all mixed up. The scientific skill of man would colonize the moon. His social and political backwardness—his cultural lag, as the sociologists term it—provides meanwhile no sure defense against a cracking of the earth, of which the moon is a satellite.

We are in the midst of a veritable explosion of technological progress, of which automation and atomic energy are only major parts. Productivity per man-hour in American agriculture increased by 87 per cent between 1947 and 1957, and in industry by 34 per cent. Our use of electric power more than doubled in that brief time. In many other countries similar change took place. For the first time in human history it is possible to produce enough to meet the basic needs of all people on the earth. But because we have not made anything like corresponding progress in methods of distribution of goods and wealth, we wring our hands over "unsalable surpluses," condemn our farmers for producing it, and watch a third of the human race continue to go hungry to bed each night.

Modern science performs miracles in conquering disease, prolonging life, and preventing infant deaths. But we do not know what to do with this longer life. We call it "the *problem*" of aging. And we look with fear upon the prospect of so rapid and great an increase in the population of the earth that its resources might be insufficient to sustain even a subsistence for the multitudes of people.

Whatever the future may hold, it is already fact that our world is a full world. No longer does a geographical frontier exist, except in the polar regions. There is no longer a "West" anywhere, television to the contrary notwithstanding. People cannot any more move away and leave their problems behind. California, soon to be America's most populous state, looks across the Pacific at overpopulated Japan and China.

At the very time when it is necessary to our survival that we learn to live together at peace, we have come to the place where we *must* stand and face and solve our problems where we now are.

Sociology, not geography, has become the key to hope. Free, unsettled, unowned land once virtually guaranteed freedom and rough economic justice in our country. Today we must protect and nurture these values by conscious, planned social action. The natural, physical influences of the frontier must be replaced by the will of the people to be free and to establish and preserve economic opportunity and justice.

For the first time in the world's history people have to settle down to the task of making a "go" of it with their present neighbors, instead of running away to find new ones.

Meanwhile all the world has in many respects become one neighborhood. There is instantaneous communication to every part of the earth today. People can know what is happening to other people everywhere else. They can know this at the very time it happens. And they can know it whether or not they can read and write. Transportation is almost as rapid as communication. International visitations and "exchanges of persons" are the order of the day. The demand for education and for literacy spreads like wildfire among peoples blocked for centuries from knowledge of the outside world. The possibility exists, again for the first time in human history, of a world-wide sharing of information and knowledge among all the nations and peoples. Not only so but one of the brightest stars of our time is the sudden enlightenment of the economically advanced nations to their evident interest and duty in sharing what we call technical "know how" with the disadvantaged peoples. The whole pattern of thought of the colonial era assumed a division of the world between technically advanced, manufacturing, and—yes—exploiting nations on the one hand and technically stagnant, agricultural, and exploited nations on the other. The new idea of "technical assistance" reverses all this and has already set up a new kind of purposeful communication.

But unfortunately it must be observed that while the science of instantaneous world-wide communication has been mastered, we still don't know what to communicate. It is as possible for a Hitler, a Stalin, or a Perón to harangue an audience of millions as for counsels of peace or useful facts or cultural experience to be brought to them. Indeed the scales are weighted *against* a worth-while use of our new communicative devices. In almost a third of the world the people are denied by dictatorial governments their elementary right to hear or read any facts or ideas not approved by those governments. And even in the so-called "free world" billions of dollars are spent yearly to reward clever experts in mass motivation for their boasted ability to make people believe anything they want to make them believe and to make them buy any product "motivators" are paid to induce them to accept. We have the means of spreading culture, beauty, knowledge, and understanding around the world. But we have barely considered whether or not we shall really try to do so. And we have yet to learn how best to use these new means or how to keep them from being prostituted to dangerous, unworthy, or at least frivolous purposes.

Out of World War II and the ferment that has followed, and as a result of the new world-wide communications and contacts, has come a change in the psychology and outlook of one and a half billion people. These are the peoples in the economically under-developed areas of the world. Through the centuries they have plodded along under burdens of unpayable debt, dying if not in childhood, then at early ages, eking out an existence which they assumed to be their only possible lot in life.

Today they no longer believe such an existence to be their only possible lot in life. They have heard of, seen some evidence of, the very different lives of people in other lands. And they believe some of this can be theirs. For the first time in thousands of years they believe tomorrow can be different from today. And they are deeply determined to make it so. One way or another they fully intend to realize their "revolution of rising hopes." Furthermore, they have already made certain progress. Hundreds of millions of them have gained political independence. Some of them have actually achieved a modest improvement in their incomes and living standards. In the United Nations, at Bandung, and elsewhere they have been and are being listened to.

The drive behind this revolution of rising hopes is the more intense because these peoples know that side by side with their still painful hunger there exist so-called "surpluses" in other lands. The tragic fact is that, despite technical assistance programs, foreign aid, and all related efforts, the technological revolution of our times has widened rather than narrowed the gap between the "have" peoples and the "have not" peoples. Productivity, since World War II, has been out-stripping population increases in the West and in Japan. But in India, for example, the population has been increasing by 2 per cent a year whereas food production has been pushed up only 3 per cent a year. And many lands have shown less relative progress even than this. Per-capita income in the United States is more than thirty times as large as it is among the billion and a half people of Asia, Africa, and some other parts of the world.

Such a situation cannot endure. Not in a world of universal communication. Mankind will not long continue half rich and half very poor, half complaining about "surplus," and half needing that surplus. The revolution of rising hopes will—one way or another—have its way.

Throughout the long history of man most of the people on earth have been unable to read or write. They have known little or nothing of events or circumstances of life beyond their own villages. In only a few countries of the West has anything resembling general education of the people ever existed up to the time of World War II. Today this is changing. Part of the "revolution of rising hopes" is a demand for education, literacy, information on the part of peoples all over the world. UNESCO works at a world-wide program for increasing literacy and educational advantages in all countries. It is part of the idea that has brought technical assistance into being that there should be assistance also in the field of education. A new type of missionary is going out to less privileged countries to help the people learn to read and write. Even before this has been achieved, people by the millions are listening to radios. Information, if not education, is penetrating to the far corners of the earth.

So it can be said that the basis is being laid, if slowly and painfully, for the operation of free and democratic political institutions by many peoples for whom this was in past ages quite impossible.

But at the same time there exists in the world today a powerful drive by mighty organized forces to bring an end to government of, by, and for the people, and to substitute dictatorship for it. The conception of the totalitarian state has been developed in our own times and is today a cardinal tenet in the creed of hundreds of millions of people. And even in nations which still retain free institutions there is a rising tide of insistence on conformity which threatens the spirit of freedom if not its substance.

Governments grow bigger and more powerful in almost all countries, if for no other reason than to counterbalance the monolithic power of totalitarian governments where they exist. Economic power becomes more and more concentrated in countries like our own until some huge corporations bear all too much resemblance to state industries of communist countries, in so far as their absolute dominance over whole realms of our economy is concerned. The press, radio, and television fall more and more under control of fewer people. And the worst of all this is that, coupled with the appalling fact of the hydrogen bomb, the average individual is in danger of losing his belief that he can in any important respect make decisions that will shape his own destiny or influence the course of history in his time.

Fifty years ago few people in the United States had ever heard of Laos or Viet Nam or even Korea. Fewer still cared very much what happened in those "far-away places with strange-sounding names." Today we are desperately concerned over events in Syria, Lebanon— even Jordan and Yemen. We fought a war in Korea and almost did so in Viet Nam. The simple reason is, of course, that the world is one world, whether we want it that way or not, and the interest and concern of our country and every other country of consequence is world-wide. Never again, as long as our civilization lasts, can any significant event take place anywhere in the world without its being known at once in all other parts of the world and affecting the lives and fortunes of all other peoples.

It may seem a paradox or contradiction to say next that the world has never been so deeply divided as it is today. But this deep division only underlines the fact of world-wide interdependence. Fifty short years ago the United States and Russia could have had the same relationship of armed hostility and bitter antagonism that they have today, without the rest of mankind being especially concerned about it. But fifty years ago the United States and Russia could have fought a war without dooming most of mankind to death. Today that is not possible.

The world is an interdependent whole in its quest for a better life for all. It is also an interdependent whole in its fear of universal death. The same science that promises the possibility of unlimited power from sea water to benefit all mankind, that same science has already created weapons which could be the means of race suicide.

Every man, woman, and child on earth has to go to bed worried every night lest war break out between the powerfully armed nations. The reason as everyone knows, of course, is that the United States and Russia are armed with weapons that for the first time in history could destroy all life on the earth if used in a full-scale war.

Never before has such a possibility existed, or anything approaching it.

The progress of the past half century—particularly the last quarter century—in technology, in physical science, in all the purely physical aspects of existence, and in weapons of war has been almost miraculous. But progress in human relations, in social science, in the development of economic, political, and cultural institutions and in the building of peace has been painfully, if not tragically, slow by comparison. The sociologists call this "cultural lag." In that cultural lag lies our problem.

Big cities, big corporations, big chains, big networks, big governments, big bombs—all these tower around us. We are not only afraid but somewhat paralyzed. Too many of us say: "What can I do about it?" Pathetically we place our hopes on personal visits of heads of state to one another's countries. Even more pathetically we send armies of correspondents and photographers along with them wherever they go. We hang hopes of peace on the inflection with which one of the "big men" utters a word or phrase or on the carefully measured breadth of his smile. We find comfort and encouragement to our apathy in platitudinous reports of conversation between heads of state and hope for further meeting between them. Apparently it does not occur to most of us that heads of state will begin to do some of the new and utterly unprecedented acts which alone can save the life of man only when the cry of millions of angry voices tells them they must.

We, the people, are abdicating our responsibility and with it, of course, our freedom.

One reason for this is that our moral vision has become blurred. We have tried to fit our mad dash for wealth and profit into the framework of religious teachings that call us to repentance, humility, renunciation, and concern for neighbor. We find little inspiration or eternal meaning in our individual lives and little in our national life for the simple reason that the mores of modern American materialism are, to put it bluntly, in basic conflict with the virtues of the Christian religion, or any other vital religion, for that matter.

Moral vision and sense of life direction have grown more and more dim as the postwar years have passed.

The chaplain for the Episcopal Church at the University of Chicago, Rev. Wm. H. Baar, writing in *Advance* magazine for December, 1957, had this to say:

"Not only in the factory and on Main Street but in our educational institutions we are enshrining a false god, technology. It is foolish to deny that the most widely accepted creed in the world today says, 'I believe that technology will save us.'

"Ruskin makes an interesting comment about the quick decline of the art of Venetians. He points out that here was uncommon skill and phenomenal technique. But there was no purpose. The Venetians had nothing to say in spite of their great talents.

"There is something here for us. We are determined to save our civilization. We need technicians and engineers. However, if we do not produce some concert pianists, some singers, some poets, some theologians, some historians, we may well find ourselves superbly prepared to defend a civilization that was dead and gone before the battle even started.

"The libraries of any university contain thousands of volumes written about civilizations that slipped away quietly in the midst of the din of big building programs, vast prosperity, and useless battles.

"But for the work of devoted librarians, these books would lie under inches of dust, because no one cares any more."

Shortly after the end of World War II a newspaper in a big American city published an editorial about the atomic bomb. It said:

We are face to face with the moral question whether our nation or any other nation has the right to possess the power to banish life on earth.

The editorial proceeded to appeal for a relentless drive, carried forward in a spirit of desperate necessity, for a system of universal enforceable disarmament and peace in the world.

A few short years later—in 1952, to be exact—this same newspaper published an editorial about the hydrogen bomb. It said:

As horrifying as the new weapon may be, its development was inevitable. It was in our own enlightened self-interest that we were the first to devise and explode the weapon. But we must realize, too, that it has increased our burdens of responsibility.

The "moral question" was not mentioned. The editorial simply concluded by saying that mankind's hope of survival must rest on the achievement of peace through "skillful negotiation." The prospect of being responsible, along with the Russians, for the probable destruction of most of mankind had by 1952 ceased to move us so deeply. We were getting used to having the power to banish life on earth.

In 1955 this same newspaper published, with great courage, a series of frank and deeply terrifying articles about the probable effects of atomic radiation on the human race. Even if most of humanity should by some miracle escape being fried in the fires of the bomb, future generations would consist of an increasing number of monsters, a decreasing number of normal human beings. So warned the articles. Then the paper commented editorially:

While viewing the radiation hazard with realism, we must not be talked into an unrealistic curtailment of our nuclear weapons program. As peace insurance for America and the free world, this country must continue atomic and hydrogen bomb tests—with traditional caution. In the words of Gordon Dean, former Atomic Energy Commission chairman, "We must hold tests to make weapons that are more deliverable, bigger, and better."

So now not only is the moral question forgotten, but so also is any attempt to find a way to end the ultimate and total danger which our generation has brought upon mankind. All this newspaper or the Atomic Energy Commission could suggest was to "make weapons that are more deliverable, bigger, and (God forgive us!) BETTER." Better, that is, than the hydrogen bomb which can destroy 3 to 5 million human beings at one blast and which killed a Japanese fisherman two hundred miles from the scene of an experimental explosion.

The years after 1955 saw some changes for the better. Here and there a voice was heard to make fun of the ridiculous pattern of conformity into which the minds of the American people had been

pushed. More articles like that of Rev. Mr. Baar were written. Sometimes people said: "The main business of our generation is to have
enough simple decency toward our children to give them a chance
to live." And asked: "What are we going to do about it?"

We were beginning to realize that we had in fact lost our way, lost
sense of moral direction, lost contact with the real messages of our
religion.

We were beginning, too, I think—or hope—to take more seriously
the inescapable fact that this mid-twentieth-century generation will
indeed decide the two great questions: Shall mankind live or die?
And if he lives, will he be free?

And we had begun to understand that all we needed to do to
decide both questions wrongly was to continue down the road we were
following.

We began to see in the late 1950's that certain things are necessary
for survival.

It is necessary to recover a sense of moral purpose, religious purpose, if you will, in our lives.

It is necessary to revive the will of the people to decide what is
going to happen to them.

It is necessary to find ways in which "little" people can retain some
dignity and significance in a world of bigness.

It is necessary to build institutions that can establish, maintain, and
enforce peace in the world.

None of these necessary tasks—necessary to the survival of free
human beings—can be accomplished from the top down. Haranguing
by "leaders" won't revive the will to be free. Enlightened despotism—
either communistic or capitalistic—won't restore dignity nor a feeling
that he "counts" to the average person. Nor can mere treaties, agree-
ments, or international machinery establish peace.

Like all human progress, the progress our times require must have
its roots in the way ordinary people fit their lives together in thousands of communities and in millions of groups around the world. It
is necessary that ways be found to enable people to *experience*
decision making, a sense of dignity and participation, and relationships with their fellows that are *actively* peaceful.

This book is about such ways and methods.

II

A NEW KIND OF BUSINESS
FOR A NEW AGE

We don't know for certain just how or when the first beginning was made toward a civilized society. But probably it happened somewhat like this:

It was a bitter cold winter day. Lightning had struck a tree and it was burning. A dozen or so fearful, furtive primitive human beings had approached the warmth of the fire from various directions. Each of them feared all the others. In fact, they were all so afraid of each other that they were prepared to let the precious fire burn itself out and die, leaving them to the cold and darkness, for they did not yet know how to start a fire.

Then a great thing happened. Someone in that number gathered about the fire, conveyed to the rest a simple proposal that contained every basic element in the civilizing process. The proposal was that they all agree to give up their practice of attacking one another and that they, instead, agree to work together to maintain the fire for the benefit of all.

Sometime, somewhere, some such proposal as this was accepted, the practice of mutual aid and cooperation was born, and mankind started on the upward path toward civilization.

From that day to this the great civilizing force, the great influence for human betterment, the principal means of solving problems, has been the practice of voluntary mutual aid among men.

The beginnings of agriculture would have been impossible without mutual aid among the first farmers. No one farmer could possibly

11

defend his crops against the plundering of nomadic tribes, but if all the farmers of a valley joined together to protect all their rude plots of growing things, then and only then did they have a chance to reap their harvests.

No frontier, including the American one, was settled without dependence of the "rugged individuals" who moved there upon the mutual aid of one another. The very building of their rude homes depended on this. So did their barns. They could not have survived without the aid of one another in warding off savage attacks or combating illness, or offering refuge from winter weather.

The riches of the knowledge and culture of the ancient world would probably have been wholly lost in the age of violence that followed the fall of Rome had it not been for the monasteries where a few men decided to live together in mutual aid and devote themselves to that task.

The nations of Europe as we now know them had their roots in the medieval cities. And those cities grew up out of the violence of the constant petty wars of the time. To have a chance to live at peace, the craftsmen and merchants had to resort to a kind of mutual aid for protection. It took the form of living close together in walled towns. And it was the people of those towns who eventually insisted, successfully, on the establishment of central governments capable of maintaining civil peace.

Countless other examples could be given, but it is probably unnecessary.

The pedigree of mutual aid and cooperation as the refuge of the people from violence, oppression, hunger, and danger is long and clear. And the best of modern sociology recognizes this fact.

In his book, *On Being Human,* Ashley Montagu says:

Man is born for cooperation, not for competition or conflict. This is a basic discovery of modern science. It confirms a discovery made two thousand years ago by one Jesus of Nazareth. In a word: it is the principle of love which embraces all mankind. It is the principle of humanity, of one world, one brotherhood of peoples.

It is certainly appropriate that sociological thought of our time follows Montagu's lead, for we have a simple choice today between cooperation on a world scale and virtual annihilation on a world scale.

Perhaps man will awaken to an understanding of his own true nature in the nick of time. At least let us hope so.

For the "nick" is not far off.

Meanwhile our heritage from the past is worth preserving, and one of the most precious parts of it is the capacity of groups of people to work voluntarily together for mutually desired goals.

Like all human impulses, mutual aid—cooperation—has been institutionalized in many ways. In the family first, then the clan, the tribe, the city state, the nation. All "peace groups" in history have depended fundamentally on voluntary mutual aid to keep the peace and to hold them together. No police force has ever been large enough to do this alone.

The cooperative businesses of our own times represent the institutionalization of the principle and impulse of mutual aid in the day-to-day economic activities of man.

And for reasons which will, we hope, become clear as we go along cooperative business enterprise, in new and modern form, is just "what the doctor ordered" for the times in which we live.

We are engaged in a grim struggle to preserve for future generations the institutions of freedom and of constitutional democracy which our forefathers developed out of "blood, sweat, and tears."

There is no assurance that we will be able to do this.

At least three factors will have to be present if we are to succeed.

First, the *right* of the people to decide their own destiny must be preserved. This means that governments based on law and guaranteeing through their constitutions the basic rights of man must continue to thrive.

Second, within the societies whose freedom is thus basically protected the people must have the *will* to exercise their right of self-determination, self-direction, and basic decision making. They must *want* to decide their own destiny.

They cannot abdicate that right and remain free people.

The most sinister influence that tends to bring about such abdication of decision making by the people is a sense of hopelessness—a growing, gnawing belief that there is no practical way for the average man or woman actually to guide his own fate or influence that of his children.

Therefore, the third necessary factor in the preservation of the best in human civilization is the existence of *practical means* whereby the average man and woman can make decisions which matter to him or her.

And in the day-to-day problems of life, at the economic grass roots of our existence out of which so many of our other institutions grow, the new type of cooperative business and economic organizations offer precisely such a means.

Owners of cooperative businesses are rendering all sorts of services to themselves and their communities in the United States today. They bring babies into the world; they bury people; they light up farm-houses, provide electricity for farm operations; they build homes; spread newfangled liquid fertilizer; service automobiles; market farmers' crops. They run supermarkets owned by consumers, and they conduct wholesaling of groceries for independent grocers. They drill oil wells; mine phosphate rock; grow seeds; grind coffee; and manu-facture hot-water heaters and milking machines. They pool people's savings together in credit unions, cooperative insurance companies, and cooperative farm credit institutions, and thus enable those same people to pay interest to themselves and invest their own money. And as we shall see they conduct health plans of every shape and size in an effort to make the marvels of modern medicine available to people generally.

Old-time cooperators, the "pioneers" of the idea, are no doubt turn-ing over in their graves over a lot of this. They're worried because some of these institutions aren't "true cooperatives." The health plans, for example, never pay patronage refunds, and that is one of the four basic "principles of cooperation." Some of the enterprises men-tioned above don't even belong to ultimate consumers, such as the retailer-owned cooperative grocery wholesales and the farmers' mar-keting cooperatives. In some states state-chartered credit unions are required to use proxy voting and to violate another basic "Rochdale principle," that of "one member, one vote, regardless of number of shares held." There are even cases, such as the Health Insurance Plan of Greater New York, where the members don't vote at all! And there are other cases, such as the changing "farm supply" cooperatives in suburban areas where a majority of the patrons—the non-farmers—

do not yet have full voting rights and are thus a sort of second-class membership.

So like the modern world itself the cooperative enterprises of today, particularly in the United States, are in a period of rapid change and evolution. They are in truth and fact a new kind of business that fits the new age in which we live a great deal better than either its most vocal friends or its most vociferous foes as yet understand.

Some people try to resolve the resulting confusion by saying that there just isn't much difference any more between a cooperative and any other kind of business.

They're wrong.

Some other people try to draw hard-and-fast lines between the cooperatives that still fit the pattern of the last century and those which, to meet new conditions and new needs, have modified their methods of operation.

They're wrong, too—or at least mistaken.

Still a third approach is to say that almost any sort of enterprise that chooses to call itself a cooperative—as a surprisingly large number of rather diverse operations do—should be so classified.

This is an even more serious error.

For there is a basic characteristic which, if present, makes a business, enterprise, or institution cooperative in nature; whereas without this characteristic no amount of sophistry can breathe a cooperative soul into a profit-seeking body.

That characteristic is to be found in the *purpose* of the enterprise and the pattern of ownership which must necessarily go along with that purpose.

It is this different purpose and it is this different pattern of ownership that distinguish cooperatives from other forms of economic organizations.

First, a *cooperative* enterprise is one whose *purpose* is to provide its *customers and users* of its services with goods or services which they *need* at the *lowest economically practicable net cost* and in the form and quality those customers desire. The only way to be sure this is done is for the customers or users of the services to be also the owners, and the only owners, of the business.

Any business, enterprise, or institution that belongs to the same group of people which it primarily serves with commodities or services and whose purpose of existence is to meet some need of that group of people can correctly be called a cooperative.

By way of comparison, any business whose purpose is to make profit for one group of people, its stockholders, out of the sale of goods and services to *other* people, its customers, is *not* a cooperative. Neither is any business whose owners are *not* the same people who are its patrons or the users of its services. All that such a business needs to do to make itself into a cooperative is for its present stock-holders to sell their stock to the customers of the business and to give control of the business to all the customers, each with one vote and only one.

This is not intended in any way whatsoever to imply that other forms of business aren't good and useful and necessary forms of business in our so-called "free" economic system. Indeed, it is not to say that other forms of business than cooperatives will not into the foreseeable future be the dominant forms in the American economy. More than that, it would be a bad thing for cooperatives if they were not confronted by the intense competition of profit-oriented busi-nesses. Were this not the case, the cooperatives would in all prob-ability go to seed.

Not all cooperatives act like cooperatives, any more than all people who ought to be decent human beings always act like decent human beings. Or any more than all members of the Methodist Church act like good Methodists are supposed to act. Or members of any other church, for that matter.

A simple illustration: A stock-insurance company is not a co-operative business enterprise because stock-insurance companies are in business to earn dividends for stockholders and because stock-in-surance companies do not belong to their policy holders. On the other hand, mutual-insurance companies are, in all technical respects, co-operative institutions. For mutual companies are in business, osten-sibly at least, to provide insurance protection for their policy owners at the lowest net practicable cost. And the ownership of all mutual companies vests in all their policy owners and not in anybody else. The fact that a majority of mutual-insurance companies don't act like mutuals or cooperative institutions is beside our immediate point.

Cooperatives, then, are consumer-owned, customer-owned, patron-owned businesses that belong lock, stock, and barrel to the same people who use their services. More than that, they are businesses of which you, whoever you are, can become an owner quite automatically simply by continuing over a short period to purchase from them.

Cooperatives are distribution-oriented, need-oriented, consumer-oriented businesses. One frequently hears it said that other businesses even outdo cooperatives in being "consumer oriented." They make all sorts of appeals to consumers, talk loud and long about how many millions they spend on research to develop new products for consumers. All this, to a degree, is true. And it's also true that cooperatives ought to be spending a lot more money than they do on new product research. Which they would do if they had the money. But the fatal flaw in all this argument is that while other businesses do a rather sensational—and sometimes a bit repelling—job of protesting their love for consumers, they do not carry this to the point of reducing prices any more than absolutely necessary. And certainly not to the extent of saying that all their net profits are the property of their customers and must be paid to them at year's end.

Cooperatives do both of these things.

They do more. They gear all their production and distribution of goods and services to what their patrons need—and say they need. Other businesses gear their production to what consumers can be persuaded to take after the business has decided what it wants to produce *and at what price.*

Cooperatives are really consumer-oriented businesses. They engage in consumer-directed production and distribution of goods and services.

This, as we shall see in more detail, is the basic reason why cooperatives are "a new kind of business for a new age."

There are, of course, other considerations so far as most cooperatives are concerned. More exact definitions of the form, principles, and practices of *most* cooperatives are possible. *But they are secondary to and dependent upon the underlying and basic characteristics so far discussed.*

In the early 1920's farmers, particularly in certain Middle Western states, were unable to obtain fertilizers either in sufficient quantity or at prices they could afford or of satisfactory quality. The fertilizer they did buy, moreover, usually had to be accepted "on faith" as to its contents. No analysis or formula was furnished to the purchaser.

Some of these farmers decided to start a new business—a cooperative business of their own. At first its operations were very simple ones. The farmers began by pooling their funds for the joint purchase of fertilizer where it could be bought on the best terms. Even this simple operation resulted in a 10 per cent drop in the price of fertilizer. As time went on, however, the farmers found it difficult to get enough high-analysis fertilizer at a satisfactory price. Consequently, the local "farm supply" cooperatives began to acquire their own production facilities. Before this could be done farmers had to be willing to invest capital funds in their cooperative enterprises. By purchasing at least one share of capital stock, they became members of the cooperative. Thus the farmers' money built the farmers' fertilizer plants to produce fertilizer for sale to these same farmers. There was, of course, no reason why they should not turn out the very best fertilizer that could be produced, since it was for their own use. The quantity of open-formula, high-analysis fertilizer was greatly increased as a result of the entry of cooperatives into the business of fertilizer production. Today such quality fertilizer of known content is general throughout the trade.

A cooperative, then, is a group of people faced with a common need who decide that the best or only way to meet that need is by organizing a new business to supply it directly to themselves. This they do by joining voluntarily together to pool their capital investments and thus to own, control, and patronize their own enterprise.

The larger the number of people who participate in both ownership and patronage of the cooperative, the better off all of them will be. If the farmers who start a cooperative fertilizer business can obtain twice as many members to own and patronize the enterprise, the volume of business will double and all will benefit. Consequently, the cooperatives have opened their membership without regard to class, creed, color, or conviction. This is principle number one. To buttress this, the cooperatives maintain strict neutrality in sectarian religious and partisan political controversy.

Cooperatives exist to meet the needs of the people who form them rather than to provide a high return to invested capital. So cooperative principles two and three logically follow. These are: each member-owner shall cast one vote and only one, regardless of the number of shares he may hold; and the return on invested capital is limited, seldom more than 5 per cent a year.

It would make little sense for farmers selling fertilizer to themselves or consumers selling groceries to themselves to try to make profit at their own expense. So the fourth principle provides for a "patronage refund." This is a device whereby cooperatives accomplish their purpose of providing goods or services to their members and patrons at cost. The funds remaining at the end of an accounting period after all costs of doing business have been paid, all necessary or prudent reserves provided for, and an allowance set aside for education and welfare purposes, are the "net savings." In an ordinary business this would be net profit and it would be divided among the stockholders in proportion to their investment. But since cooperatives do not exist to make profit either for themselves or their stockholders, all net savings must be distributed among the patrons in proportion to their patronage. That is, each patron receives the same percentage of the net savings as his purchases bear to total purchases. The patronage refund idea was the unique contribution of the pioneers of Rochdale, England, when they started their little store in Toad Lane in 1844. William E. Gladstone, the great liberal prime minister, called it the "greatest economic invention of the nineteenth century."

So much for the basic principles. Their application to a business enterprise distinguishes a cooperative from businesses organized for different purposes and under different conditions.

It is from these basic principles also that the taxation status of cooperatives is derived. Cooperatives pay their taxes in the way they do, not because they have any special privileges or operate under special tax laws, but simply because they must conduct their business in a certain manner.

Cooperatives pay all the taxes their competitors pay and, with minor and inconsequential exceptions, under the same exact tax laws. In many a rural community a cooperative business will be the largest taxpayer in town. Cooperatives pay school taxes, excise taxes, social-security taxes, property taxes, and all other kinds of taxes just as their competitors pay them. In fact, because their operations are necessarily made a matter of virtual public record in the annual membership meeting, their taxes are likely to be actually heavier than those of other businesses on the same volume of business and the same valuation of property.

On every cent of profit a cooperative business makes—and some of them do make profits, though it is not their purpose—a full federal income tax is paid. But an unbroken series of court decisions has properly held that patronage refunds which any business—cooperative or otherwise—is obligated to pay to its patrons is not income to that business but is the property of the patron and taxable against the patron to the extent that any taxable income would be involved to any taxpayer.

The reason for this is clear. Liabilities are not assets. Money which a business owes to someone else cannot at the same time be taxable income to that business. The basic method, as we have seen, whereby cooperatives achieve a non-profit operation with their members, and in many cases with all their patrons, is by obligating themselves to refund what would be profit to another business to their members and patrons in patronage refunds, proportional to their patronage. These obligations are binding liabilities upon the cooperative businesses. They cannot escape those obligations and remain cooperative in nature or qualify for charters as cooperatives. If cooperatives pay less income tax than other businesses, it is because they have less income to tax. And the reason they have less income to tax is because the bulk of that income belongs not to the cooperative but to its patrons. It is the patron's income to do with as he will. The cooperative does not have the disposal of that money. Such money cannot therefore be the cooperative's income.

No one suggests that a business which loses money should be compelled to pay an income tax on profits it might have made but did not make. Neither should it be proposed that businesses like cooperatives, whose owners deliberately decide to conduct them on a non-profit basis, should be penalized for that decision. To tax cooperatives on their patronage refunds would constitute precisely such a penalty.

It would be a penalty tax levied against the right of American citizens to conduct business on a non-profit basis. No such tax could be tolerated in a truly free nation.

It is true that if patronage refunds were subjected to such a penalty tax cooperatives would have their remedy. Existing as they do to benefit their members rather than themselves as business entities, they could and undoubtedly would attempt to sell at cost and thus have no patronage refunds to pay. But in the process their unique cooperative character would be destroyed.

The principles of cooperation are fundamental, especially the fourth principle of the patronage refund.

There are also certain practices which cooperatives are supposed to follow and which most of them do follow. The first practice is cash trading. This is logical for any business that wants to save its customers money, because the extension of credit is a costly matter. The nation is dotted with cooperatives which do not even come close to observing this cash trading policy. And in certain lines the credit arrangements offered by competitors have made it essential for cooperatives also to provide arrangements for paying over time. But the practice of cash trading remains the one that can make possible the greatest savings and the greatest advantages from cooperative businesses to their patrons.

Second, cooperatives usually, as a matter of prudent policy, sell their goods and services at the market price and then return any surplus through the patronage refund. Cooperatives might fail in their early years if they tried to sell at an estimated cost price. They might guess wrong and suffer critical operating losses. They find it better to give members the benefits of business at cost after, rather than before, the costs are known.

Third, cooperatives can hope for success only when they are expanding in a healthy manner. "Dead level" operations are more dangerous to a cooperative, which necessarily depends upon the interest and loyalty of its members, than they are to ordinary businesses. Constant expansion is recognized as a desirable cooperative practice, and most successful cooperatives have been built on it.

Fourth, continuous education has been found by long experience to be essential to the business success of cooperatives. Unless their members—and the general public—understand their methods of operation and are able to evaluate them fairly and properly, there is certain to be difficulty, especially when margins are small.

Here, then, are the cooperative principles:

1. Open membership.
2. Democratic control—one vote for each member-owner, regardless of the number of shares held.
3. Limited return on invested capital.
4. All net savings distributed in proportion to patronage.

And here are the cooperative practices:

1. Business for cash to the extent practical.
2. Sales at going market price.
3. Constant expansion.
4. Continuous education.

Cooperatives following these principles and practices have been doing business in many countries for more than one hundred years.

Why, then, do we speak of cooperatives as "a new kind of business for a new age"? Partly we do so because America has never yet really "discovered" cooperatives. At least urban America has not done so. And partly because the best of our cooperative businesses today are a very different sort of enterprise from their predecessors of the depression years.

But the main reason we have titled this chapter as we have is because of certain alarming though little-heeded trends in our country's economy. Some of those trends give the reasons why cooperative businesses have been organized. And why cooperatives are needed as a voluntary, "free-enterprise" kind of counteractive and corrective force for the trends that threaten both our welfare and our freedom.

III

THE HEALTH OF THE PEOPLE

In every time and every place through man's history the nursing of a neighbor back to health has been looked upon as an act of fundamental goodness and charity. Such acts created warm human relationships and were first steps toward developing true communities on the frontier. They have the same effect today. But in modern America and other complex societies they are far less common, even in the country. And in our huge cities they seldom happen any more.

There are reasons for this change, not all of them bad reasons either. The main one is that modern medical science can perform miracles of healing. The average person can't.

Fifty years ago a sick person's chances of recovery were almost as good if he never saw a doctor at all as they were if he did. Moreover, almost any good doctor knew nearly as much about the healing arts as did the next one.

Neither of these facts is true today. If one can only find the right doctor, skilled in the right specialty, the difference between seeing him and not seeing him when one is ill may well be the difference between life and death.

Given a full opportunity for treatment and care under good conditions, modern medical practitioners can not only cure almost any disease, but they can maintain health in people.

So it is hardly remarkable that neighborly help—so often futile—in time of sickness has been replaced wherever possible in our modern society by the calling in of skilled doctors, nurses, and other professional technicians.

Socially, something precious has been lost. But physically, in the sense of life and health expectancy, much has been gained.

Indeed were there enough good doctors, enough nurses, enough public-health workers, enough of the manifold men and women of greater and less technical skill who assist and supplement the work of doctors and nurses, our nation might achieve a hitherto-un-dreamed-of level of good health.

If the people could afford to pay for these services.

Unfortunately, neither of these conditions yet prevails.

Between 1900 and 1950 the number of doctors in the United States increased by only 58 per cent, while the population was increasing by 100 per cent. And this trend still continues. It is true that the increase has been far more rapid in the number of professional nurses, pharmacists, and other health workers. So it can be said that each doctor's time is better used. But the need and the human demand for more and better health-care service far outrun the supply. And Congress continues to debate legislation to encourage the training of increasing numbers of people capable of rendering such care.

One reason for the shortage of doctors is, in turn, the inability of millions of families to pay the cost of modern medical care, especially when such payment is made on an emergency-fee-for-service basis. Many rural areas, for example, lack doctors because it appears unlikely that a good income could be earned by a doctor settling there. On the average, American families are spending about 5 per cent of their annual income for medical and health care. But because of the hit-and-miss way in which most of this money is spent, and also, of course, because of the low incomes of many millions of families, we remain no better than a moderately healthy nation.

There is every reason why something should be done to improve this situation.

One such reason has to do with the sweeping changes which are taking place in the pattern of employment of the American people. Probably for the first time in history we are confronted by the fact—and the problem—of widespread and accelerating technological unemployment in the mass-production industries. Indeed this is true of practically all phases of our economy that produce things as contrasted to services.

A few examples will suffice.

Every major air line in the country has been in process of reducing the number of pilots in its employ. The reason? The huge jet planes carry twice as many people from place to place in half the time. With no allowance for increased traffic, this means one-fourth as many pilot flying hours.

The automobile workers' union had almost one and a half million members a few years ago. Its plans for the future are based on the assumption that there never will be more than 1 million people employed by the automobile industry again.

The number of textile production workers in the United States was 1,146,300 in 1947; 947,000 in 1954; and 820,000 in March, 1958. It is still going down.

Should our rate of economic growth be slowed we would be faced with a tremendous volume of technological unemployment. Indeed, unless that rate is increased, this problem will become more and more serious.

Furthermore, the prospect of re-employing any large percentage of those displaced workers in the manufacture of more physical products for sale to consumers is probably hopeless. Unless we learn rather quickly that our children, in simple justice, are entitled to a good education in uncrowded classrooms, taught by decently paid and not overtired teachers; unless we begin to conceive slum clearance and urban redevelopment as somewhere nearly as important as paving a quarter of the country with concrete highways; unless we give earnest attention to expansion of health service; unless we begin to see that "reasonably full employment" will from now on depend upon sharp expansion of work in fields directly servicing the general welfare, we are in for serious trouble.

No great civilization has ever been built on an unlimited increase in the consumption of material gadgets and satisfactions. Our country will be no exception.

What more logical or broadly acceptable way of expanding employment could be conceived than to do it in the field of health services and the improvement of health standards of the American people? Obviously, displaced textile workers can hardly all expect to become doctors. But whereas in 1900 three out of every five professional health workers were doctors, by 1950 only one out of five people working in the field of better health for their neighbors was a physician. The business of maintaining and improving health is one that employs a whole spectrum of people, from most highly skilled physicians to the unskilled orderly.

At least one key to expanding health services and improving health standards is to be found in a modern application of the same socially-invaluable motive that led the pioneer woman to go to the neighbor's cabin to help nurse a sick child. That key can unlock the door to understanding of ways in which the same amount of money now being spent for medical care by the American people can actually purchase far more effective service and far better sustained health.

That which individual families cannot possibly do alone, groups of families, willing to cooperate together, can and are doing very well indeed.

But they must first *decide,* both the well and the sick among them, to pool together their present needs, their possible future needs, and part of their monthly income.

This is what people do when they join or subscribe to a group health plan. Some such plans are properly called cooperative plans; some are called community plans; some, labor health plans. But all of them have certain basic characteristics in common. And all of them lead to a better way of spending the health dollar.

The story is told that the people in Chinese villages once observed the custom of paying so much to the village doctor if the family had been in good health during the preceding year. But proportionately less was paid if there had been sickness in the family. The idea was to reward the doctor for keeping them well.

Whether or not this story is true, it illustrates the basic difference in point of view between the business of curing sickness and the plans to maintain health.

This chapter is about the plans to maintain health, and to improve it. It is about what groups of people on their own initiative can do to that end. It is about the application of a few reasonable methods toward enabling more and more people to be able actually to afford the best of modern medical care. It is also about the cooperative health movement in the United States. More commonly it is called the group health movement. And "group health" is the term used in practically all the legislation and by most of the organizations involved in these efforts. Group health as contrasted to individual health.

But since this is a book about the values of cooperation in modern life, we'll speak of the "cooperative health movement." And we'll be accurate in doing so. For the whole fine enterprise depends upon the basic decision of a group of people to act together, to cooperate, in order to guard the whole group from the economic disasters of costly illness and to improve their health standards at the same time.

Out of that basic decision there comes the opportunity of these cooperative groups to decide for themselves all sorts of related questions. Questions like these: How much shall we pay for drugs and prescriptions; shall we provide dental services for ourselves; what group of doctors do we believe can serve us best and with most interest; what should be done to make certain that those doctors can practice the best of medicine under the best of conditions and with the best economically practical rewards; what can be done about health problems of aging people; what must we charge ourselves per month in order to assure ourselves of the health care we need and still keep our plan economically solvent? Shall we build our own hospital, make arrangements to use community hospitals, or require our members to carry Blue Cross insurance?

Cooperative health plans make it possible for groups of people to decide for themselves a lot of vital questions about their family health. This is good for the people and good for their health.

Where did this movement start, how widespread is it, what forms has it taken, and what is its future likely to be?

It's difficult to date the beginning. Perhaps it should be said that when Benjamin Franklin organized the first mutual fire-insurance company in America in 1752 he persuaded the policy owners to join together to guard their health against fire. He certainly did persuade them that whereas they couldn't fight, or prevent, or pay for fires individually, they could do so if they joined together to spread the risk and to pay for joint protection. In 1851 French immigrants in San Francisco organized the French Mutual Benefit Society, built a hospital, and established a prepayment plan. The German immigrants in San Francisco and the Cuban-Spanish in Tampa did likewise a few years later. All these plans are still in operation. In all of them fraternal groups, drawn together by nationality ties, buy together their health care and their health protection.

Or maybe the beginning should be said to be when the first of the railroad hospitals was established—back in 1882 by the Northern Pacific Beneficial Association. For while they had probably never heard of the Rochdale Weavers in their lives, these railroad men went as a group to their employers and, using their group needs and group strength as bargaining power, obtained agreement to have hospital services provided for them as part of their compensation. No one railroad man could have done this alone.

In 1913 the International Ladies Garment Workers Union in New York City set up for its members the first union health center in United States history. It was a place where union members' money was used to provide outpatient care for any ambulatory ailments any of them might suffer. It and scores of centers like it are in operation today.

Or perhaps we should mark the beginning in 1929 at Elk City, Oklahoma. Then and there a doctor named Michael Shadid put four and four together in his own mind and persuaded others to do likewise. First, the farmers of western Oklahoma were hard pressed. They could rarely pay their doctor bills, especially big bills to meet emergencies. Second, there was no hospital within a radius of many miles. Third, the doctors had no assurance whatever of being able either to make a decent living or to practice the kind of good medicine they wanted to practice. Fourth, the people were "taking it lying down."

So Dr. Shadid suggested that all four of these conditions be attacked at once, beginning with the last one. If the people who needed, *or who might need*, medical care would agree to become members of an association to provide themselves with hospital and medical care in an orderly manner, they probably could do it, even with their small resources. If they would agree to pay an original membership fee to get the enterprise started and then a few dollars each month to cover cost of at least the most necessary types of care, then they might persuade doctors to associate themselves with them to provide such care, and to have some assurance of a dependable income. Maybe they could even build a hospital that would belong to the members and become a medical center for the whole area.

They did.

It wasn't easy. But with the help of a substantial loan from Dr. Shadid himself, the first cooperative health plan—so designated—in the United States was brought into being. It has lived a stormy life. Even today there are features of Community Hospital-Clinic of Elk City that draw criticism from some students of health problems.

But the cooperatively owned hospital at Elk City, staffed by competent doctors, is the medical center of a several-county area in western Oklahoma. Some of its doctors are officers of the county and state medical societies.

And lots of people in that area have been enabled to pay for good medical care for their families.

In the years that have followed, all sorts of plans have developed in all sorts of places among all sorts of people. Some of them, like the pioneer big-city plan—Group Health Association of Washington, D.C.—and Group Health Cooperative of Puget Sound, and Community Health Association of Two Harbors, Minnesota, are in most respects true cooperatives even in a technical sense. Membership is open to anyone who wants to join; control is by the membership, each exercising one vote; ownership of all facilities vests in the membership; and of course the plan is operated on a non-profit basis. Even in these plans, however, no patronage refunds are paid to members when the year's operations show a surplus. This is a distinction between the health plans and all other types of cooperatives. In other kinds of cooperatives that which would be profit to a conventional business belongs instead to the individual members and patron-owners and at year's end is divided among them in proportion to patronage. But ethically health plans cannot be operated for the financial gain of anyone, not even their members. If there is a surplus, then either the monthly subscription charges are reduced, or new services are added, or doctors and other staff people are better compensated, or the money is put into a fund for a new wing on the clinic.

Besides these "pure" cooperative plans there are a wide variety of others, all with two basic common characteristics. In all of them a group of people have decided to pool their need for health care, to pay for it as a group with sick and well paying the same amount, and to arrange with groups of doctors and other professional and non-professional people to provide the health care they need. In the second place, all these group health plans are based on some rather logical thinking.

Here is the essence of it.

(1) The problem of health economics is actually the most serious problem the American family faces today, aside, of course, from the danger of atomic war. This is partly because of the pain and suffering that ill health brings, and partly because of the rapidly rising and quite unpredictable cost of adequate medical care.

(2) But much of this sickness could actually be prevented if families had the right kind of medical care whenever needed, including preventive care. And much of the economic disaster to families could be avoided if they were able to pay for health care on a budgeted, periodic prepayment basis.

(3) Few families can afford to pay, in addition to the family doctor, the fees of the specialists who might be brought into a difficult case. The average family cannot have the advantage of medical specialization unless it can get it through group practice by balanced teams of physicians.

(4) Neither can the average family afford modern medical care if it tries to pay for it on an emergency fee-for-service basis. Under this system there is no control of costs nor even any predictability of costs. This is why, even though on the average they spend plenty of money for the purpose, most of the people are not getting adequate medical care today.

(5) The American people are actually paying as much for emergency medical care after they are sick as they would have to pay for comprehensive care to keep them healthy, if only the money were spent in the right way. Figures developed by the President's Commission on the Health Needs of the Nation and other reliable authorities show that we spend approximately 5 per cent of our income for medical care. Five per cent of an average family income of $5,000 is $250.

(6) The simple outline of a solution is, therefore, a system of prepayment whereby people can pay a fixed amount each month in

return for the care they need, when they need it. And $250 a family per year is enough to pay for quite complete and comprehensive medical care if the money is spent in the most efficient way—through a group practice prepayment health plan.

(7) Prepayment for hospital care is a good thing, but it is even more important to have prepayment for the services which, given in time, can make hospitalization unnecessary. In other words, we need prepayment for comprehensive care, to keep people out of hospitals and thus reduce the cost of medical care. We ought to give our doctors a chance to practice preventive medicine by seeing them regularly for periodic checkups and examinations, and by consulting them for small as well as serious symptoms. But we are likely to do this only if we have already paid for such services through a group health plan.

(8) No such plan is possible unless a fairly substantial and representative cross-section of the community bands together. No plan can succeed if its only subscribers are those who are in immediate need of medical service. You have to have the healthy people, too, and in considerable numbers.

(9) In a democracy it is good to develop and rely on the initiative of the people in solving their own problems. It is not good to depend upon the government any more than necessary. It is best to do things for ourselves. Some consumer responsibility and consumer control over economic aspects of medical care, its cost, and methods of paying for it are therefore a good method.

(10) When group practice, prepayment, comprehensive care, sharing of risks, and consumer initiative are brought together to make a group health prepayment plan, the problem of medical economics can be largely solved. Modern medicine can be brought even to the small communities, and it can be put within the reach of modest family budgets.

The story of how the people and some of their doctors have moved toward cooperative action in the field of health is one of struggle, conflict, doubt, disappointment, and gradually increasing success.

The news of what the Oklahomans had done spread quickly across a depression-ridden land. The next important plan to be organized was the Group Health Association of Washington, D.C. It was founded in 1937 by a group of government employees. From the beginning it has been thoroughly cooperative in all its aspects. Anyone may enroll in the plan. It is controlled by its members, each with a single vote. The members own all its facilities, elect its board of directors. In 1960 its large and competent staff of general practitioners and specialists provided comprehensive medical care for some forty-five thousand people in the Washington area. Included are the members of the large Transit Workers Union who, after considerable negotiation, were blanketed into the plan in 1959. The union built a new branch clinic for GHA to take care of the increased membership.

Group Health Association has had its battles, however. In its early years the medical society black-listed all the doctors who had become associated with the plan and denied the use of hospitals to either GHA doctors or their patients. A five-year lawsuit, finally decided by the United States Supreme Court, held the medical society to be engaged in monopolistic practices, and required readmission of the GHA doctors to the society and restoration of hospital privileges. This decision rendered in 1943 has proved a precedent for an unbroken series of victories for group health plans whenever they have had to go to court to combat discrimination against their doctors by "organized medicine."

The decade of the 1940's saw citizens of dozens of small rural towns on the Great Plains organizing cooperative hospital associations. A number of these hospitals were actually built—too many of them in some areas such as West Texas. In some cases prepayment plans were organized as well. But almost always the monthly dues were set at too low a figure. The facilities were by no means always well constructed or well planned. Medical-society opposition scared doctors away. In consequence, most of these hospitals have been transformed into community-owned facilities, most of the prepayment plans have been abandoned, and the hospital buildings alone remain as reminders of noble efforts too hastily entered into and with too little forethought or planning.

So except for Elk City and Washington, D.C., practically all of the development of cooperative health plans has taken place since World War II. It is a young movement born out of an increasing health consciousness on the part of the American people and their recognition that the rising cost of medical care constitutes their number-one economic hazard. Half a million American families incur medical bills each year which add up to their entire annual income. Another million have medical indebtedness equal to half their incomes. To millions of people Blue Shield, Blue Cross, and commercial insurance have sold health insurance of one kind or another. By 1958 almost three quarters of the population had some kind of health-insurance coverage.

But total payments from such insurance met less than one-fourth of the medical bills of the American families who thought they had "protected themselves" by buying health insurance. This is certainly better than nothing. But it isn't very good protection, and it does little to *improve* health. On the other hand, the families who are members of cooperative-type prepayment group practice health plans receive their benefits not in the form of cash payments, but of doctors' and nurses' care. And the attempt is made to provide that care for as many types of illness and as many measures of prevention of illness as possible.

In 1944, in the small town of Two Harbors, Minnesota, a cooperative plan was started largely by railroad and steel workers. It saved from abandonment the only hospital in town, went on to enroll two-thirds of the town's families as members, succeeded in attracting enough courageous doctors to care for the people, and at last won medical-society recognition with membership for its doctors in 1956.

Nineteen hundred and forty-five saw the organization of Labor Health Institute in St. Louis. This plan, limited to the members of a single local labor union and their families, provides the most comprehensive care for its 15,000 enrollees of any labor-sponsored plan in the United States. A health and welfare fund contributed to by employers supports the plan. LHI found that it could pay the hospital bills of its members for less money than it cost to purchase Blue Cross insurance for them, because people who have access to constant medical care whenever needed have to go to the hospital less frequently than does the population in general.

Hardly a surprising fact, when you stop to think about it.

In 1946 the United Mine Workers' Welfare and Retirement Fund began receiving forty cents for every ton of coal mined. The money was, and is, contributed to the fund by the employers. But the miners dig the coal. Various methods have been tried to assure the miners and their dependents of high-quality medical care and to prevent waste of the Fund's money. In the end it was found that the Fund simply had to select the good, dependable, and conscientious doctors and leave out the ones who were careless or who were overeager to operate. This rather logical decision caused a furor among some state medical societies. A couple of state legislatures came close to passing laws that would have put doctors in jail for caring for miners and receiving payment from the Fund for doing so.

But no such law has been, and none is likely to be, enacted.

For one reason, because the Miners' Fund has done too much downright good for the health of people in some of the least medically advantaged areas of the whole country. A network of ten beautiful hospitals has been built in the Appalachian Mountain country where once no good hospitals existed at all.

Nineteen hundred and forty-seven was an important year. For in that year the Health Insurance Plan of Greater New York began to provide services to subscribers. And across the continent Group Health Cooperative of Puget Sound was organized. Today both these plans are providing comprehensive medical care for about 5 per cent of the population in their respective areas.

The Seattle plan is a true cooperative like GHA of Washington, D.C. It owns and operates its own clinics as well as a beautiful new hospital—both financed mainly by investments of the membership.

HIP, as the New York plan is popularly known, contracts with groups of doctors throughout the greater New York area to provide such services as are needed by its more than half million subscribers. The groups are paid on a capitation basis—so many dollars per year for each person choosing that particular group.

As the years have passed some of the most farsighted labor unions have multiplied the number of health centers where their members can obtain diagnosis and care for ambulatory ailments.

In 1951 the A.F. of L. Medical Services Plan of Philadelphia broke the barrier that had limited union health plans to members of single unions. From the start this plan was set up to serve any local union that decided to participate in it. By the end of its first eight years of operation more than thirty local unions and some 60,000 people were receiving care from this plan.

And in the middle fifties a similar plan—Union Health Services, Inc.—began operation in Chicago.

As this book is being written a group of leading citizens in Detroit, spearheaded by the United Automobile Workers, are striving to develop a community-wide prepayment health plan that will use the services of a number of groups of doctors and of the hospitals already in existence.

By 1960 upward of five million people in the United States had fairly well solved the problem of medical economics for themselves by the application of the broad method of cooperation.

No two of these plans are alike. Some of them have open membership for either individuals, families, or groups. Some have closed membership, their services provided only to members of a single local labor union. Most of them provide service benefits; but one or two pay cash indemnities and have an agreement with doctors to accept the amount of the indemnity in full payment for their services. Some of them exclude from the care provided a number of ailments; whereas others will meet almost any medical need of their members or subscribers. Some are democratically controlled by their members; others by boards of directors which are representatives of, but not elected by, the members; others by the trustees of labor union health and welfare funds. A few are "producer cooperatives" owned and controlled by groups of doctors. Some have been started by groups of people who needed health services; others have been started by labor union officials; others by public officials; still others by doctors. Not one of them pays patronage refunds.

Thus it is evident that "cooperative" health plans are only more and less cooperative in the strict sense of that word. Some at least violate the cooperative principles of open membership; some violate the principle of democratic control; and all of them fail the patronage refund test.

But fundamentally they are cooperative in their essential nature just the same, for they all have the one most essential characteristic of cooperation. *They are enterprises whose owners are the same people who are the users of their services.* They therefore exist not for the financial gain of any individual or of the enterprise itself. They exist to provide a service—in this case health care—to a group of people, their owners, at the least practicable net costs. They are an expression in practical form of the idea and principle of mutual aid.

In some ways they are the most dramatic of all expressions of that principle, for in a group health plan the basic essential of success is that there be enough reasonably healthy people paying into the common fund to make possible payment of costs of taking care of their sick fellow members.

And this, when you stop and think about it, is a rather good idea. In fact, a noble one.

Briefly, these plans make it possible for a family to spend money to maintain health instead of always having to spend it to cure sickness. The objective of such plans is to prevent people having to go to the hospital, rather than merely to pay some part of the bill after they are in a hospital. Since hospital costs have risen about three times as fast in the past thirty years as have medical costs generally, it is obvious that the best single way to reduce family expenses for medical care is to keep people as well as possible and out of the hospital.

But most commercial health insurance—and also Blue Cross and Blue Shield plans—actually encourage people to go to the hospital, because in most cases they can collect from their insurance only when they are in the hospital.

The cooperative-type health plans work in just the opposite direction. Since they undertake to provide medical care, not money, where, when, and as needed, they naturally strive to keep their subscribers as well as possible, to care for them without hospitalization to the extent that good practice dictates, and, above all, to prevent serious illness by maintaining health.

The facts are simple and convincing. In 1956 Blue Cross subscribers nationally used an average of 995 days of hospital care per 1,000 persons covered. And in Michigan the figure was 1,100 days per 1,000 persons covered. But the members of Group Health Cooperative of Puget Sound needed only 562 days of hospitalization per 1,000 members; and at Group Health Association of Washington, D.C., only 546 days. Ten out of 100 Blue Shield subscribers in New

York City are hospitalized each year on the average, compared to only eight out of 100 subscribers to the direct-service Health Insurance Plan of Greater New York.

Furthermore, such plans are able to control costs in other ways. For example, about 21 per cent of the total bill for medical care consists of payments for drugs and medicines, and this percentage is rising steadily. A large proportion of this bill consists of extortionate markups in price which have nothing whatever to do with the quality of the medicines or the employment of people or the expansion and improvement of service.

These drugs and medicines don't need to cost anything like as much as they do, as hearings before the Kefauver Committee of the United States Senate in 1959 and 1960 so convincingly showed.

Cooperative health plans can do something about it. For example, Group Health Cooperative of Puget Sound runs its own pharmacy. Average cost of subscriptions filled by that pharmacy in 1958 was $1.15 compared to a national average cost of $2.62. The members of this cooperative saved themselves more than half of the expense for drugs and medicines that they would otherwise have had to pay. They did this by *deciding* to go into the prescription business *for themselves*.

If only half as much has to be spent on drugs for the same medicinal value, then that amount of money is available to be spent for more preventive care, more rehabilitation services, more dentistry or psychiatric services, or whatever will contribute to better health for the group involved.

One Wednesday afternoon a lady in a well-to-do suburban community cut her hand severely on a can opener. She tried to call a doctor. But while this community has about twice as many doctors per capita as does the nation as a whole, Wednesday is their day off when they all play golf. The lady managed to talk to one doctor's secretary on the telephone and was advised that the only thing for her to do was to drive herself ten miles to another suburb where there was a hospital and where presumably professional people would be on duty, even on Wednesday afternoon.

Had this lady lived in the small, rather low-income community of Two Harbors, Minnesota, she need not have driven ten miles with blood streaming over her hand. The chances would have been two out of three that her family would have been member-owners of the Community Health Plan of Two Harbors. But whether she had been a member or not she could have called the cooperative clinic and a doctor would have been on duty or readily on call.

As *some* doctor always is every hour of the year wherever such plans exist.

The difference? In the wealthy suburb the old fee-for-service, emergency treatment, every doctor and every-patient-for-himself system still prevails. But in the far poorer steel and railroad town on the bleak shores of Lake Superior a smaller number of dollars spent on medical care is buying more dependable and probably better medical care for the people.

Because the people have seen the value of mutual aid—of spending their health-care dollars together, through a health plan of their own.

In 1958 average family expenditures for personal-health services were $294, according to the Health Information Foundation. For this amount most families were receiving only fair health care. They were paying for it on an emergency basis, almost always *after* they had become too ill to neglect seeing a doctor any longer.

But $280 will pay the total annual subscription cost for membership in the best and most comprehensive cooperative health plans in the country. In some plans the cost is considerably less than $280. In few of them is it more.

Better health care for great numbers of the American people and access to the marvelous benefits of modern medical science, these wait not for more money to be spent nor for the government to pass a law.

They wait only for people to become wise enough, farsighted enough, community minded enough, to pool both their need for health care and their money to pay for it—together.

These benefits wait indeed for more of us to apply to our own actions the modern version of the motive that sent the pioneer woman to the neighbor's cabin to help nurse a sick child.

There exists a national organization dedicated to bringing about this very result. It is called Group Health Association of America. Its members are the major cooperative, community, and labor health plans of the country. Its program is promotion of group practice, prepayment, comprehensive direct service care, and consumer initiative. In all probability the progress of Group Health Association will measure the progress of these very sensible steps toward a more healthy America. For GHAA, as it is generally called, became in 1959 the principal spokesman for the interest of consumers of medical care. In fact, it is the only such spokesman with a broad popular membership. In that year two organizations joined to form GHAA. One was American Labor Health Association, whose membership included administrators and representatives of nearly all of the labor-union-sponsored health plans of the United States. The other, and older, parent organization of GHAA was the Group Health Federation of America, founded under the name Cooperative Health Federation in 1946 and composed of some labor health plans and all but one or two of the more significant cooperative and community health plans of the United States and Canada.

IV

HOMES AND
NEIGHBORHOODS

The appearance of economic health in our economy today is deceptive. American industry is generating nowhere near enough mass buying power to form a market for what it is producing at the prices it insists on charging. The gap between total prices and total effective demand is wide indeed. That gap is *caused* by monopolistic, "administered" overpricing of most industrial goods in our economy and the practice of internal financing of capital expenditures, the cost of which is added to the price consumers pay for the goods.

United States Steel Corporation, itself, in a statement entitled: "Steel and Inflation: Fact and Fiction," says 88 per cent of all prices in our economy are administered.

Where investment in plant is financed from "internal" sources—that is, out of corporation surpluses arising in the course of business—the simple fact is that such plant is being paid for by consumers of the products of the industries. The cost of the new plant has obviously been added to the prices of the goods sold. Otherwise, the surplus could not have been accumulated. Monopolistic profits measure the gap between total prices of goods produced and effective mass buying power of consumers. And the cost of plant financed without the raising of additional capital is a factor in that gap.

The gap is currently being somewhere nearly filled by the sum of all military expenditures, plus the increase in consumer debt, plus a considerable portion of the increase in mortgage and long-term debt, plus local, state, or federal governmental deficits, plus the losses taken by small and competitive businesses when they are forced to sell below cost of production as farmers in general are compelled to do.

Despite this gigantic subsidy it is necessary for our manufacturers to resort to fantastic excesses of advertising and sales pressures to dispose of the flood of things they are pouring out.

The end is in sight. But for the astronomical burden of consumer debt and the rapid population increase we would have reached it already. American families may be—probably are—conformist enough to think they must own two automobiles, a couple of television sets, a fancy refrigerator, and an overpriced suburban home. But few families will buy—now or ever—three or four cars, or four or five television sets, or more than one refrigerator, or a home costing more than fifty thousand dollars. The luxury market has its limitations. One such limit is the limit to which the average young couple can expand the burden of family debt. Another limit is a healthy, normal revulsion, signs of which are now unmistakable, against the ridiculous worship of material things into which our present economy has driven many of us. Still another limit so far as automobiles are concerned is the virtual impossibility of finding a place to park them, so that increasingly people use public transportation and—God save the mark—even walk!

Fortunately there is a corrective for much of this unbalance which has already proved its effectiveness. That corrective is the extension of business ownership to many millions more people. It is a way the people can own some of the industrial plants for which they are actually paying. It is the organization of business enterprises by groups of people for the explicit purpose of meeting their own needs. It is *consumer-directed production* and distribution of goods and services. This corrective is the generation of more and more of a kind of competition that monopoly can't frighten or buy out but which can correct the worst of the abuses of the present situation for the simple reason that it exists to serve people's needs, not to exploit their whims. This corrective comes into play through the form of business organization called cooperative or mutual business.

Let us illustrate.

On February 16, 1960, Nelson Rockefeller, governor of New York, announced that 6,300 home units would soon be built on the site of the Jamaica (Long Island) race track. He announced that this group of homes would be named Rochdale Village, in honor of the twenty-eight poor weavers who founded the first Consumers Cooperative at Rochdale, England, in 1848. Mortgage financing for the project, said the governor, would be provided mainly from three sources: the state teachers' retirement fund, $28 million; the state employees' retirement funds, a like amount; and the state division of housing, $19 million.

Sponsor, builder, and developer of this, the largest single cooperative housing project in this country and perhaps in the world, would be United Housing Foundation.

Within twenty-four hours after Governor Rockefeller's announcement more than two thousand applications had been received by United Housing Foundation. They came from people who wanted to live in and own, together with 6,299 other families, the Rochdale Village. These people had never seen plans or pictures of the buildings. They had been told only approximately what the down payments would be or the monthly payments once they were living in their new homes. But they were ready in most cases to make their down payments right then.

Why did this happen?

Partly because good homes in good neighborhoods are the outstanding unmet economic need of middle- and lower-income families in the United States today.

And partly because Rochdale Village was to be another project of United Housing Foundation. Which meant that the homes would be built not for sale at a profit but to give as many families as possible good homes in good neighborhoods at costs they could afford. People had confidence in United Housing Foundation.

And people in New York City had learned from experience that consumer-sponsored cooperative housing is built to meet the needs of people for homes—and for no other purpose. Such housing represents one of the most dramatic examples of what we are going to call "consumer-directed production." Goods or services so produced are already in effect sold before they are even produced. Just as was the case with the homes in the yet non-existent Rochdale Village.

Let us explain.

Some 14 million American families are living in substandard or slum homes today. And many families have escaped this fate only by spending far more in purchasing their homes than they could safely afford. Yet in some of our major cities there is considerable unemployment in the building trades.

The reason for all this is twofold. First, we have not been building enough new houses nor doing nearly enough to cure big-city blight. Second, the houses that have been built have been mostly luxury housing. Comparatively few of them cost less than $15,000 and a family should have an income of at least $7,000 in order safely to afford a home that expensive. But only a minority of American families have incomes of $7,000 a year.

Our construction industry is building the kind of houses it wants to build, at prices it wants to charge, without much direct reference to what people generally need or can afford.

So a few intelligent people have had the idea of reversing this process and building the kind of homes the people do need at prices they can afford. The surest way to be certain you are doing this is to let the people who need the homes do the decision making. In other words, to organize a cooperative of the home needers, build homes tailored to their needs and pocketbooks, and enable them to own their own homes, cooperatively, after they are built.

Under such circumstances no high-pressure sales efforts are needed. The houses belong to the families who are going to live in them before they are even constructed!

A whole section of New York's lower East Side has been changed from a slum into a beautiful lawabiding community of neighbors by this method. And the cost of this housing is 25 per cent to 30 per cent less than comparable commercially built housing. Average monthly charges including all costs in these cooperatives is $60.00 to $70.00 for four-room apartments. That is, $720 to $840 a year. Families with incomes as low as $4,000 can afford such costs for their homes without incurring burdensome debt.

But project this a bit further. Suppose in every major city there were competent service organizations, as there are in New York, ready and able to guide and advise groups of people needing homes so they could get them through cooperative housing. All that cooperative housing would be built to the specification of the people's needs and pocketbooks. What would other builders do? They'd compete. They'd start trying to do the same thing—to go the coops one better. Some of them would succeed in all probability.

And there would appear a solution to the housing problem of the American people without subsidy from government and by the people's own effort, investment, and use of intelligence.

Moreover, we would achieve the kind of balance between supply and effective demand which could reasonably assure full employment in the construction industry into the indefinite future.

Price inflation would be effectively prevented because part of the competition in the industry would come from businesses belonging to the people who were going to pay the bill for its product!

Cooperative housing got its start in the United States in 1926—not long ago. It began with a remarkably logical decision on the part of some members and officials of the Amalgamated Clothing Workers' Union. They were hard pressed at the time just as the twenty-eight Rochdale weavers were when they started the first consumer cooperative in Rochdale, England, in 1848, and just as Connecticut dairy farmers were when they started the first farmers' marketing cooperative in the United States in 1804.

The clothing workers figured up how much they were paying in rent on the rather shabby apartments their families occupied. They capitalized this amount. They investigated costs of construction of apartment buildings in the New York area. They found out how much mortgage financing would cost. They concluded from all this that if they could become their own landlords, that is, build and own their own homes, they could save money and have far better homes besides. They appointed a committee to plan further and especially to see if money could be borrowed. Fortunately they selected as manager of the enterprise a tiny man with a giant's vision, Abraham E. Kazan.

Kazan, now president of United Housing Foundation, has been the genius and spearhead of American cooperative housing ever since.

The result of the pioneer effort was Amalgamated Housing Corporation, builder and sponsor of an apartment building on the border of Van Cortlandt Park. An understanding and sympathetic bank agreed to loan the money for the mortgage. It turned out to be a gilt-edged investment and the daddy of a number of other similarly gilt-edged investments in later years. Not once has a single one of the New York cooperative housing associations failed to pay interest and principal in full on time.

The Amalgamated project turned out to be a brilliant success. Not only did it provide good housing at considerably reduced cost, it created a true neighborhood in the midst of America's largest city. It brought into being a neighborhood in which forums and lecture courses would be held on all manner of subjects, where nursery schools and summer camps would be organized for children, where cooperative food stores, credit unions, and insurance services would be organized by the neighbors for mutual benefit of the neighbors. Gardens and shrubbery and vines on the brick buildings have come to be prized by these families. And pride in appearance and in "keeping up" the cooperatively owned properties have held maintenance costs to half what they normally are in either conventional "landlord's" rental housing or in publicly owned housing.

But what is perhaps most remarkable—though hardly surprising, really—about the Amalgamated homeowners and other similar groups who have followed in their footsteps has been the record of unbelievably low incidence of crime or delinquency among them. Seventy-five per cent of the families now resident in the Van Cortlandt Park homes are either the same families or direct descendants of the families who went to live there in 1926. And there has yet to be recorded a single case of major crime or even of serious juvenile delinquency among them!

Cooperative home ownership at its best engenders pride in one's neighborhood. The spirit of mutual helpfulness in providing good homes and environment appears to create a group morale and group standards of conduct whose social value is hard to measure.

Amalgamated Housing Corporation (the correct name for the pioneer project) has added a number of buildings to the original group as the years have passed.

Encouraged by the success of the first venture there followed, slowly at first, similar ventures in other parts of New York City. The early ones were sponsored by Amalgamated Clothing Workers and financed by savings banks whose complete confidence Kazan had gained.

Not until the post World War II years did the tempo of development become more rapid. Then other strong labor unions such as International Brotherhood of Electrical Workers and International Ladies' Garment Workers became interested. So did some of the larger credit unions and other membership organizations. And not only was this interest in the sponsoring of projects, but in their mortgage financing as well. Some insurance companies also joined in financing some of the projects. Several of them centered in the Corlears Hook section of the lower East Side, where by 1960 a whole area, once a miserable slum, had become known as Cooperative Village, with 5,000 family-owners of the apartments, a number of credit unions serving these family needs, a fine cooperatively owned supermarket for their shopping, and excellent playgrounds for the children.

Even before World War II broke out cooperative housing had been established in the minds of New Yorkers as a good idea.

The war years, of course, saw little housing construction. The need increased with each passing month. So did the savings of many families. And as the peace finally came, the stage was set for a surge of activity. It centered, still, in New York City. Tenants in government housing, built for war workers in Dayton, Ohio; South Bend, Indiana; Dallas, Texas; and a couple of other places, organized cooperative associations and bought the homes they had been renting from the government. But nowhere else were the laws as favorable as in New York. Nowhere except in New York had there been demonstration of cooperative-housing success from bare land to happy neighborhood, and nowhere else was there an A. E. Kazan.

Interest was fairly widespread and attempts were made to form one organization for the promotion of cooperative housing. But this proved too much to expect. Two points of view emerged. On the one hand were A. E. Kazan and his close associates who were rigidly unwilling to compromise any of their thoroughly cooperative principles, who knew how to do the job, and who refused to be pushed into so broad a program as to endanger their established standards for every project they undertook. Their world was New York City. On the other hand stood people who, while recognizing the extreme value of the accomplishments of the Kazan group, felt that attempt should be made to extend the benefits of cooperative housing beyond New York, and who, in general, were less insistent on application of pure cooperative methods so long as more and more and more housing could be obtained.

The net result was three organizations, all centered in New York, but all working independently of one another and in somewhat different ways.

The first and strongest of these was United Housing Foundation of which A. E. Kazan was to become president. It proceeded along the lines that had already been proved so successful to develop one housing cooperative after another in metropolitan New York. Much of the activity centered in the lower East Side of the city.

By 1959, 12,000 families in New York were housed in beautiful, and remarkably inexpensive, apartment buildings, which they themselves owned as a result of UHF activity. It was evident that within a very few years this number would be trebled. Other labor unions besides Amalgamated Clothing Workers took an interest. International Ladies' Garment Workers union sponsored and provided a $15,000,000 mortgage loan for a lower East Side project known as ILGWU Village. At its dedication in 1956 there were present both United States senators from New York, the mayor of the city, the president of the Borough Council, several congressmen, the president of the American Federation of Labor, Mrs. Franklin D. Roosevelt, and many other state and national leaders. Cooperative housing, à la the United Housing Foundation, was definitely accepted as a most important constructive factor in American urban life.

Not the least reason for this was that monthly charges, including the upbuilding of equity ownership were, and are, in such projects between 20 per cent and 30 per cent less than simple rentals would be in comparable commercial housing. And a basic reason why these savings are possible is that cooperative housing is consumer-directed production of housing. It is production geared to real needs by the people who have the needs.

It is true that in New York cooperative housing can have some tax abatement along with any other type of non-profit housing. Few other states have the same type of law. Nor is there anywhere any special tax provision for cooperative housing. It pays the same taxes exactly as do other kinds of housing. But in New York any kind of non-profit housing, including cooperative housing, can qualify for tax abatement for a period of twenty-five years. This is in no sense a tax exemption. But under New York law, non-profit housing is permitted to pay the same taxes for a period of twenty-five years as were collected upon the same property before the new construction took place. This, of course, is some help in keeping the monthly charges low, but it is no "special privilege" for cooperative housing. It *is* a special provision of New York law for any non-profit housing.

But in this postwar period the United Housing Foundation people were not working alone. The Middle Income Housing Corporation got its start by guiding construction, development, and occupancy of Morningside Heights Housing Cooperative, sponsored by a number of religious and educational institutions. It followed with Chatham Green housing cooperative sponsored by city and state credit unions. William Reid, national credit union leader and later to become chairman of the New York City Housing Commission, became president of the Middle Income Housing Corporation.

The Foundation for Cooperative Housing provided in many respects the counterpart to United Housing Foundation. FCH was fathered—and largely financed—by Winslow Carlton, public-spirited civic leader and president of a consumer-oriented health insurance company. FCH looked far and wide across the nation and thought generally about the national housing problem. It equipped itself to assist and counsel in the development of cooperative housing almost anywhere. It worked less intensively than United Housing Foundation, and was less insistent on application of all the cooperative principles to the projects with which it worked, but it spread its work and influence more broadly. And it converted to cooperative ownership houses in Bridgeport, Connecticut; Greenbelt, Maryland; Kansas City, Missouri; and dozens of other places. The Bridgeport conversion was made possible by purchase of the homes and resale to the tenants by Nationwide Insurance Companies.

In 1950 an event took place in Washington which was to confront all three of the organizations just described as well as the Cooperative League of the United States and everyone else concerned with the cooperative movement with an almost overwhelming challenge. In that year Congress enacted into law section 213 of the Federal Housing Act. It provided for insurance by FHA of loans to cooperative housing projects. Such projects, as the law came to provide after some amendments, could be sponsored either by the consumers or by builders or by investors. Amortization and interest terms were among the more favorable ones provided by the national legislation.

The result was that "cooperative housing" of many shapes and sizes began to spring up all over the nation. Some of these projects were genuinely cooperative in their major aspects, particularly some of those guided by one or another of the service agencies mentioned above. Others were purely luxury apartments as to which the "cooperative" section of the act offered the most convenient method of financing.

Most of them were projects that developed something like this. Builders or investors saw in section 213 their best opportunity to build housing, sell it expeditiously and under the most favorable financing arrangements. So many families needed housing that they readily bought shares in cooperative housing of this type—particularly since down payments were in many cases quite small. Few of these people understood well what they were doing. Few of them knew, despite information sheets prepared and recommended by FHA for distribution among them, just what a cooperative was or what their obligations and responsibilities as cooperative owners entailed. Still fewer of them realized the potential values and benefits of cooperation, not only in home ownership, but in neighborhood development and in the obtaining of needed supplies, services, and recreational facilities.

By 1959 there were some three hundred cooperative housing projects in the United States, 150 of them in New York State, with perhaps four hundred thousand people living in them. Some of them were thoroughly cooperative communities, both economically and socially. Some had hardly any of these aspects. In these latter cases the families had new houses to live in. And that was good. But the task of helping them to realize what cooperative ownership could mean to them remained almost wholly to be done.

Who was going to perform this task?

A start had been made by the Cooperative League in 1958 when the first national conference on cooperative housing had been convened by that organization in Washington, D.C. So much interest was shown that the League immediately announced that such conferences would be held annually.

But two days of experience-sharing and discussion among a group of cooperative housing leaders once a year, is hardly adequate to convey to several hundred thousand resident-owners the meaning and value of cooperative housing.

A three-day training institute for cooperative housing managers sponsored and conducted by the Cooperative League dug somewhat deeper and brought demands for more of the same kind of activity.

It was, however, evident that the answer to the over-all problem could be found only in a national organization of cooperative housing associations. Such an organization could set standards of proper cooperative operation for its membership. It could provide assistance and advice in problem solving. It could work at the development of more "United Housing Foundations" and "Foundations for Cooperative Housing" in other parts of the country. It could conduct training conferences and institutes. It could do its best to insist on adequate educational programs for owner-occupant-members of cooperative housing projects.

All this a national federation for cooperative housing could do *if* the diverse element in the field could be reconciled, the various viewpoints brought into reasonable harmony, and *if* enough of the cooperative homeownership groups could be persuaded to join and to pay dues to finance the work of the national organization. Throughout most of 1959 and early 1960 work to these ends went forward, through initiative of the Cooperative League, UHF and FCH.

On May 11, 1960, a meeting of established cooperative housing leaders was held in New York City and the National Association of Housing Cooperatives became a reality.

The scope of the work of such a national organization will be limited only by the available resources, for there is no longer any doubt at all that "cooperative housing" in all its aspects and all its various degrees of real cooperation will dot the nation in the years ahead.

Indeed at the annual Conference on Cooperative Housing held in Washington in February, 1960, the conservative commissioner of the Federal Housing Administration stated in his address that for millions of families in the nation in the middle- and lower-income groups the one real hope of homeownership and good housing lies in cooperative housing. The executive secretary of the National Association of Housing and Redevelopment Officials declared at the same conference that cooperative housing is the master key to good urban renewal programs.

At this conference, also, Mr. Ira Robbins, a member of the New York City Housing Commission, made an announcement that could have tremendous portent for the future of the use of cooperative ownership in securing good homes for American families. Mr. Robbins stated that the New York City Commission had decided to build eight projects with homes for more than seven thousand families, and instead of maintaining them as publicly-owned housing, to sell them as cooperatives to the families who would live in them. It was well known that serious social problems had been arising in connection with so-called "public housing." Perhaps some of these could be solved by a new and extended use of cooperative methods and co-operative ownership. At least the municipality would collect some $50 million in taxes which it would not otherwise get, and since the equity down payments would be made at the outset, some $20 million of the estimated $138 million cost would be immediately recovered for use elsewhere. No subsidy would be involved. But the borrowing power of the city would make possible less costly financing and could thus bring the monthly charges to the new cooperative owners within range of lower-middle income families. This was important, for a 1 per cent decrease in the interest rate can reduce monthly charges by as much as $2.25 per room.

The decision of the New York City Housing Commission opened a huge new door for cooperative housing. If cooperation were to be employed by municipal authorities to meet as much as possible of the housing needs of groups heretofore requiring partially subsidized public housing, there could be a very great increase in cooperative housing in this most critical field.

As was said at the beginning of this chapter, it is probable that good housing at costs they can afford is the most serious unmet economic need of Americans today. This, then, is the kind of situation in which cooperatives have their clearest reason for existence, their best opportunity to show the benefits they can bring to a whole society, and the best opportunity to win broad public acceptance.

That cooperative housing will become an increasingly important factor in the economic and social life of our country is hardly to be questioned. The only question is: To what extent will the full potential values and benefits of cooperation in its best and fullest expression be realized?

V

HOW ELECTRICITY CAME
TO RURAL AMERICA

"Why should the rural electric cooperatives be allowed to take business away from the power companies?"

"Aren't these coops socialistic?"

"Why should they get government loans at a lower rate of interest than the government has to pay when it borrows money?"

"What excuse do a bunch of farmers have for getting into the power business?"

"What if the electric cooperatives took over the whole power business of the country?"

"—and why in hell don't they pay their taxes?"

These are some of the questions that are in the minds of many people—particularly those who read the metropolitan newspapers.

This chapter is about those questions.

In 1935 less than one farmer in ten in the United States had electric lights in his home or electric power in his barn. The basic reason was that the power companies regarded rural business as unprofitable. They believed, and said so, that farmers never would be able to afford electricity. Studies conducted by the commercial utilities brought forth estimates that the average farmer would have to pay seventy-five cents per kilowatt hour for energy if the companies were to make their established rates of profit from serving him. Farm families were told that they would have to pay $200, $500, sometimes $2,000 to the power companies just to get a line built to connect their farm.

The point was that the commercial power companies were in 1935—and still are—in business to make a profit, as good a profit as possible, out of each customer served.

Had no other economic motive been called into action America's countryside would probably still be using candle and lantern light. The production miracles performed by United States farmers during and after World War II would have been quite impossible. American agriculture would remain a backward industry instead of the most progressive one in the entire nation. A multimillion-dollar rural market for electric appliances would not exist. Rural living would still be relatively primitive and difficult compared to urban living. Electric power rates would be twice what they are now in rural and suburban areas.

And the problem of technological unemployment in the electric power and appliance business would be far more critical than it is.

But another motive was called into action with great effect. Another form of economic organization was born into the electric power business.

What the profit motive couldn't or wouldn't do the service motive and the mutual-aid motive did do. What commercial business couldn't do cooperative business accomplished brilliantly. In place of artificial scarcity of electric power in rural America there was developed a system of cooperative generation and distribution which has made the farms and villages the most rapidly growing market for electric energy and appliances in the nation. Jobs were created by the hundreds of thousands during the depression and additional jobs in the whole electric industry have continued, ever since, to be created each year.

For example, farmers used 14 per cent more electricity in 1958 than they had in 1957. Average consumption jumped from 415 to 472 kilowatt hours a month.

In the first twenty-five years of rural electrification rural people spent more than fifteen billion dollars for electrical appliances.

By 1958 more than 95 per cent of American farms were electrified.

And all this has happened because the competition of rural electric cooperatives has changed the course of the entire industry from one of artificial scarcity and high rates to one of adequate service at reasonable rates. Because there was room in our American economic system for businesses started by groups of people to meet their own specific economic needs, the health of the basic industry of modern economic life was restored, at least in the rural areas.

True, public power developments like TVA have had much to do with restoring a measure of competition in the power business. But this would have had relatively little effect in the countryside had it not been for the rural electric cooperatives.

The story of rural electricity since 1935 is thus one of the best illustrations of the benefits to an entire nation that can flow from consumption-oriented or consumer-directed production and distribution. This story can teach us much about how to overcome the menace of technological unemployment, as can also cooperative housing. For instead of restricting employment and production in order to maintain artificially high prices as is so often done where proprietary business gains monopolistic control of an industry, cooperative or consumer-directed business by its very nature produces and distributes what people need and does so with the *purpose and motive* of fully meeting these people's needs at the most reasonable practicable net cost.

In 1935 the depression was deep over the land. Some 14 million workers were unable to find employment. Farmers and other small businessmen were bankrupt or close to it. Congress and the national administration were seeking to stimulate economic activity and restore employment opportunities. Partly for this reason and partly as an aid to agriculture, the Rural Electrification Administration was established by executive order in 1935. The Norris-Rayburn Act was passed by Congress in 1936, and became known as the Rural Electrification Act. It provided, in brief, for a new agency in the government, the Rural Electric Administration. It provided that the agency could make loans to promote the servicing of farmers, rural people, and rural institutions with electricity. Requirements were that borrowers from REA must agree not to serve communities of more than fifteen hundred persons and must agree to serve any farmer or other consumer in the area who asked for such service no matter whether it was or was not profitable to do so. The authors of the legislation expected that the bulk of the loans would be made to established electric power companies, which were, are, and always have been eligible to borrow from REA. But this did not happen. Instead, in the very earliest months after passage of the act nothing much happened at all.

But then farm people began to think. If the power companies weren't going to do anything about rural electricity, then why shouldn't the farmers do something themselves?

Fieldmen from the REA did what they could to plant and nourish this question. And to suggest that, once they had organized themselves cooperatively so they could pledge their credit as a group, farmers could borrow from REA to build the necessary lines.

Furthermore, there had been pioneers already. In fact, the first rural electric cooperative of which we have record was organized in 1914 at Granite Falls, Minnesota.

In 1919 a man by the name of Clyde Groer owned a small hydroelectric plant near Viola, Wisconsin. He lacked adequate market for the power generated by his plant. He began to propose to farmers that they form a cooperative. Unlike the large utility companies, Mr. Groer told the farmers he believed they *could* afford electricity and that he could sell wholesale power to them with mutual advantage to them and to him. Forty-three farmers agreed to join the cooperative. A four-man crew spent six months building eighteen miles of line to reach these forty-three farms. This small cooperative was still in existence when the events of 1935 and 1936 took place.

In succeeding years successful experiments with cooperative electrification were made here and there. In northeastern Mississippi the Alcorn County Electric Power Association, financed largely by a loan from TVA, had cut the cost of electricity in half during its first year's operation and was an established enterprise before the REA came into being in 1935.

And so there began in 1935 and 1936 one of the most remarkable organizing campaigns in the history of our country. The men and women who carried on that campaign are honored today in hundreds of rural communities. Their names are etched in the cornerstones of beautiful little stone and brick buildings in hundreds of rural towns. More than that, *those who remember when the farms still operated by candle and lantern* honor these organizing pioneers as the founders of modern agriculture and modern farm living in the United States.

One of my most vivid memories is that of sitting in a meeting at Oconto Falls, Wisconsin, which marked the twenty-third anniversary of the organization of the electric cooperative which serves the surrounding area. The big tent pitched for the meeting was filled to capacity. Two men—one a minister, retired, the other the president of the cooperative—were eulogized by men and women with tears in their eyes and voices, for they had been the ones who had traveled farthest and oftenest through snow and biting cold to tell the hope of cooperative rural electricity from farm to farm in the winter of 1935–1936. The account was told, simply but with deep drama, of the meeting on December 9, 1935, where twelve men had put their names to the incorporation papers for the Oconto Electric Cooperative Association and sent off an application for a loan to REA in Washington. The most attractive building in Oconto Falls is the headquarters of the electric cooperative. And appropriately so. For along with other cooperatives it is the one type of business which the local people of that area are sure to continue to own as an important locally-owned industry through the years. Given, of course, their will to do so.

But what did these pioneers of the middle twenties organize? A cooperative business association, of course. But what was its substance? Not much, one may say. For all it possessed was a comparatively small group of members who had each paid a $5.00 membership fee. It had in addition, of course, the hope of a loan from REA. But these would have been of little consequence had there not been organized into these cooperatives two intangible things of priceless value and deep strength. The first of these was a common need of a group of neighbors. This was the first thing that had to be organized. In fact, these electric cooperatives—as well as almost any kind of cooperative that is well conceived—consist basically of the organization of a common need of a group of people. Plus, of course, a reasonable faith that that need can be met by cooperative action.

The second element that was organized as farmers put their signatures to the papers by lamplight was the credit of the members—their promise to pay on schedule the money they hoped to borrow. Many of these farmers were at the time near bankruptcy. But they were honest men. Their pledge of their good names was a better security than a lien upon their farms. *Provided they made the pledge together, as an organized group.*

No one farmer could make an electric system out of his need for electricity. But groups of farmers—once their need was cooperatively organized—could do so. No one farmer could hope to monetize the credit of his single good name, but groups of farmers could do this. The bringing of electricity to rural America is thus another demonstration of the basic fact of life that what one of us cannot do alone a number of us cooperating together can frequently accomplish.

Mutual aid is a good method of solving problems.

It has worked brilliantly in giving some 4,500,000 farmers and rural people ownership of a part of the key industry of modern economic life—the power business.

It is not necessary to recount the details of the story here. Before 1935 was out rural electric cooperatives had been organized and received loans in Indiana, Ohio, Texas, Wisconsin, and Mississippi. In the months and years that followed the country became dotted with a nationwide system of electric cooperatives. It was they, with their simple method of organizing need and pledges to pay their debts of honest people, that did the lion's share of a job on which America's future was to depend. It was not the rich and powerful utilities. Not till the cooperatives had demonstrated that farmers could afford electricity—at decent rates; not until the cooperatives had shown the vast market for electric appliances that lay latent in the countryside; not until the record of repayment of their loans (99.9987 per cent, to be exact) had been established; and not until the competition of the cooperatives had brought about rate reductions of 40 per cent, 50 per cent, sometimes more; not until all this had taken place did the commercial utilities begin really to try to serve rural America with electricity.

The utilities fought the REA program and especially the cooperatives from the start. Their principal Washington lobbyist is paid several times the salary received by the general manager of the National Rural Electric Cooperative Association. This was true even when, by 1959, NRECA had a membership of more than four million five hundred thousand consumers of rural electricity and was one of the most significant national organizations in the nation. But only after the cooperatives had demonstrated that serving rural areas with electricity could be "good business" did the utilities begin in earnest to try to take the newly developed business away. Their methods were many and various. Expensive national advertising programs warned of the "dangers of socialism" represented by the electric cooperatives. "Spite lines" were built in attempts to skim off the most thickly populated parts of a cooperative's territory. Carefully planned campaigns were conducted to try to induce the owners of the cooperatives to sell them out to the dominant commercial utility in the region.

All these methods plus ever-increasing pressure upon Congress have been used with ever-increasing intensity as the years have passed.

Here and there they have been successful.

Most of the electric cooperatives are strong organizations with loyal, proud memberships, their annual meetings attended by hundreds, sometimes thousands, of members. One coop in Iowa prides itself that no less than 10,000 people attend regularly its annual meetings. These meetings are the outstanding event of the year in the county where they are held.

But there are elements of weakness in some of the electric cooperatives. In some of them the manager has worked himself into the position of a virtual dictator and runs the organization with an iron hand. In others the membership among suburban people, accustomed to the blessings of electricity all their lives, now outnumber the farmers. As the years pass, the number of members who vividly remember the day when their cooperative first brought electricity to the farm dwindles. In their places are people who take electric service as a matter of course. Where no educational program has been carried on, no newsletter sent to the members, and little effort made to develop pride of ownership, the blandishments of the power companies have their best chance to bring about a "sellout."

The electric cooperatives must serve all who need service in their area. This is often extremely expensive. The average number of customers per mile of line is only three for the coops compared to twenty-five for their powerful competitors. The ratio of investment in plant and equipment to gross revenue of electric cooperatives is three times that of the commercial utilities. The coops, therefore, face a most difficult competitive situation, to say the least. But in the face of these facts political attacks upon them increased during the 1950's and centered in demands and proposals that they be denied opportunity to borrow from REA and forced, instead, to seek financing in the commercial money markets.

The other prong of the political attack on electric cooperatives through the years has been an effort to persuade Congress to *forbid* loans by REA to finance cooperative generation and transmission facilities.

This is both understandable and critically dangerous to the cooperatives. It is understandable because if the rural electrics were in effect forbidden to develop their own generation systems where necessary, they would lie at the mercy of their competitors, the power companies.

It is not necessary for the distribution cooperatives to generate all or even a major part of the power they use. The fact is they were generating only about 15 per cent of it in 1959. But they must generate some of it, as they discovered from painful experience very early in their history.

Indeed, one of the main problems which the cooperative distribution systems faced, after their lines were built, was that of obtaining wholesale power at fair rates. There were exceptions, particularly in areas where there were sources of public power. But generally speaking the commercial utilities demanded somewhat more than a pound of flesh to supply power to the bright new lines which the farmers had strung because they had organized their need.

So, like the petroleum cooperatives had had to do, and like every kind of cooperative will have to do when they become strong enough to exercise effective competition, the electric-distribution cooperatives began to develop in certain areas their own independent sources of power. It was not enough to demonstrate that a lot of average people could organize, own, and operate successfully electric-distribution systems. It was also necessary to prove that in generation of electricity as well the people could "do it for themselves" if they had to and if they applied the method of cooperation.

The story of Dairyland Power Cooperative is typical. It had its origin in 1937, in a meeting of representatives of ten electric distribution cooperatives. They met because the commercial power companies in Wisconsin would supply power to them only at the exorbitant rate of two and one-half cents per kilowatt hour—wholesale. They thought they had better have their own source of wholesale power. They formed Wisconsin Power Cooperative.

A loan of $650,000 was obtained from REA and a year later seven northern Wisconsin cooperatives were supplying farmers with power not only over their own lines but from their own diesel generating plant at Chippewa Falls.

Meanwhile, distribution cooperatives in Iowa, Minnesota, and southern Wisconsin had found, like their northern neighbors, that wholesale power at reasonable rates just wasn't to be had. So they organized Tri-State Power Cooperative and completed a steam plant at Genoa, Wisconsin, in 1941.

Shortly before this plant was completed, three of the commercial utilities in the area made a new offer—an offer of wholesale power to the electric cooperatives at a much lower cost than they had originally demanded. Their pencils somehow had become a good deal sharper.

Why?

For the simple reason that the farmers were about to prove that they could generate power for themselves—and to find out from practical experience how much it really needed to cost to do so.

In October, 1941, Wisconsin Power Cooperative and Tri-State Power Cooperative were merged to form Dairyland. In the months and years that have followed new plants have been built, new connecting lines constructed, new economics of operation introduced. Most of the plants are steam plants that use coal that comes up the Mississippi in barges from Illinois and Kentucky mines. But one is a hydro plant on the Flambeau River which cost more than six million dollars, largely because of delays brought about by bitter opposition from forces that seemed to say: "It just isn't decent for a bunch of farmers to build a power plant. Only big companies with offices in big cities have a right to do such things!"

But the farmers did it. Over and over, as power use increased on the farms and in the rural areas, Dairyland increased, doubled, trebled its capacity. Each time the opposition cried that Dairyland would never in the world have a market among its members for all that power. Over and over it was proved that the expansion wasn't enough to meet the demand.

In the year 1950 alone $2,000,000 was saved to the members of Dairyland. By which we mean that they got their wholesale power from their own system at a cost of $2,000,000 less than it would have cost to buy it from commercial utilities at the best rates they had offered.

It pays to do it yourself, with your neighbors.

Indeed by 1958 when more than one hundred thousand farmers and other rural customers were owners of Dairyland, it could be shown that while the cost of living index had been rising 30 per cent over the preceding ten years, the cost of power from Dairyland had been reduced 35 per cent. Wholesale power was being delivered by 1959 at slightly less than one cent per kilowatt hour!

Independence worked. It worked not only in Wisconsin but in central Iowa and in Kentucky and in Missouri and a dozen other places where the distribution cooperatives joined together and built their own generating cooperatives.

The utilities' lobby screamed to Congress. It urged that legislation be passed forbidding REA to make any loans for generation and transmission of power. It wanted the electric cooperatives to be dependent on their competitors—competitors who had fought and hated them from the start—for every kilowatt of power they might need.

Congress has not listened.

Independence worked in other ways, too. With courage and foresight Wisconsin Electric Cooperative contracted with an independent aluminum company to break the shortage of materials and cable in the postwar period and to bring down monopoly-fixed prices for these essential items in rural electric expansion. This was a very risky venture, but it paid off. It paid off not only in the freeing of the expansion of the electric cooperatives but in the freeing of aluminum markets generally from some of the worst aspects of monopoly influence.

Throughout the years of the 1950's the attacks upon rural electric cooperatives—as well as other mutual and cooperative enterprises— were being intensified. Full-page advertisements paid for by their competitors attempted to paint the electric cooperatives as recipients of huge subsidies from government, as costing taxpayers large amounts of money, as unfair competition, as something out of line with "American ways." Highly paid lobbyists, supported by the national administration then in power, demanded curtailment of loans for generation and transmission projects, a sharp increase in REA interest rates charged to cooperatives, even the abolition of REA. It was said that the electric cooperatives should go to the banks and insurance companies and investment houses for their financing—should get it through "normal channels." Employees of the private utilities proceeded en masse to undermine the loyalty of electric cooperative members and induce them to vote to sell their systems to the utility combines. The complaints that the cooperatives are "tax free" was voiced even more stridently despite the fact that in many counties the electric cooperatives are among the very largest of all taxpayers.

The National Rural Electric Cooperative Association, which since 1942 has served the electric cooperatives as their national service federation and public-relations and legislative defender, and to which former Congressman Clyde T. Ellis has given such dynamic leadership, faced its severest test and challenge.

And all this came at a time of stress and change and hardship for American agriculture, when the number of farms was decreasing, when lines between farm and town and even city were becoming blurred, when 400,000 meters installed by electric cooperatives stood idle because there were no longer any people on those farms.

One wonders why all the criticism. It must be because people generally do not know the facts. Or do not think about them.

The United States has made money out of the rural electrification program. The cooperatives are well ahead of schedule on repayment of their debts. The interest rate—2 per cent—is ample to cover all costs of administering the program.

The cooperatives pay every kind of tax which their competitors pay and are, as has been said, in many cases among the chief contributors to the tax revenues of the states and counties where they are located. True, there is an exemption from federal income taxes for the electric cooperatives—an exemption which no other type of cooperative has. It is provided partly because electric cooperatives cannot serve any consumer unless he is a member of the cooperative. It is an exemption granted because the cooperatives must be organized as non-profit enterprises, all the earnings of which are the property of their members, not of the cooperative. Those members are liable for income-tax payments to the full extent that their incomes are increased or their costs of doing business decreased by the patronage refunds received from their cooperatives. Sometimes these are paid in cash. More often in "capital credits," which are certificates of ownership in the cooperative power systems, evidencing the equity in those systems in the hands of their members. By 1959 these members had built up an average equity ownership of about 17 per cent in the electric cooperatives of the nation. But this is still a long way from the 50-per-cent equity ownership which most lenders would demand as a condition of financing the mounting need for financing of these rapidly expanding cooperative utilities. Loans at even "normal" rates could hardly be expected.

Furthermore, the lower interest rates charged by REA are part of a contractual agreement required of the cooperatives. The lower rates are the other side of the coin that requires electric coops to provide full area coverage to all who need the service, regardless of cost and which shuts them out of markets of high customer concentration— indeed prevents them from offering service to any community of more than fifteen hundred population.

These are a different kind of American business institution—these electric cooperatives. They are entitled to a fair deal. They have brought light and power to farms and rural homes and schools and churches where there was no light or power before. They have made possible the decentralization of our industry into rural areas. They have opened up a vast new market for all sorts of electrical goods and services.

They have done a greater thing, for power is the life blood of modern economic life. Without it no industry or business, or city or town, can operate at all. Who controls the supply of power controls the nation.

Power should not be a monopoly in the hands of anyone—least of all a private empire.

Why, then, should the great utilities in whose hands is 85 per cent of all our power business inveigh with such vehemence and attack so cleverly and with so many resources the electric cooperatives whose share of total national business is comparatively very small indeed?

Is it not a matter of great pride to every thoughtful American that ours is a country where groups of almost bankrupt farmers could rise out of the Great Depression and build electric-power companies for their own use out of their good names and the method of cooperation and mutual aid? Should we not be glad that healthy competition has been injected into an otherwise monopoly-ridden industry by this fact? Is it not true that the only policy that can be defended in reference to an absolute necessity for all life and commerce is one that brings about abundant production and distribution at the lowest economically practicable cost? If so, then the electric cooperatives deserve the thanks and approbation of all Americans.

And is it not significant that the opposition to the electric cooperatives—as is true of other cooperatives as well—comes always from far away, never from the people in the areas where the coops live and serve, not even from the most conservative business people in those areas?

For they have seen a modern miracle of change and transformation. They have seen, as one Georgia rural mail carrier put it: "The countryside changed from a malaria-ridden, cotton-picking backwoods area to a modern farming section, where folks subscribe to daily newspapers, send their children to college, read by good light in the evening, and where the mother has time to be a mother."

One of the glories of the American system is that 4,500,000 farmers and rural people own part of the key industry of this great industrial nation. The story of rural electric cooperatives proves that our system can be made to work for the benefit of everyone. It proves more. It proves that the people *by their own efforts* can make it work that way. It proves that cooperation is good for our country— all our country, including the competitors of the cooperatives.

For the cooperatives showed that farmers *could* afford electricity *if it was offered to them on reasonable terms,* and thus opened a vast new market not only for their own services but for those of their competitors as well.

The handicaps and limitations under which the electric cooperatives operate are more than ample justification for both their interest rate and their tax status. But despite those handicaps and limitations, the electric coops have injected a new dynamic into what was largely a stagnant industry. They have prevented monopoly in that industry from causing technological unemployment to spread. The virulence of the attacks of their competitors is the best of proof that they are successful, significant, and permanent factors in the economic life of rural America.

The outlook for electric, as well as other cooperatives brightened markedly as the new president John F. Kennedy took office in 1961. For, in contrast to the outgoing administration, Mr. Kennedy and his appointees showed clear understanding of the needs, problems, and values of the electric cooperatives of the nation.

VI

MONOPOLISTIC POWER AND
THE HOPE OF FREEDOM

Much has been made, in postwar America, of the steady rise in living standards, the blurring of class distinctions, and a broader distribution of wealth, ownership and income. In the immediate postwar years there was substantial evidence that all three of these trends were strong. Factories surrounded by automobiles belonging to the workers are still one of the great American showpieces for foreign visitors. In other countries the automobiles would be bicycles—or nothing.

But while living standards continue to rise and stenographers continue to be indistinguishable from wealthy women in dress and appearance, the third boast is hardly borne out by the facts. Instead, economic power becomes more and more concentrated in fewer and fewer hands. More and more industries are falling under dominance of "big threes" or "big fours." Equity ownership of industries is effectively held by a tiny fraction of the population. And small business, *truly independent of the industrial giants,* has a more and more difficult time of it to survive.

In 1952 there were 3,750,000 families in the United States one or more of whose members owned one or more shares of corporation stock. After four years of a rather intensive drive to spread ownership and make a "people's capitalism" a partial reality, there were, in 1956, 4,500,000 families with stockholders in them. But this left some forty million families with no stock ownership whatsoever. Only about one family in ten shared ownership to even the extent of one share in any of the corporations of the United States.

By contrast, one family in every four owns one or more shares in one or more cooperative businesses. Cooperatives with about 2 per cent of the business of the country have made business ownership available to two and one-half times as many families as have all the registered corporations in the country with 85 per cent of the business.

Something to think about. Especially if we are in earnest about actually achieving a "people's capitalism."

A recent article in the *American Economic Review* by Victor Perlo pointed out that the Du Pont family owns $4 billion worth of corporation stock, the Rockefellers and the Mellons, $3 billion each. But *all* United States wage earners put together own less than $750 million worth of such stock.

From the 1929 crash until about 1949 there was a trend toward wider distribution of wealth and property. Then a reversal set in and by 1953 less than 2 per cent of the people owned 30 per cent of the nation's personal wealth. They owned 80 per cent of all corporate stock and virtually all state and local government bonds. These facts are from the National Bureau of Economic Research.

The Special Committee of the United States House of Representatives on Problems of Small Business found that in 1952 the 500 largest corporations in the country owned $51\frac{1}{2}$ per cent of all manufacturing assets. Only three years later, in 1955, the committee found this percentage had jumped to 57 per cent. The committee did a little projecting and came up with the sobering statement that if existing trends continued, these 500 firms would own all the factories in the United States by 1978.

With concentration of ownership goes concentration of control and of decision making. In March, 1959, the *Wall Street Journal* reported the president of Chrysler Corporation as saying that Chrysler's decision about making a small parkable automobile would depend on what General Motors and Ford decided to do. He did not say so, but the fact is that the *price* at which such a small car would be sold was also dependent on what General Motors did about pricing.

Once in a while a small businessman seems not to comprehend

how American business is supposed to be conducted under the new dispensation.

In 1957 a small baker who had a loan from the Small Business Administration decided to bid on the contract to furnish bread for one of the large army commissaries. Up to that time only four very large bakeries have ever gotten the contract. Their bids had always been identical, with one exception. They had always bid seventeen and a half cents on white bread and corresponding amounts on all other types of bread, except rye. Apparently they drew lots to see which one of them would bid one cent below the others on rye bread. The lowest one of the four naturally got the contract.

The small baker bid twelve and seven-tenths cents a loaf, which was way below the amount the Army had been paying. Immediately, however, one of the big bakeries proceeded to bid ten and a half cents, about a 40 per cent reduction under what all the big bakers had been bidding. It got the contract.

About 85 per cent of all research and development work in the United States today is carried on by only 375 of the largest companies.

And 94 per cent of all defense contracts go to the same group of giant concerns.

Monopoly marches not only in manufacturing but in other lines of business as well.

There were 387,000 retail food stores in the country in 1939 and only 279,000 in 1954, a 39 per cent decline. Furthermore, by 1954 6,000 of the 279,000 stores were making one-third of all the sales.

A member of the Federal Communications Commission informed the 1958 Public Relations Conference of the Cooperative League that only two television networks have 90 per cent of the viewing audience and that only eighteen New York City agencies handle 80 per cent of all radio and television advertising.

Competition among newspapers is almost a thing of the past. About fourteen hundred cities in the country have daily newspapers. But in less than three hundred of them are there even two separate and distinct companies or individuals owning and operating papers. In all the others a complete monopoly of public information exists so far as the press is concerned. Freedom of the press is reduced largely to the "freedom" of a very few individuals possessed of enough capital to own the press to say what they want to say. One of the most distinguished and universally respected members of the United States Senate, running for re-election to his third term in 1960, expected to have the support of no more than one or two newspapers out of hundreds in his state. He belongs to the political party that is not favored by the "power elite" of the nation. The largest city in this senator's home state has a normal Democratic majority of about two to one or three to one. But all of its four newspapers are stalwart Republican organizations, for the simple reason that their owners are Republicans. The press is not prejudiced. It does not have to be. It is simply the property—almost all of it—of people who have one point of view. And competition of varying ideas and points of view is virtually a thing of the past. The press conforms, and admonishes everybody else to do likewise.

Some of the results of this tremendous concentration of economic power are evident enough. *Fortune* magazine's annual survey of the 500 largest corporations shows their average rate of profit to be between 10 per cent and 12 per cent per year. In the first six months of 1959 United States Steel made a profit of 10 per cent on *sales* and 17 per cent on invested capital.

Not that profit making is a bad thing, but the average profits of small businesses are somewhere around one-fifth to one-tenth as large as those of the giants.

The reason is that the big companies are in position to "administratively determine" what the prices of their products and services are to be. In the summer of 1958 Nelson C. White, vice president of International Minerals and Chemical Corporation, put it this way: "No single one of industry's activities is so misunderstood as its pricing operations. It is essential that we meet criticism. It calls not so much for defense as for explanation. Each company uses pricing as a means of attaining its corporate objectives. The result is pricing by policy, by plan, and not by accident." And as noted in a previous chapter, one reads in a pamphlet issued by United States Steel Corporation and entitled *Steel and Inflation: Fact vs. Fiction*, that 88 per cent of all prices in present-day United States are administered prices.

"Administered prices" are prices that can be and are fixed by administrative decisions of managements of companies. This practice is possible only where the company in question has monopolistic control in its industry—usually along with three or four other huge companion companies. Administered prices bear no relationship to economic conditions in general nor to supply-and-demand situations. Ralph A. Young, research director for the Federal Reserve Board, commenting in early 1959 on increases in steel and automobile prices, succinctly said: "They don't make economic sense."

They don't.

Both steel and automobile prices were increased in 1959 despite the fact that supply was far in excess of demand. The steel industry at the time was operating at only about 50 per cent capacity. Automobile sales were far below expectations, yet prices were raised, not lowered.

All through the 1950's there was loud outcry about inflation and the danger to the buying power of the dollar. But few of those who viewed with such alarm had the courage to point out where the inflation came from.

It came straight out of monopolistic industrial power. There would have been no inflation of prices whatever in the 1950's had all our industries operated as the competitive ones did. Farm prices actually *fell* by 5 per cent, and so did textile prices from 1953 to 1958, to give two examples from industries which are still competitive. But meanwhile steel prices were increased 37 per cent; automobile and machinery prices were increased 22 per cent; tobacco prices were boosted 15 per cent; and the same was generally true of all industries where monopolistic control made administered pricing possible.

The result: We had an 8 per cent increase in the wholesale price index in those five years, despite the sharp decline in farm and some other prices.

Monopoly took its toll.

And monopoly takes another toll that is even more serious. Monopolistically placed industries now finance a great proportion of their expansion, not by selling stock but by what is called "internal financing," that is, using earnings to pay for new plants or to buy out competing businesses.

What this actually means is that both capital and labor in the monopolistic segment of our economy are refusing to pass on to the nation as a whole the benefits from increased technological efficiency. If they were doing so, they would either lower their prices or provide better products at the same prices. They would not be maintaining such exorbitant profit rates as to make possible the building of new plants and the purchase of whole businesses without the sale of new stock issues. They would not be charging consumers of their products the cost not only of those products but of the new factories they want to build in addition.

As long as such practices continue, technological unemployment will increase, the competitive industries such as agriculture will suffer, and the rate of growth of the American economy will lag.

Something has to be done. For as the Union Oil Company has been saying in recent institutional advertisements: "Any concentration of power in the hands of a few—whether they be businessmen, financiers, industrialists, government officials, or labor leaders—is inevitably at the expense of the majority of the people."

Something has to be done or economic freedom, economic enterprise, and economic growth in the United States are likely to be slowly strangled by the restrictions on production which are the inevitable handmaiden of administered pricing.

But what?

What can be done?

One alternative that must at least be considered is to let matters go along on their present course until the whole of our economic life is subject to monopolistic control by a few corporations, until price competition has completely disappeared, and until entry of new companies into all industries is as impossible as it is today in automobiles, steel, farm machinery, or chemicals. It seems almost incredible that the people of a country whose founders braved stormy seas to find freedom would permit such an end to freedom. But unless public lethargy changes to indignation pretty soon, this very result is altogether likely to take place.

Another alternative is actually to enforce the anti-trust laws. This has never yet been done since the Sherman Act was passed. To be effective, the laws would have to be amended so that a showing that monopolistic power does in fact exist in a certain industry would be sufficient to enable remedial action to be taken, regardless of how such power was acquired.

Then the very thorny question arises as to just what the remedial action could be. Could General Motors, General Electric, General Foods, or any of the other "Generals," be forcibly broken up? And if they were, would they *stay* broken up? Would the resulting smaller companies actually compete—in pricing especially?

Such questions are hard, indeed, to answer.

A wide variety of proposals have come from members of Congress who have taken the trouble to look at the facts about the spread of monopoly in our economy. One suggestion is to require prior announcement of price increases in basic industries. This might put some hesitation into the minds of men able to "administer" price increases at will. Another long-standing proposal—first advanced by Senator O'Mahoney of Wyoming—is for the licensing of all corporations doing interstate business by the federal government. This would make it possible to reveal facts more readily. But it would hardly, in itself, provide the answer as to how to act upon these facts.

The most logical and effective counteractive to the perils of monopoly is organization of consumer buying power. This has been accomplished to a sufficient extent in countries such as Sweden, so that no anti-trust laws are needed. The national interest in economic pricing, good quality, and, above all, in full production, is protected by consumer-owned cooperative businesses. Not only are they in position to bargain on reasonably equal terms with highly organized producers, such consumer-owned businesses are also able to enter manufacturing themselves, to supply their own cooperative stores, and to break the grip of monopoly by the most logical method of reintroducing effective competition. But this is the subject of a later chapter.

And meanwhile there is action which small business itself can take now and directly.

A couple of examples will make it plain.

A short time ago an earnest, thoughtful man in his late fifties came to the offices of the Cooperative League. He started out by saying: "The days of the small, independently owned business are numbered. I just don't know how much longer I can continue. Before many years all the businesses on Main Street in our smaller communities are going to be absentee owned by large national concerns."

The man who said these things to me in our Cooperative League offices was no radical. He was a successful owner and operator of a department store in an Illinois rural town. His business, he said, was still doing well, but he saw handwriting on the wall. And he didn't like what it said. He believed in local ownership of local business. He believed in healthy competition. He didn't want a national chain to swallow his business if he could help it.

There was one way he had discovered whereby this could be prevented. And prevented not only temporarily but for time to come.

That was why he had come to see the Cooperative League, why he had visited local cooperatives in southern Wisconsin and a regional wholesale cooperative in northern Illinois.

He wanted to turn his business into a cooperative. Because if he did, it would always have to be locally owned by local people in the town where it did business. Cooperative businesses, he recognized, are the one kind of business that can stand and live and keep their independence in the face of the drive for monopolistic economic power.

Already this gentleman had called together some of the influential citizens of his town and discussed his idea with them. They were interested, he said.

We assured him we'd come to help whenever he asked us to. He was provided with such of our literature as he felt might be useful. He left for home to talk further with his fellow townsmen and gauge their interest in buying his business as a cooperative and keeping its ownership at home. It will be good for his town if he succeeds.

To give just one other example among many that could be mentioned, a small manufacturer from Iowa came to see us one day to inquire about the organization of cooperative service businesses.

His reasons were these: He contended that in his particular line of manufacturing the small company was every bit as efficient as the big one. There was no problem about competing in the actual *manufacture* of the goods.

But in this day of national advertising—and even of advertising of national advertising!—it is, so said this man, utterly impossible for the small company to *market* its product in competition with the big one. It is impossible for the small company to afford national advertising or a huge sales force. Hence it cannot build acceptance of a brand name or develop market outlets satisfactorily in the present-day business world.

So what this man had in mind was a cooperative marketing and promotion agency which would belong to a number of manufacturers of the same product. Such an agency backed by the combined resources of several small manufacturers might be able to compete with the sales and promotion department of a large competitor. One brand name and designation might be agreed upon and market acceptance developed for the products of all the small manufacturers together.

Cooperation makes it possible for many small units to retain their basic independence but voluntarily to act together so their combined position in the economy will be competitive with that of huge concerns. The cooperatives are the "little man's" chance in a world of bigness.

Indeed a good many thousands, not to say millions, of those "little men" have actually taken that very chance. Independent grocers are one of the best examples. When you consider the tremendous competitive advantages of the national chains, you wonder how any independent one, two, or three store grocers survive at all.

But thus far, at least, thousands of them have survived.

How?

Donald P. Lloyd, manager of Associated Food Stores, Inc., a retailer-owned cooperative wholesale company in Salt Lake City, told a congressional committee about it in June, 1959. Here is part of what he said:

"Cooperative Food Distributors of America is a trade association, representing approximately twenty-seven thousand small business retailers who sell direct to the public. These retailers are the sole owners of approximately one hundred wholesale warehouses or units, known as retailer-owned wholesale grocery companies. While our yearly sales of dry groceries are in excess of seven billion dollars, nevertheless we are small business, that is, 27,000 small business organizations. Through our 100 wholesale houses we perform exactly the same functions as any wholesale grocery, with one exception. We are not in business to make a profit in our wholesaling functions. We are in business to get the benefit of mass purchasing power for our individual retailer members and the consuming public.

"Retail food and grocery stores of this country do a volume of about fifty billion dollars a year. Nearly two-thirds of this volume is done by individual store operators (those operating single stores or small chains). The other third (37 per cent actually) is done by chain stores (operations that have eleven or more stores). We believe it is generally conceded that individual operators in our business have been able to hold their position largely because of organizations like ours that have made it possible for relatively small stores to buy and sell on a competitive basis."

Mr. Lloyd pretty well tells the story. There can still be economic freedom, there can still be effective competition, there can still be a chance for the "little man" if the cooperative method of economic organization is used. Many small independent firms owning together their cooperative source of supply can stand in the market place against very large and powerful competitors indeed.

In 1954, the United States Department of Commerce reported, co-operative retailer-owned food wholesalers had sales of $1,300,000,-000, or 17.7 per cent of the total sales volume of general-line grocery wholesales.

And the trade publication, *Progressive Grocer,* estimates that co-operative grocery wholesales owned by independent retailers increased their sales by more than 200 per cent between 1948 and 1957.

Many consumer-owned cooperative food stores are members not only of their consumer-owned cooperative wholesale organizations, but also of the retailer-owned wholesale in their area.

Mutual aid is a good principle not only for individual persons but for small business firms as well.

So far as we can determine this type of cooperation first appeared in America in 1804 with the organization of a cooperative marketing association by some Connecticut dairy farmers.

One of the first comparable actions by other small businesses took place in 1887 when a few New York druggists met in a back room and decided to pool their orders for a barrel of Epsom salts. Even before that the Chicago Printers Cooperative Association was securing and assigning to its members book-and-job-printing business.

Hundreds of years earlier the Craftsmen's Guilds of the Middle Ages had many of the aspects of a modern cooperative. Certainly both have been rooted in the mutual-aid principle.

Today there are more than one hundred thousand independent grocers who are members and owners of cooperative wholesales. And more than eighty thousand druggists buy supplies cooperatively through their regional wholesale warehouses. Hardware merchants are not far behind, though for some reason the word "cooperative" seldom appears in the names of their thoroughly cooperative wholesale service agencies.

Most of the newspapers of the country are member-owners of the Associated Press, which is conducted as a pure cooperative on a non-profit basis and with no taxes whatever paid on any "profits."

All of this does not prevent newspapers which are themselves bene-fiting from their Associated Press cooperative from inveighing against any other group of people—farmers or consumers, for example—who presume to apply the same principles and practices toward meeting *their* needs and problems.

Indeed some of the members of cooperative hardware and drug cooperative wholesale agencies are vehement in their attacks on co-operatives of consumers and farmers.

But no one suggests that they stop using cooperative methods them-selves or that they change the proper tax status which these wholesales have always had.

Patronage refunds which cooperative businesses are liable to return to their customers are liabilities of those businesses, not assets or income to them. They are the property of the customer-owners and taxable against them to the extent that taxable income is involved. And this is true whether the cooperative is one of consumers, farmers, newspapers, grocers, druggists, or hardware merchants.

The degree of economic freedom and of healthy competition which still exists in the United States despite the march of "bigness" is due in no small part to the cooperative businesses which smaller enter-prises have organized for their own protection. This is a very-little known, but patently a very important, fact about our American economy today.

The largest, most important, and most disadvantaged group of small businessmen who suffer from monopolistic controls in our economy is the farmers. It is no wonder, therefore, that cooperative businesses are far more deeply rooted and of longer standing and of greater relative strength among farmers than in any other population group. The farmer's cooperatives enable him to gain some degree of economic bargaining power. Without cooperative ownership of related businesses, farmers as small individual producers have precisely no economic bargaining power whatsoever. Cooperatives *can,* if large and strong enough, restore some economic strength to the farmer's position.

More will be said of this in the following chapter.

But here one simple truth must be set forth. The metropolitan press never tires of complaining about the "subsidies" which are paid to farmers. And probably a majority of city dwellers believe that the rest of the economy is subsidizing the nation's farmers. In fact, the reverse is true. The really *big* subsidy is the other way around. If a family can buy food and textiles for less than they really ought to cost, it is then in position to pay more for automobiles and electricity than they ought to cost. The subsidy which the farmers contribute to most of the rest of the economy is far greater than any price support payments they may receive. In general farmers are selling their crops at below cost of production if *all* their costs are taken into account— return on investment, wages, salaries, depreciation, for example. And the fact that agriculture and the few other industries where competition still exists are forced to sell either below cost or at small margins is the basic reason why the "administered price" industries are able to exact inordinately high prices for their products. If the competitive industries such as agriculture did not receive so few consumers' dollars for their products, there simply would not be enough such dollars available to pay the very high prices for metal products, chemicals, tobacco, and the like. Not unless there were great monetary inflation.

The heavy price that farmers pay to provide this subsidy to General Motors *et alia* and the story of the measures taken by farmers to protect themselves are the subject of the next chapter.

VII

THE ACHILLES HEEL OF MODERN AMERICA

Through most of the history of mankind primary producers have been exploited largely because other people or firms have done all the buying and selling, manufacturing, and processing of primary products.

A relatively obvious way to end such exploitation is for primary producers to organize their own agencies to do their own buying and selling and at least some of the processing and manufacturing of their crops.

Farmers' cooperatives are agencies of this kind.

Abraham Lincoln's classic remark was: "No nation can continue to exist half slave and half free."

From the experience of the 1920's we should have learned that the American economy cannot continue to exist part prosperous and part depressed.

But we did not learn that.

After World War II we tried once again to see whether the rest of the population cannot enjoy prosperity while our agriculture and the people who work in it struggle in depression.

It never has worked.

It will not work now.

It should not work.

Every nation that has ever tried to make this unjust imbalance work has suffered disaster.

History does not record a single case of a nation, once great, which permitted deterioration of its farming life and loss of independence of its farm families and retained its greatness.

We shall be no exception.

The root of the so-called "farm problem" is this: Each farm operator is compelled, in trying to support his family, to do the very act which, done by all farmers, brings about disaster to agriculture generally. That act is to increase production just as much as possible.

The lower the price goes per unit, the greater the pressure on each farmer to produce more units. When all farmers do this the result is further depression of prices. This, in turn, brings about even greater pressure for more production. And the vicious circle is complete.

Even all this might not spell approaching disaster for our agriculture were it not for the fact that hardly any of the rest of our economy operates under the same conditions. If the businesses to which farmers sell were truly competitive and actually free to bid for the farmers' crops, the price might, sometimes at least, go up. And if effective competition existed among firms selling to farmers, then farm costs might be expected to go down. If there were not monopolistic bottlenecks, "economic tollgates," between the farmer and the consumer, the low prices received by farmers would be reflected in lower prices for food for consumers, and a broadening of the market. But this does not take place either. All that happens is that the profit margins of a few processors and "branders" and packagers become more and more swollen.

Individually the farmer is helpless in the present-day economy of the United States. Only if farmers join and act together can they possibly hope to gain a measure of economic bargaining power and some hope of escaping ultimate ruin.

That is why farmers have formed cooperatives. They began a long time ago. The first farmers' marketing cooperative of which we have record was organized by dairy farmers in the Connecticut River Valley in 1804.

In the latter half of the nineteenth century the Grangers spearheaded formation of both marketing and consumer cooperatives among distressed farmers on the prairies and elsewhere. At least one of these is still in business—at Cadmus, Kansas.

It was not until the turn of the century, however, that cooperatives for the marketing of agricultural crops began to be developed on a large scale. And it was a quarter century later before the cooperatives which provide necessary farm and home supplies began their substantial growth.

The marketing cooperatives were formed to protect farmers against the harsh effects of the speculative market. Before the coming of the cooperatives the farmer was forced to sell his crop—frequently to but one or two available buyers—at whatever price the buyer was willing to pay and under whatever conditions the buyer laid down. The larger the crop, the lower the return. Farmers had no way of storing their crops, or avoiding a temporarily glutted market. They received none of the advantages of rises in prices which so frequently took place after the crop had been purchased by middlemen or processors. They needed their own storage facilities and marketing agencies. Marketing cooperatives were the result.

Marketing cooperatives have brought better and far more stable prices to farmers, and it is doubtful that costs to consumers have been increased as a result. What has happened has been that a larger share of the consumer's dollar has found its way back to the farmers and the rural community than would otherwise have been the case. Furthermore, the marketing cooperatives have helped to improve the quality of food products reaching the consumer. They have stressed grading and labeling and by this means have raised standards of the food-distribution system all along the line. A hundred trade names of cooperatively marketed farm products—such as oranges, milk, raisins, potatoes, eggs, poultry, butter, and cheese, to mention only a few—stand today for dependable quality wherever American consumers find them.

There is a natural difference in viewpoint between marketing cooperatives and consumer cooperatives. Practically all the enterprises discussed in this volume are essentially consumer cooperatives. The farmers' marketing cooperatives and the small businessmen's cooperatives are the main exceptions. Consumer cooperatives are established by their members to *supply themselves* as abundantly as possible with some kind of goods or services. The larger the volume of general production and distribution and the greater the number of its patrons, the better for the consumer cooperative. Marketing cooperatives, however, exist to *sell* their members' products to other people. From their viewpoint there *can* be too many producers of that product and more production than can be readily marketed in orderly fashion.

In the past—though far less so today—this has probably been the reason why some marketing cooperatives have been reluctant to identify themselves closely with other cooperatives. But it is no reason to regard marketing cooperatives as "monopolistic" enterprises or as anything but desirable institutions. Like labor unions, they enable large groups of producers, who individually would be economically helpless, to protect to some degree their incomes, living standards, and purchasing power.

There are nearly seven thousand marketing cooperatives in the United States. They market annually for their farmer members fourteen major categories of products with a total value, after allowing for duplication, of between $9 and $10 billion. About a quarter of all United States farm products are handled by marketing cooperatives at one or more stages in their progress from farm to consumer's table.

Some dairy and poultry products and some fresh fruits and their by-products leave the cooperative ready for the consumer. But a negligible amount of even these products is sold directly to consumers by farmers' cooperative marketing agencies.

The historic function of marketing cooperatives has been to gather the products of their members in a local area and to sell them in an orderly fashion but in their raw state. As packaging and processing have been added to this basic function, and as local marketing cooperatives have become federated for regional or national marketing, the "spread" between the price received by farmers and that paid by consumers has been narrowed and the farmer has received a larger percentage of the consumers' dollar.

Dairy products account for about one-third of all cooperative marketing. The 1958–9 value of dairy products marketed through some 2,000 cooperatives ran close to $3 billion a year. In some cases products are sold and delivered directly to consumers or at least to retail stores. The bulk of the dairy products marketed by cooperatives, however, is still sold to large-scale dealers and processors. The dairy cooperatives are federated nationally in the National Milk Producers' Federation. In recent years there has been increasing discussion of nationwide cooperative marketing of dairy products.

Second in point of value of products marketed cooperatively are grain and soybeans, amounting to about $2 billion a year. Some soybean products are sold to farm supply cooperatives. And most of the grain is marketed by regional cooperatives—terminal elevators— with which most of the 2,700 local cooperative elevators are affiliated. As yet the grain cooperatives do comparatively little processing. Most of the grain-marketing cooperatives are affiliated with the National Federation of Grain Cooperatives with Washington, D.C., headquarters.

Livestock and livestock products sold for farmers through cooperatives have an annual value of about $1.6 billion; fruits and vegetables, about $1 billion; cotton and its products, over $400 million; poultry and poultry products, $350 million. In all these cases cooperatives are the best reliance the farmer has in securing a fair and proper grading of his crops for both better quality and better prices. Some fruit and vegetable marketing cooperatives are factors of prime importance in both regional and national markets.

Measured by dollar volume of business, the agricultural marketing cooperatives are by far the largest single type of cooperative business in the United States. But the basic problems of American farmers remain unsolved. What would happen, however, if farmer-owned cooperative businesses processed, packaged, advertised, and sold through nationwide marketing organizations can only be surmised. Certainly the benefits and protections would be vastly greater.

And if a considerable proportion of farm crops could be sold directly by farmer-owned enterprises to consumer-owned ones, the "spread" between what farmers receive and what consumers pay would amount simply to the costs of processing, transportation, and sale.

Imagination and capital put together in proper mixture could still, through cooperation, change the outlook for the American farmer.

While cooperative marketing has not yet been fully effective in protecting farmers with fair prices when they sell their crops, the farm-supply cooperatives have demonstrated a remarkable ability to reduce farmers' costs of production and to give them real bargaining power as purchasers of necessary farm and household supplies.

In many respects the sheet anchor of American cooperative development is the 4,300 farm-supply and rural "general-store" cooperatives found in most Midwestern towns and in many other parts of the country.

With a membership of more than 3,500,000 in 1959 and a business volume of about $2.4 billion, these cooperatives supply 20 to 25 per cent of the major farm and home needs of America's rural population. They enable farmers to control and reduce production costs.

A typical cooperative of this type will do business in an area covering all or a major part of a county. It will operate a general store, a feed, seed, and fertilizer depot, a petroleum bulk plant and filling station, and frequently a farm-machinery display room, and a coalyard. Located generally in the principal trading center, it may operate branches in some of the smaller outlying communities. In growing numbers these stores serve some non-farm people.

Linked with strong state or regional wholesale cooperatives, many of these 4,000 rural cooperatives provide an assured source of high-analysis fertilizer, dependable good-quality seeds and feed, hardware, farm machinery, building supplies and paint, electrical appliances, petroleum products and fuels, insecticides and sprays, and often groceries, clothing, and many other items. About a quarter of the mixed feeds, about a fifth of the fertilizer, and about 20 per cent of the petroleum used on farms is supplied by these cooperatives.

Most of these commodities are "high-margin" items, so the cooperatives have been able to show fairly consistent records of paying patronage refunds and of keeping prices down for the benefit of rural people. Since their expansion began in the late twenties, the rural supply cooperatives have been able to build up a substantial volume of retail and wholesale business. Significantly, their business has increased fastest in periods of "hard times."

In practically every section of the country retail farm supply and rural consumer cooperatives own or are affiliated with regional wholesale and production cooperatives.

Among the more important of these regionals are: Cooperative Grange League Federation, Ithaca, New York; Southern States Cooperative, Richmond, Virginia; Eastern States Farmers' Exchange, West Springfield, Massachusetts; Midland Cooperatives, Inc., Minneapolis, Minnesota; Consumers' Cooperative Association, Kansas City, Missouri; Illinois Farm Supply Co., Bloomington, Illinois; Indiana Farm Bureau Cooperative Association, Indianapolis, Indiana; Farmers' Union Central Exchange, St. Paul, Minnesota; Farm Bureau Cooperative Association, Columbus, Ohio; Farmers' Cooperative Exchange, Raleigh, North Carolina; Missouri Farmers' Association; Washington Cooperative Farmers' Association; Pennsylvania Farm Bureau Cooperative Association; Central Cooperatives, Inc., Superior, Wisconsin; Pacific Supply Cooperative, Walla Walla, Washington; Fruit Growers' Supply Co., Los Angeles, California; Farm Bureau Services, Lansing, Michigan; Tennessee Farmers' Cooperative; Farmers' Union State Exchange, Omaha, Nebraska; and Utah Cooperative Association.

These regional wholesale cooperatives supply their member retail associations with most of their needs for fertilizers, stock feed, seeds, auto supplies, hardware, petroleum products, and insecticides. Increasingly, though not yet to the extent that the times demand, these things are produced and manufactured by regional cooperatives in their own plants or in plants jointly owned by several regionals. More than one hundred fertilizer plants, for example, are operated by these cooperatives. There are more than two thousand cooperatively owned oil wells and ten coop refineries.

By entering production, cooperatives have been able to provide their patrons an assured, full source of supply of commodities often difficult or impossible to obtain. Moreover, far greater savings in cost can be made for cooperative patrons through production activities than are possible through retailing and wholesaling alone. Cooperatives engaged in production can provide their members more substantial patronage refunds and give them more property ownership than would otherwise be possible by simple merchandising of products produced elsewhere. Howard A. Cowden, founder and president of Consumers' Cooperative Association, largest of regional supply wholesales, has stated that for every dollar of savings made for its patrons through wholesaling, CCA has been able to make a nineteen-dollar saving on the commodities produced in its own factories.

Two national wholesale supply cooperatives are owned by certain of the regionals in the United States and Canada. These are United Cooperatives in Alliance, Ohio, and National Cooperatives in Albert Lea, Minnesota. National Cooperatives manufactures milking machines and hot-water heaters as well as carrying on its procurement and distribution functions.

Most farm-supply regionals are members of the American Institute of Cooperation and the National Council of Farmer Cooperatives. Many are members of the Cooperative League of the United States and of state associations and councils of cooperatives.

Outstanding needs of farm-supply cooperatives, both retail and regional, which became clear during the "awakening fifties," were these:

1. Further modernization and expansion of services and business volume, including in many cases the development of patronage from non-farm or part-time farm or suburban people;
2. Member education to bring about greater member participation, since this is the unique business asset of cooperative enterprise;
3. Further development of production, back to basic raw materials;
4. Integration and in some cases merger of operations to achieve greater efficiency and economic strength and to add new needed services to farmers;
5. Adequate sources of financing on favorable terms to carry out these objectives and meet these needs. Banks for cooperatives and cooperative insurance companies can supply some of this need. It is apparent, however, that additional sources of capital, to finance new, integrated and expanding services, are also needed.

Steps to that end were under discussion as the 1960's opened.

For the same problems and elements of injustice which caused farmers to form their cooperatives a half and a quarter century before appeared in aggravated form in the decade of the 1950's.

The numbers of purchasers of farm products declined sharply. By 1960 seventeen huge buyers made 80 per cent of all purchases of groceries and meats in the New York Market. Ten buyers controlled the Seattle markets, eight the ones in Portland, fewer still in Omaha. In 1948 independent grocers handled 50 per cent of the nation's food, the chains, 29 per cent. Ten years later the chains were up to 38 per cent, the independents down to 30 per cent. In 1960 the big packers, Swift, Armour, and Cudahy, asked federal court permission to open and operate retail food stores.

As monopolistic controls were being extended more and more broadly and into more and more industries, the plight of those segments of the economy which remained competitive became more and more serious.

This was the trouble with small business.

It was the trouble in agriculture.

In a sentence: Most of United States industry, including nearly all of it with which farmers have direct leadings, has become monopolistic in character. Price competition is a thing of the past and prices for industrial products which farmers must buy are "administered" upward quite regardless of economic conditions, including supply-and-demand relationships. Production is controlled in order to protect the price.

In contrast, agriculture remains a competitive business. No one among the 4,000,000 farmers of the nation can possibly affect total volume of supply to any measurable extent. All of them know this. Furthermore, farmers, like other people, have to make a living. The wherewithal for that purpose is measured by the number of units sold times the price. The lower the unit price, the harder farmers necessarily will try to produce more units. Lower prices for farm products do *not* tend to reduce, but rather to increase, the so-called "surplus." Obviously, too, farmers have to plant and plan production many months before harvest. They cannot control production to maintain price levels, and probably wouldn't even if they could.

Hence, prices received by farmers tend downward; prices paid by farmers tend upward. Prices received by farmers are the result of full production sold at whatever price the market will bring. Prices paid by farmers are mostly fixed—largely by administrative action.

This is why the parity index hovers around 80—which means agriculture suffers a chronic loss and injustice of about 20 per cent of the share of national income to which it is entitled. It is why, between 1947 and 1957, the prices of industrial products rose 26 per cent while farm prices *fell* 5 per cent. And this despite the fact that production per man-hour was going up 90 per cent in agriculture compared to only 24 per cent for all non-farm industry. The benefits of greater technological efficiency have been passed on to buyers by agriculture. Had this also been done by other industries including those with which farmers deal, the parity index would have been 100 or thereabouts and farmers would have little legitimate complaint. Instead, in November, 1959, the ratio between prices received by farmers for their crops and prices paid by them for supplies and services dropped to 77, the lowest point since 1940.

In general, agriculture in the United States is conducted on a full-production, market-determined-price basis. Except where price-support programs come into play, farmers take for their abundant crops whatever the market will bring. This full-production at freely determined prices for consumers is the basis, and the only basis, on which, in a free economy, we can expect to build full employment, adequate growth, and general price stability. Because so much of our economy has been allowed to become monopolistic, farmers suffer economically for the very reason that they operate in the manner best calculated to serve the nation's best long-run interest.

For unless, as technological progress continues, the benefits are passed on to the nation as a whole, as consumers, there cannot take place a broadening of the market nor enough expansion of production to prevent mass technological unemployment from becoming rampant.

This simply is not happening in most United States industry. And to compound the tragedy of our agriculture, it is not even happening with respect to the ultimate *consumers* of farm products. Only the middleman processors and marketers of farm products get the benefit of the low prices farmers receive. Thus by taking lower prices, farmers do *not* build for themselves a broader market. They only line the pockets of processors and marketers of food products. Costs of food to consumers go right on up. Between 1950 and 1958 the cost of food to the average family went up $122. But farmers received $12.00 *less* for this food in 1958 than they had eight years before. Processors and middlemen got $134 more. Farmers' share of the consumers' dollar spent for food dropped to thirty-eight cents in 1959. Middlemen got the other sixty-two cents. And the outlook was for a continuance of the same trends.

Furthermore, United States Department of Agriculture statistics showed that whereas the retail market value of farm crops sold domestically went up from $42.8 billion in 1951 to $51 billion in 1959, the gross payments to farmers were actually $200 million less in 1959 than in 1951. But the "marketing charges" between the farm and the retail store rose from $22.8 billion in 1951 to $31.2 billion in 1959.

Little wonder there were 3,900,000 fewer people living on farms in 1959 than there were in 1950.

Let's take one state as an example to see a little more exactly what the plight of American agriculture is.

Minnesota's farms are among the most productive in the world. No finer agricultural soil exists than the band of level land that stretches across southern Minnesota and northern Iowa and through the Red River Valley of North Dakota and northwestern Minnesota.

To find out the facts about Minnesota's agriculture, her governor, Orville L. Freeman, later to become Secretary of Agriculture in the Kennedy Administration, appointed a special study commission.

These facts are revealing and alarming. They ought to make people with a sense of justice deeply angry.

For total farm production in Minnesota has been increasing at the rate of 9 per cent a year since 1932—more than twice the rate of increase of industrial production in the nation. Moreover, this was *not* because of an increase in corporation farming. Quite the contrary. The percentage of family-type farms increased from 61 per cent in 1939 to 67 per cent in 1956. Average total investment per farm increased from $10,000 in 1939 to $30,000 in 1956.

In the year 1955, 63 per cent of Minnesota farm operators had incomes of less than $2,000. Average per-capita farm income in Minnesota is only 43 per cent of average per-capita income of urban people.

In plain words, although they are investing three times as much in their business and producing at an almost unbelievably increasing rate, farm families in one of America's richest agricultural states receive on the average considerably less than half as much as urban families do. Why?

The fundamental reason, as should be plain by now, is that farmers as individuals simply do not possess enough economic bargaining power either when they sell or when they buy. And the only method of gaining such economic bargaining power that has thus far proved really dependable has been the organization of cooperatives.

But the coops just are not large enough or strong enough as yet to meet the problem.

The farmers' cooperatives have accomplished a great deal. Controlling only about 20 per cent of the fertilizer business, farmers' cooperatives have shown that they can compete successfully with giant chemical companies. The result? While chemical prices generally rose 4 per cent from 1953 to 1958, fertilizer prices, owing largely to coop competition, actually fell 2½ per cent. And from farm electricity, credit, petroleum, insurance, similar examples can be given of the effectiveness of the competition of cooperatives in reducing farm costs and adding to farm income part of the profits of related industries.

But what cooperatives *could* do for American agriculture if they were to achieve a very substantial growth can be shown by the following facts and figures:

Let's take 1955, about an average year for the postwar period. Let's also take one Middle Western state where a good pattern of cooperatives exists. The county cooperatives owned by the farmers in turn own the statewide wholesale and production cooperative. Farmers thus produce and refine part of the petroleum products they need; produce, mix, and distribute part of the feed and fertilizer they use; and market and, to an extent, process the poultry products and grain they sell. In 1955 the return in patronage refunds to farmers on the supplies obtained through this cooperative system was 6 per cent. And the increase in income from the products marketed cooperatively over what that return would otherwise have been was 2.7 per cent.

Now if *all* farmers had been owners of cooperative businesses like these in 1955 and had used their services fully—which, of course, was very, very far from the case—but if it had been the case, then

$800 million would have been added to farmers' incomes from co-operative marketing and $1,800,000,000 would have been subtracted from their costs as a result of cooperative farm-supply business. Farmers' net income in that year would have been 17.8 per cent more than the $11 billion which it was.

If anyone sincerely wants to find a way to restore health to American agriculture without dependence on government action, here is where he can find it. But he will have to be willing to encourage in every proper way the rapid growth and more effective integration of the farmer-owned cooperatives. And he will have to do some new thinking about consumption standards in an age of abundant production.

One kind of expansion of business of farm-supply cooperatives that was already taking place in the late 1950's grew out of the economic and sociological changes then taking place in the American population. Wise managers and boards of directors were actively seeking the patronage of suburbanites and part-time farmers. They had to. The case of a "farm-supply" cooperative near Milwaukee is typical. Only a few years before, this cooperative was surrounded by an important agricultural area. As the cities spread, they swallowed farms. They also produced families whose need for fuel oil, automobile supplies, hardware, tools—even seeds and fertilizers—was only somewhat less than that of farmers. The cooperative went out after this business. And got it. The cooperative continued to flourish as it could not possibly have done had it continued to limit its business to full-time farm producers. In the process it gave up any opportunity it might have had to qualify for the one remaining special tax consideration—exemption of money used to pay dividends on shares—which some purely agricultural cooperatives were still eligible for. It also gave up its opportunity to borrow from the Banks for Cooperatives, described in Chapter ten, which can at present lend only to cooperatives a high percentage of whose business is with full-time farm producers. But it was worth these sacrifices to stay in business, and to achieve steady, substantial growth.

The total business of producing, processing, packaging, and delivering food to consumers is a very prosperous one. Every part of it is prosperous except farm production itself. Farmers need to get into the prosperous parts of the food business. They need to own a segment of the prosperous parts of the food business themselves. There is a way to do this, as we have seen. Let us examine how that method, the cooperative one, can deal with the basic causes of our farmers' problems.

There are three basic causes of the present distress of American agriculture. The first is related to the way our agriculture is organized —or rather the way it isn't organized. The other two have to do with the market for farm products.

First, American agriculture lacks rational vertical integration. It has some of this, but not enough.

Steel companies use a lot of coal, so they go out and buy and own and operate coal mines. Automobile companies use a lot of steel, so they buy and own steel mills and iron mines. Farmers need feed and seed, and electricity and credit—among other things. There is no more reason for steel companies to own coal mines than for farmers to own oil wells, fertilizer plants, electric systems, and banks. But the only way farmers can do it is through cooperatives. If we are going to continue to permit vertical integration of industry, which we almost certainly are, then if we are in earnest about solving the problem of agriculture, we must develop as rapidly as possible effective vertical integration for agriculture.

Some integration has taken place already. One kind has been carried on by agencies outside agriculture which have integrated the farmer into their operations. Feed companies are the outstanding example so far. But processing corporations and chain stores are likely agents as well. The results of this sort of integration have been ruinously low prices for the farm products involved—broilers, as an instance—and the reduction of the farmer to the status of a wage worker with no source of income except that allowed for prescribed routine operations.

The other kind of integration is the best hope of restoring prosperity to agriculture, of increasing farmers' incomes, of making possible the survival of the American pattern of rural living. This second kind of integration takes place through the organization of cooperative businesses by farmers whereby they themselves can own a portion of the businesses related to agricultural production, either as suppliers or as processors and marketers. The principle of cooperation is applied to enable a large number of weak economic bargaining units to become strong, by joining together in mutual aid of one another. Thus it becomes possible for farmers to add a small percentage of the earnings of the very prosperous petroleum industry to their incomes by the simple process of owning some of the businesses which supply farmers with petroleum products. It becomes possible for farmers through their cooperatives to own and operate part of the fertilizer business and to run it for the benefit of farmers—at full production at the lowest economically sound cost. The result of this particular operation has been that whereas between 1953 and 1958 prices paid by farmers for all inputs for their farms went up 5 per cent, costs for fertilizer went *down* 2½ per cent. This was because about 25 per cent of the fertilizer business is cooperatively owned by the people who use the fertilizer.

Cooperative ownership by farmers of part of the industries that supply farm inputs gives to farmers some degree of control over their costs of operation. Such cooperative action by farmers enables them to gain a degree of economic bargaining power without which their cause is quite hopeless in the kind of economy we have today.

To be effective, this integration has to reach back to primary sources of supply, such as basic fertilizer ingredients, electric-power generation, and crude petroleum.

Loans at the lowest possible rate of interest ought to be made available to any cooperative willing to move toward greater economic strength for American agriculture along these lines.

Expansion of cooperatives enabling farmers to buy and manufacture for themselves the supplies and services their operations require will not only reduce costs of production but will add to the income of agriculture some of the earnings from these related industries.

The other field in which these same results can be obtained is in enabling agricultural primary producers to process, package, promote, distribute, and sell direct to consumers their farm products while still owned by farmers. Here we come to the second major cause of the problem faced by our agriculture. That cause is that when prices received by farmers go down, the prices consumers pay for the same products do *not* go down but frequently rise instead.

Almost one-fourth of all farm crops are marketed through co-operative marketing associations. But a real approach to a solution of the so-called farm problem will come only as farmers begin to share with consumers in both income from and control over the processing, packaging, and distribution of food products. Were a portion of farm products processed, packaged, and distributed from farm to consumer's table by businesses cooperatively owned by either farmers, consumers, or both, the situation where low farm prices are not reflected in lower costs to consumers could be cured. The competition of such cooperative businesses would result either in better incomes to farmers or lower costs to consumers, or probably both. A yardstick of cooperatively owned enterprises which could carry raw products clear through to the consumer's table under ownership of farmers or consumers would bring about direct dealing between farmers and consumers. And this would mean that if consumers paid higher prices this would result in bolstering agricultural income; and that if farmers' prices fell, the market for their products would actually be expanded because prices paid by consumers would go down. Meanwhile, again, a portion of the earnings of businesses related to and dependent on agriculture would be added to the income of rural America, thus restoring economic balance and improving general economic health.

Practically everybody is suggesting decentralization of industry, establishment of more small industries in rural areas, as a practical answer to the agricultural problem. But few of them include in their suggestions the one feature whereby such decentralization would contribute toward a basic, lasting solution.

That feature is local ownership, by farmers and rural people, of these industries. This means cooperative ownership. And it should extend not only to fertilizer and petroleum and electric systems, not only to marketing agencies, but also to processing and packaging plants. If one reason for the big spread between prices received by farmers and prices paid by consumers is the cost of processing and packaging, then one answer to it is for processing and packaging plants to be owned by cooperatives of farmers and/or consumers.

If there were this kind of decentralization of industries related to agriculture under cooperative ownership by farmers, then indeed there would be another basic step taken toward solving the farm problem.

The "farm problem" will never be solved as long as it is considered as a problem related only to the farm itself. Especially not if farmers are simply told to try to make a "free market" work in agriculture when no such "free market" is at work anywhere else. The problem is a problem for all rural America. And one basic solution of it is rural, local ownership, through cooperatives of industries intimately related to agriculture and the adding of that income to the income of agriculture.

Such a solution involves neither dependence on government nor the pushing of smaller farmers off the land, nor attempts at artificial reduction of production. The cooperative solution has no minus factors in it.

The third basic cause of agricultural distress is our refusal to think in terms of abundant production *and consumption*.

Instead, we insist upon "thinking" in 1890 terms about the 1960 world.

It won't work.

American farmers are geared both technologically and psychologically to produce an abundance. Nothing probably is going to change this.

What can be and must be changed are certain habits of thinking. Some people—in fact, a good many people—still retain the idea that it is good for other people's character if they are somewhat hungry now and then.

There is no doubt that privation and sacrifice develop character—when they are necessary. If there is not enough to go around, then the finest people are the ones who deny themselves in order to leave more for others.

But it is an entirely different matter to insist that other people be in want when there is or could be enough for all.

In the May 22, 1960, issue of the New York *Times* there was hidden away in the inside pages an article that indicated a break in the old pattern of scarcity thinking. The article was headlined "Wheat Glut Held Fortunate Now." Instead of the weeping and wailing about the high crimes and misdemeanors of wheat farmers in producing so efficiently and creating such an "awful problem" here, the *Times* special writer J. H. Carmichel had this, in part, to say:

The harvesting of another bumper wheat crop in the United States is just getting under way. At a time when the international political situation appears to be approaching a crisis this may prove to be most fortunate to the free world.

With the carry-over from other crops, the supply of wheat in the United States for the next season, which starts on July 1, promises to exceed 2,500,000,000 bushels, the largest amount ever held by this or any other nation. Representing some four times the quantity that will be needed for home consumption in the United States before the 1961 crop is harvested, this record supply gives added assurance to the free world of necessary food in an emergency.

At the same time, the surplus may act as a deterrent to any group considering waging war against the free world. Although warfare may have been changed because of nuclear weapons, a nation or group of nations would be most hesitant in going to war against a nation with an assured supply of food for years.

Peculiarly, this record supply of wheat was not wanted by this country. The Government has restricted the acreage to be seeded to wheat for years. But research and technological development have steadily increased the yield of wheat to an acre. As a result, this year's crop, which is expected to be about 1,225,000,000 bushels, will be produced from about 62,500,000 acres. In 1939, when World War II started in Europe, American farmers produced only 740,000,000 bushels on virtually a similar number of acres.

Another factor in the present international situation is that the communist world has not been nearly so successful in the production of wheat. Despite the desperate efforts to increase production, recent reports indicate a short crop in the Soviet Union this year as well as in Poland and in one or two of the other satellite nations. A few years ago Russia had to import wheat to supplement local supplies, and observers in the trade are confident that some foreign purchases by the Soviet Union may be necessary this year.

With its record supplies the United States is encouraging the sale of wheat to other nations in the free world. Only recently the United States Government signed an agreement with India through which 588,000,000 bushels of wheat would go to that country over a four-year period. This would be at the rate of 147,000,000 bushels a year and would be paid for in Indian currency.

There have been reports that similar deals are pending with other nations, one of which is Pakistan. Many nations have insufficient foreign exchange to pay for wheat to be used largely as a reserve. Such nations, by paying for the wheat in their own currencies, are aiding their economy instead of weakening it, for the funds received by the United States Government are in turn loaned to the governments buying the wheat to carry through various projects.

Are we beginning to realize that nothing is really "surplus," much less the staple food of all mankind, so long as there is unmet human need for it? The early actions of the Kennedy Administration seemed to indicate so.

We have to learn to think in terms of distribution and consumption of an abundance of food and fiber. The Wallace-Homestead poll of farmers recently showed that farmers are already doing this. In this poll farmers were asked which of six so-called "farm" programs they would most favor. Fifty-three per cent of them put at the top of their list the following measure: "Make the school lunch program reach twice as many children as now." Forty-one per cent said the same should be done with the special school milk program, and 38 per cent proposed adoption of a food-stamp plan to put food surpluses within reach of needy people. These three measures led all others by a very substantial margin. No other proposal received support from more than 29 per cent of the farmers answering the poll.

The fact is that if all the 8 million United States families whose incomes are less than two thousand dollars a year had had adequate diets, their added consumption would have equaled all the so-called food "surpluses" of the three years, 1957–1959.

And what about the 1 billion people in the rest of the world who are downright hungry every day? Obviously the United States cannot sprinkle its agricultural surpluses over other countries just to be rid of them. It is no simple matter even to give food away—and not always even wise. But it does not seem beyond reason to believe that with chronic hunger on the one hand and chronic surpluses on the other some rational plan of bringing the two together through some world food plan could be devised.

But it won't be done until we start preferring abundant production and consumption—and learning to live with them—instead of apparently preferring an artificial scarcity. Especially since attempts to impose artificial scarcity on United States agriculture have never succeeded, and probably never will.

The cooperative method of attacking the problems of our agriculture could, if broadly enough applied, render such attempts largely unnecessary. Especially so, if we conceive cooperation in its broader meaning—that of working with people all around the world for the relief of human need.

So clear are the sociological and moral values in the cooperative approach to solution of the problems of farmers that the churches of the nation began at mid-century to advocate this approach in forthright fashion. On June 4, 1958, the General Board of the National Council of Churches of Christ in the United States adopted a statement entitled "Ethical Goals for Agricultural Policy." In that statement the following paragraph appeared:

The encouragement of voluntary association, cooperation, and mutual aid among farm people. Christian tradition has always emphasized mutual aid and cooperation as practical expressions of the command to love God and neighbor. One of the finest things farmers have done has been to associate themselves together in voluntary organizations for mutual aid and cooperation. Such associations should be encouraged, with the opportunity it provides for character growth through independent judgment, decision-making, responsibility-bearing, and the like. The churches should encourage full membership participation in such organizations of mutual aid and cooperation as a genuine contribution to both Christian and democratic ideals for society.

In 1960 the National Catholic Rural Life Conference made of the October issue of its official magazine *Catholic Rural Life* a special supplement entirely devoted to cooperatives and their value to the farm family and to rural life generally. In the lead article of this special issue the Most Reverend Leo A. Pursley, bishop of Fort Wayne–South Bend, wrote this paragraph:

The solidarity of the human race and the organic structure of society give rise to the principle of social justice, according to which each individual must do his part to promote the common good. Through cooperatives we can avoid handicapping one another by unrestrained and unjust competition. We can put into practice the plan of life intended by our Maker. The cooperative movement takes its origin from the assumption that all classes are bound together, that the interest of one class is the interest of all, that no class can prosper unless the others do. Cooperatives help diffuse the ownership of things among a greater number of people. Ownership brings with it responsibility and stability. Thus, cooperatives become a bulwark of Christianity and democracy, a means of strengthening the solidarity of the race and the dignity of the individual.

VIII

THE PEOPLE IN THE OIL BUSINESS

There was a time when emphasis in the oil business was on production, exploration, and control of crude oil. But today, with some 85 per cent of all known crude reserves in the hands of the major companies, and with world production in excess of demand, the drive is to control marketing outlets. Without such outlets, independent producers and refiners are going out of business.

Nineteen hundred and fifty-seven saw fourteen smaller marketing companies merged with, or acquired by, larger integrated companies. In 1958 the number was eight. And in 1959 no less than thirty-six smaller firms disappeared by the same route.

As 1960 dawned people on the inside of the oil business predicted that the days of independent marketers as well as the days of independent producers and refiners were indeed numbered. Fancy prices were being offered by the majors for the properties and good will of established marketing concerns. Names have seldom been changed. The consumer may think he is buying from an "independent" dealer, but the chances are increasing each month that he is actually patronizing an outlet of a major company. Concentration in the oil business marches on.

A prominent Texas oil banker was quoted by *Petroleum Week* (November 6, 1959) to the following effect:

Not too many independent operators realized it at the time, and some still don't, but the instituting of proration actually gives all the crude market to the majors. Compare oil and gas producers today. The gas producer has a contract. In most cases that contract specifies a minimum take and a firm price, and it usually runs for twenty years. The oil producer has no contract. He can only market through a major oil company, and that major can change the price when it wishes, and it can quit taking the oil tomorrow if it wants to. Oil has been in such big supply that the major, outside of some premium offered above the posted price occasionally, to change a connection, hasn't had to offer any inducement to the producer.

The independents have actually forgotten that there could be cooperative marketing. There is no reason, legal or moral, why the independents couldn't form cooperative marketing associations.

Whether or not the remaining independent oil companies will use the method of cooperation to stay in business remains to be seen. But several million consumers of petroleum products have done so with considerable success and with benefits to themselves and to all consumers of oil which would be difficult accurately to measure.

It was said some years ago that the three strongest organizations in the world were the Roman Catholic Church, the Standard Oil Company, and the French Army.

World War II took the French Army out of the list.

The Catholic Church, of course, holds as strongly as ever its authority over hundreds of millions of devout members.

And the Standard Oil Company holds a radically different kind of authority over the pocketbooks of an almost equal number. Despite the rise of other major oil companies, "Standard's posted price" is still a guide and verdict for most of the petroleum businesses of the United States and much of the world.

Occasionally a "price war" flurries among the retail filling stations of a city or two, but it does not last long. And crude prices and refined product prices are kept well under control by the "good fellowship" that exists among the major oil companies. There are even indications that the results of anti-trust action of half a century ago may soon be reversed. Some of the Standard Oil companies that succeeded the single trust are discussing merger. And in the drastically different temper of our times such action would probably be accepted with but feeble popular protest.

It is a documented fact that seven companies control the production of petroleum throughout the world outside of the United States of America and the communist bloc. But the Department of Justice dropped its anti-trust suit against the American companies in this group. Just why this was done has never been explained, but perhaps the answer is suggested by the fact that whereas almost every other nook and cranny of American life has been the subject of a congressional investigation, no inquiry of any sort has disturbed the oil business in more than thirty years. The voice of oil is not loud, but it speaks with unchallenged authority.

In no industry is it more true that the regulated control the regulators. The Bureau of Mines uses the figures furnished it by the major oil companies to estimate the volume of petroleum reserves in the United States. And the Bureau has yet to issue—and stand by—an important decision or even publication that displeased the industry.

It is freely and widely predicted that the time is not far distant when all "independents" will have been eliminated from the petroleum business and there will remain only the cooperatives as competition to the major companies. The president of the Independent Oil Refiners Association, speaking at the dedication of a new unit of a cooperatively owned refinery, stated that the major oil companies should be very grateful to the coops for entering the business. Their presence in it had been the main factor, he thought, in preventing the government's being forced to drastic action to correct an obviously monopolistic condition. This particular gentleman had reason to speak with feeling, for in the town where he spoke (Cushing, Oklahoma) there had been no less than fourteen oil refineries, most of them independents only a few years before. At the time of his address there were but two—one owned by a major company, the other by a cooperative. So there was good reason for these remarks.

The competition of cooperatives is of a unique sort. It is competition that does not sell out. The reason coops entered the oil business in the first place was not to "make money" but to save money for badly overcharged farmers. As the cooperatives grew and integrated their operations, the objective broadened. It became one of strengthening the economic position of their members by enabling them to own a part of a great industry. Selling out to the majors, however attractive the offer, would render impossible the achievement of either of these objectives.

Plenty of drama surrounds the beginning of the people's venture into the oil business. The coming of the tractor in the twenties had much to do with it. Tractor fuel cost a lot of money. And farming was far from prosperous. Up in Minnesota a group of farmers huddled around a kitchen stove and talked themselves into investing some hard-earned cash in a filling station and bulk plant. By operating these themselves as a cooperative they could supply their own needs and those of their neighbors for oil products and find out how much such products really needed to cost. This was in 1921 at Cottonwood, Minnesota. It was the first step of the people into the oil business. It was a successful step from the first day.

The Cottonwood people found out very quickly that an isolated retail operation was in a badly exposed position, to say the least. So did other local petroleum cooperatives that were beginning to operate in other communities. At times it became strangely difficult to get supplies. And so on a shoestring, a prayer, and a lot of faith, Midland Cooperative Wholesale was organized in 1926 to provide petroleum products to the local coops in the area.

In the early years patronage refunds to members of oil cooperatives averaged around 16 per cent.

Meanwhile, Ohio and Indiana and Illinois farmers wondered why it should cost seven cents a gallon just to deliver tractor fuel from tanks in town out to the farm. They found out it actually needed to cost less than half that much. They found this out by organizing their own oil-product distribution cooperatives, as the farmers up in Minnesota had done. Here, too, it soon became apparent how necessary it was to have one's own cooperative wholesale source of supply. And in all three states the Farm Bureau sponsored state-wide cooperative wholesales to pool the demand of the county cooperatives and try to supply it.

But wholesales, too, were subject to strange and sudden "shortages" on the part of their suppliers, who were also their integrated competitors.

There were times when the fainthearted counseled that it would be better to sell out. But they didn't prevail.

Instead, out on the plains of Kansas there arose in the late twenties the first cooperative oil refinery in American history. It was followed by others in various parts of the country, built or purchased by various cooperatives belonging mostly to farmers. The Department of Justice had to be called in to threaten an investigation of why it seemed so impossible for the Kansas refinery to obtain a dependable supply of crude oil. Only then was it able to operate with reasonable efficiency.

But still the people's oil business was neither integrated—as it *had* to be to survive—nor independent—as it could be only through complete integration.

The people had to prove they could do the *whole job* for themselves.

They did.

In the winter of 1939, again on the Kansas plains, a small group of men from Consumers' Cooperative Association stretched their hands over a fire. All night they waited there. At last, as the morning came, their anxiety was rewarded. For the first time oil flowed from the ground to be owned by the very people who needed to use its end products. For the first time the great reserve of energy which the processes of God's nature had stored in petroleum for the benefit of all men was piped directly into facilities designed directly to meet these men's needs.

In 1943 Midland Cooperatives purchased a refinery at Cushing, Oklahoma, which paid for itself out of three years' savings.

No need to prolong the story. Today cooperatives supply from oil well to bulk plant and filling station about 18 per cent to 22 per cent of the petroleum used on farms in the United States. In the states of the upper Middle West the percentage is considerably higher. In some counties as much as 40 per cent to 50 per cent.

The rate of growth has been encouraging. For example, in 1950 cooperatives supplied 16 per cent of all petroleum products used on farms in the United States. In 1957 this percentage had risen to 20.4 per cent. Net value of petroleum products handled by cooperatives increased 33.7 per cent in those seven years, whereas total expenditures of all farmers for oil products went up only 14.4 per cent in the same period.

Most of the products sold by cooperatives to their members and customers at retail come from their own refineries. In 1957 coops sold 1,957,000,000 gallons of liquid petroleum fuels; cooperative refineries turned out 1,873,000,000 gallons. The product of some two thousand cooperatively owned oil wells is ultimately sold to consumers through some twenty-seven hundred local petroleum cooperatives operating 2,700 bulk plants and 2,000 filling stations.

Cooperatives own about two thousand oil wells. They operate *ten* refineries, only about half what they once owned, but with substantially more total capacity. Coops distribute—through their own pipelines, trucks, wholesale and retail outlets—about 2.2 per cent of the nation's total supply of petroleum products. They refine about 1.6 per cent. Their weak link is that they supply less than 15 per cent of their refinery capacity from their own wells. For balanced and reasonably secure operation they need about 50 per cent.

Even with this small proportion of the great industry's business, the cooperatives have accomplished much. They have returned in patronage refunds to farmers and to farm income and to rural towns and their income tens of millions of dollars. These refunds represent the savings made from retail and wholesale distribution—the difference between actual cost and going market prices. They represent also the savings made from production and refining. They mean that part of the lush profits that otherwise would have been made *out* of farmers and rural people have instead come back to them through their cooperatively owned oil wells and refineries.

The greatest benefits, however, have been indirect and intangible. By 1959 the index of prices paid by farmers for necessary supplies and inputs had risen to 275 from the base period 100 for 1910–1914. But for the two commodities where cooperatives are strongest—petroleum and fertilizer—the index was only 175 and 152, respectively.

In Minnesota, Wisconsin, and some other states it could be shown in 1959 that the cost of gasoline had risen only about two-thirds as much as commodity prices generally since the low point in 1934. To what extent this fact was owing to the competition of the strong cooperatives in this area it was, of course, impossible accurately to determine. But certainly this competition was one major factor in the result.

The economic motivation of cooperatives is simple and clear. It is to supply their customers, *who are also their owners,* with the best-quality products at the lowest economically practicable net cost. There is no logic in taking advantage of oneself. Hence the constant effort of petroleum cooperatives to improve quality of product for their patron-owners' benefit has been an influence, again hard to measure, upon the whole industry, and has brought indirect benefits to untold numbers of people who do not even know that oil cooperatives exist.

It is questionable whether there are any more efficient oil refineries than some of the cooperative ones, such as CCA's at Coffeyville, Kansas; Midland's at Cushing, Oklahoma; or the refinery at McPherson, Kansas, operated by National Cooperative Refining Association. NCRA is a central facility owned and operated jointly by some seven regional petroleum cooperatives. Its capacity is 26,000 barrels a day.

It is a little-understood law of the operation of cooperatives that they tend always to diffuse their benefits, which once only their members enjoyed, among the population as a whole. Comparatively few people remember that seven cents per gallon charge that was made thirty years ago for delivering fuels from town to farm. One reason is that after cooperatives found that such charges could be reduced to two and one-half or three cents—and *did* so reduce them—the whole industry followed suit.

The oil business as a whole is one of the most profitable ones in the American economy. And some of the benefits flowing to the 2,000,000 or more cooperative owners of part of that industry are quite apparent.

To illustrate, let us take a typical street intersection in a middle-sized Middle Western town. It has three filling stations on three of its corners. One belongs to a major oil company, the second one to an independent contractor, and the third to a cooperative.

Obviously, the second and third stations are locally owned enterprises, whereas the first one is absentee owned. Furthermore, none of the earnings—from retail-profit margins, delivery charges, wholesaling, refining, or production—made at the major oil company station remains in the community where it is located. Only the actual wages paid to the workers do so. With respect to the second station, owned by a local man who contracts with an oil company for his supplies, the situation is somewhat different. Here not only the operator's wages but also the profits from *retail* sales remain in the community. Here again, however, none of the earnings of the supplying oil company is returned to the owner of the station.

The cooperative is a different kind of business; it is and must always be the property of the people who use its services and buy its products. They are local people—farmers and townspeople. Moreover, their local cooperative owns its share in regional wholesale and production cooperatives. Not only do the salaries and wages paid to the people who run the station remain "at home" in the community, so does a proper proportionate share of all the margins of earnings (or savings, as cooperatives term it) from delivery, wholesaling, refining, transportation, and production. For these earnings are returned by the wholesale and production cooperative, in patronage refunds, to its local cooperative members each year. They find their way, again in proportion to their patronage of the station, into the pockets of all the community's residents who are customers and owners of that station.

Time was when the number of such people was limited because the cooperative station was less attractive, less orderly, less clean, less well painted than its competitors. In some communities this is still the case. One manager of a local petroleum cooperative is reputed to have expressed his opposition to a new sign by saying: "Why fix up a sign? The members all know where it is and no one else cares."

Probably they didn't.

But times have changed. Beginning in the early 1950's, petroleum cooperatives began to put on a new face—not only at their shiny, always efficient refineries, but at their local stations and bulk plants as well. Regional wholesales paid for professional development of product and facility identification programs. In place of the dingy, poorly located, unattractive cooperative filling stations there have been appearing bright, nicely decorated, clean, attractive general-service facilities capable of bringing in not only the members' business but that of many chance customers as well. One of the finest filling stations in the country is operated directly by Midland Cooperatives, Inc.,

in metropolitan Minneapolis—partly as a demonstration of what cooperative service at its best can offer.

The people entered the oil business back in the twenties largely to
ease the economic pressure on farmers and agriculture. Even today
most of the cooperative business in oil products is owned by farmers
and serves farmers and rural communities. But the nation has become
more and more rapidly urbanized since World War II, the cities have
spread into the countryside, and the absolute number of farmers has
declined.

The oil cooperatives have read the signs of the times. They have
begun to expand their business in the towns, especially in heating
oils and automobile supplies. They have acquired filling stations in
suburban communities and in one or two cases in the heart of cities.
Meanwhile, consumer cooperatives, city based, have followed marketing trends and added filling stations and complete automobile services, purchasing their gasoline and oil from the regional cooperatives
that once supplied farmers almost exclusively.

Cuyahoga County, Ohio, offers an interesting example of these
trends.

In 1934, when the county Farm Bureau Cooperative was organized,
there were 1,230 farms in Cuyahoga County. In 1959 there were
barely one hundred farms of fifty acres or more, but a considerable
number of five- and ten-acre garden and small farm plots, practically
all belonging to people with city jobs. Full-time farm families make
up considerably less than one-fifth of 1 per cent of the county's population, which includes the city of Cleveland.

The Farm Bureau Cooperative could have gone out of business
without half trying. All it had to do was stick to its farm-supply
business to bring about that result. But its board and manager were
farsighted people. As sale of farm fertilizers declined, they pushed
lawn seed and garden fertilizer. As farm-equipment sales went down,
sales of garden tools and home appliances went up even more sharply.
Most important, however, has been expansion of petroleum business,
in gasoline and fuel oil among town and city customers. Sales of
petroleum products were $26,800 in 1936; $502,000 in 1958. In
1953 automatic fuel-oil delivery was begun and this, of course, has
been responsible for much of the increase.

Total sales of the cooperative have climbed from a bare $17,000 in 1934 to almost one million dollars in 1958.

The farmers still cling to control. Urban people, while receiving their full share of patronage refunds, can be "associate" members only, without full voting rights. But time will no doubt change this situation, too. For the common interest of farm and city people as consumers of needed commodities has been recognized in very practical fashion by this cooperative.

The people are in the oil business to stay. Their cooperatives in this industry are as efficient, as well operated, as any elements in the industry. And the very prosperity of the industry means that substantial profits are made by commercial companies and hence that substantial patronage refunds can be returned to owner-customers of its cooperative segment. There is need for even further integration among these cooperatives. There is need, on their part, for ownership of a much larger proportion of their needed supplies of crude oil.

But even if, as now seems likely, major company acquisitions eliminate practically all other competition from "independents," the cooperatives, the people in the oil business, will not sell out, for to do so would be to deny every aim and objective that took them into the business in the first place. It would be to bring to an end one of the most significant demonstrations of the vigor of the American democratic tradition.

That is the truly grand spectacle of some two million average American families, owning together a fairly substantial segment of the most highly integrated industry in the United States and successfully competing with some of the mightiest economic giants in the world. And all because they *decided* that this was a wise thing to do, and because the existence of the cooperative method of organizing a business made such a decision possible.

IX

THE PEOPLE'S MONEY

It is the people's money.

All of it is—or once was.

All the money and credit in existence is the result either of the savings of the people or of the use of those savings by banks, insurance companies, and other financial institutions, or of the monetization of the people's credit by banks or government, or of the use of the people's credit by governmental or private agencies.

An insurance company, for example, is nothing more or less than a group of people who are willing to share together common dangers and hazards of life and who pool some of their savings to meet those disasters when they arise. On those savings of the people the whole empire of insurance rests.

Banks loan money to farmers and homeowners and businessmen and take mortgages on farms, homes, and business property as security. In such cases the bank has not loaned these people *its* money or credit. What it has actually done is to monetize the credit of farmers or homeowners or businessmen—credit they already had but which they had no means of turning into money.

When rural electric cooperatives borrow money from the government they are not borrowing anyone else's credit. They are borrowing their own credit. For certainly these 4,500,000 rural citizens and farmers have borrowed no more than their proportionate share of the credit of the whole people, which they, by their productiveness, have helped to create.

So at one point or another in the process all the capital, all the money, and all the credit in our economy have been in the hands of plain, average citizens, a few of them rich, a great many of middle income, a majority of them rather poor.

None of which, of course, is really surprising when you stop to think about it. The only surprising thing is that so few people *do* think about it. But some of them do. And some of them act accordingly. What such people do and why is the subject of this chapter.

This chapter is about the people's money, credit, and savings. It is about banks and insurance companies and credit institutions. It is also about *people's* savings institutions, *people's* insurance companies, and *people's* credit agencies.

It is about how the people's credit is used—and abused; made into a dynamic instrument of modern life—and turned into a means of controlling the lives of the very people whose credit it is. And we will touch briefly on the fact that the frightful scourge of unpayable life-time debt is the major millstone about the necks of people in most so-called "less-developed" countries.

These are matters about which the average citizen has repeatedly been told—and usually persuaded—that he can have no adequate understanding. This mistaken idea of a supposed incurable ignorance is a major source of our most serious economic problems.

As President John Adams, certainly no radical, once wrote: "All the perplexities, confusion, and distress in America arise, not from defects in our Constitution or federation, not from want of honor or virtue, so much as from downright ignorance of the nature of coin, credit, and circulation."

What President Adams said is still true today. So let's begin with savings, for here all economic progress begins.

Savings are the gateway to all economic progress—for families, for communities, for nations. Man has never taken a step in economic progress unless he first set aside the savings that could make that step possible.

Until a primitive man had gathered in his cave at least a little more food than he needed for immediate consumption, he could not progress at all. But when he had even one day's food supply already on hand, then he could spend that day making a crude slingshot so he could kill more game or planting wild seeds so he could raise a crop of grain.

Stored food was the first kind of savings.

With stored food in his cave, primitive man could take time to fashion rude stone tools, or to build shelters for himself and maybe for others of his tribe.

Then savings took the form of the stone tools, the shelters, and the food.

Later, savings were made in the form of metal tools or of the metals themselves from which many things could be made.

All these were savings of real wealth, of things used in sustaining and protecting life. These savings meant freedom from immediate want. They meant freedom to do new things, freedom to progress.

Without any savings at all man is the slave either of other men who do have savings or else of his own basic need to find food to sustain life.

Only people who possess savings can be free.

And so it is that control of savings is the gateway to freedom just as savings themselves are the gateway to economic progress.

In all ages and in all societies people have made some savings. In most ages and in most societies the shrewd and clever ones have taken from the rest, if not their actual savings, then at least effective control over them.

In societies ruled by chiefs or kings or dictators with absolute power over the people, the evidence of that absolute power has been the privilege of the ruler to control the savings of the people and take them away when it pleased him to do so.

In our own day the same principles apply. Only the methods are different. In the main, we make our savings in the form of money. Without the use of some such savings we can make no economic progress either as families or as communities or as nations. Neither can we make provision for our families' needs of tomorrow, unless we have savings available for that purpose. If we have no savings of our own, then we must attempt to borrow those of other people. And at that point we are not really free, because we must pay whatever price, in interest, is asked of us, and usually risk some of our property in addition.

In our society, as in earlier ones, most of the people make savings from time to time. And again, as in earlier societies, most of the people fail to keep control of their own savings—and thus become dependent upon those to whom they have given control over those savings.

There are ways to change this. There are ways in which groups of people—even those who are able to set aside only very small savings indeed—can keep control of their own savings and gradually build a firm basis for their freedom and financial security.

But no one can do this by himself. It can only be done by groups of people joining together in mutual aid of one another and using the right kind of tools to make their mutual aid effective.

Among such tools are credit unions, cooperative-type mutual insurance companies, cooperative farm-credit institutions, mutual savings banks, savings and loan associations, mutual-investment funds, and similar mutual-aid agencies.

The opposite side of the savings coin is borrowing. If people will save together—pool their savings and their credit—then they can borrow together and invest together. This is the cooperative principle applied to finance.

When a family breadwinner dies or a child goes to college, or the washing machine breaks down, or illness strikes suddenly, the average family needs a source of credit to tide it over the crisis. Credit unions have grown out of this need. Before the introduction of the credit union it was possible for families to borrow. But legitimate banks were not, generally, willing to make small loans on the personal notes of people having little security—the very people whose need for the credit was the greatest. The alternative was the finance company, which often charged a very high rate of interest, or the loan shark, for whom the sky was the limit.

The credit-union idea injected into this situation was the soul of simplicity and the essence of cooperation. Although no one family had any chance of bringing down the interest rate of finance companies or of inducing the banks to provide a small loan service, a considerable group of such families—even poor ones—did have means of solving the problem *if they joined together to do so*. This was done by combining the need for credit with the practice of regular savings. By utilizing the people's own savings, it became possible for the whole group to meet the credit needs of individual members as they arose. If enough people in a group are willing to purchase $5.00 shares in a credit union, then when any one of them is in need of a loan he can borrow from his own group at reasonable rates, repay his own group, and receive his share of the earnings.

The membership of a credit union is built around some common interest of the group such as the same employer, membership in the same church, labor union, or other organization, or residence in the same neighborhood. All credit unions are supervised and examined by either federal or state authorities, their investments checked and limited to securities that will assure financial soundness.

In 1921 there were only 199 credit unions in the United States. By 1960, credit unions in the United States numbered almost twenty thousand, with a membership of more than eleven million and assets of close to 5 billion dollars. More than a thousand new credit unions are being organized in this country every year. Credit unions provide about 8 per cent of all installment credit in the United States.

The origin of the credit union, like that of other cooperative institutions, is buried in the sands of very ancient times, for such institutions are as old as mutual aid among people. And since mutual aid is the basic civilizing influence in all history, that is very old indeed.

Institutions similar to credit unions probably have existed in India and some other countries for centuries. But Germany is the birthplace of credit unions as we know them. Almost simultaneously in the middle 1800's Herman Schulze-Delitzsch in urban Germany and Frederick Raiffeisen in the country were trying to do something about the age-old problem of poverty, debt, and the usurious interest rates that made the debts almost impossible to pay. Raiffeisen was mayor of the little German town of Flammersfeld. Out of his despair over the people's plight there developed in his mind one of the most dynamic ideas of modern times. It was the idea of cooperative credit. He saw that no one of the debt-ridden farmers could expect to borrow on any better than existing terms. But if a group of farmers would pledge together unlimited liability for repayment of one another's debts, then something might be done. He tried. He talked. He finally formed a union, largely of farmers, who were willing to make the pledge and then pool their credit in cooperation with one another. Then he went out and raised a small fund of money as the seed of the first credit union. It proved successful. The loans were made at decent interest rates, old debts were paid off, the loans were repaid on time. Today thousands of "Raiffeisen" societies serve the rural people of German-speaking nations as village banks and savings and loan associations.

The similar work of Schulze-Delitzsch among city workers was honored by the German Federal Republic in 1958 by the issuance of a commemorative postage stamp.

During the last half of the nineteenth century the rural-credit development in Germany served as a model for a similar one in Italy. There, it had the support of the Catholic Church. Today one of the principal social tenets of this church in all countries is encouragement of credit unions.

For many years the practice of unlimited liability was adhered to. In some parts of Italy it still is. But gradually it was abandoned as experience showed it to be unnecessary. The personal endorsement of a fellow member replaced it. Luzzatti, the Italian pioneer, called this "the capitalization of honesty."

United States credit unions owe an incalculable debt to the credit societies of India, as we shall see. But the American credit union as we now know it came from these European beginnings through Canada. The great leader and father of the Canadian credit unions was Alphonse DesJardins, a Quebec journalist. In 1909 he also organized in the Sainte Marie parish of Manchester, New Hampshire, the first credit union in the United States.

The first general credit-union legislation in this country was passed in Massachusetts after an investigation by Pierre Jay, state banking commissioner. It revealed not only the need for a weapon to fight loan sharks but what the best weapon was. DesJardins came down from Canada to testify.

Edward A. Filene, millionaire Boston merchant, also testified. He related that on a trip to India he had met W. R. Gourlay, employed by the British government to form credit societies in Indian villages. Filene had traveled with him awhile and was deeply impressed by the soundness of the idea, and the present and potential services these societies rendered to the desperately poor Indian people. He infected the Massachusetts legislators with his enthusiasm, and this played a major part in getting the law passed.

From then on, until his death in 1937, Filene's wealth and driving interest were largely responsible for the growth of United States credit unions. His work started in earnest in 1921. In that year he set up the Credit Union National Extension Bureau with the help of Roy F. Bergengren, whom he chose as Bureau secretary. Meanwhile, three more workable state credit-union laws had been passed and 199 credit unions organized.

The Bureau's purposes were: to get needed enabling laws; to organize credit unions as examples; to increase the number of credit unions to the point where it would be possible to organize self-sustaining state leagues and a national association of those leagues. These four goals were achieved in 1934 when the constitution of the Credit Union National Association was drawn up and signed.

Roy F. Bergengren was managing director of the Credit Union National Association from its organization in 1934 to 1945, when he resigned. In 1946 he was made managing director emeritus. Thomas W. Doig, a pioneer credit-union leader and organizer, succeeded Bergengren, serving until late 1955, when his health failed. H. B. Yates, Texas credit-union leader and former president of CUNA, filled an interim period as managing director until the selection of H. Vance Austin in 1957.

Since 1934 progress has also been made along all the fundamental lines of credit-union objectives. Congress, nearly every state legislature, and all Canadian provincial governments have passed credit-union enabling acts. These are constantly being improved. The state leagues and the National Association generally tend to increase the scope and effectiveness of their operations. Offices in Canada and Washington supplement the work of the head office of the Credit Union National Association in Madison, Wisconsin. Thanks in part to the activities of the office of Federal Credit Unions, the number of United States credit unions more than doubled between 1934 and the beginning of World War II, when the total was 10,456. At the beginning of the war membership had reached 3,532,006 and assets totaled $322,515,000.

It was not until after World War II, however, that great expansion began. By 1958 there were 25,000 credit unions in the world with almost 13,000,000 members, and assets of about $4,700,000,000.

Most of these were in the United States and Canada. By the end of 1959 the United States alone had 19,800 credit unions with a membership of 11,300,000, assets of $4,382,000,000 (mostly members' shares), and outstanding loans to members of $3,700,000,000. But increasing interest in credit unions was being shown in practically all Western Hemisphere countries and in many other parts of the world as well. To serve this growing need for credit-union benefits, CUNA organized its World Extension Division in 1954.

The simple principle of the credit union is that a group of people having common ties and interests keep control of their own savings and their own credit and use them for mutual benefit of the group.

And what may be called the "gospel" of credit unions says something like this: A woman or a man is to be honored and respected not for what he *has* but for what he *is*. Therefore loans shall be made to credit-union members not because they have so much security that they do not really need a loan but simply because they *do* need the loan, because their name is a good name and because their fellow members honor that good name. This principle and this "gospel" have at many places and times worked near miracles. They will work a lot more.

In Nova Scotia during the depths of the depression some Scottish Catholic priests from St. Francis Xavier University showed fishermen how they could first organize credit unions among themselves and then build their own marketing cooperatives, lobster "factories," and other means of getting a decent return for their catch. The simple but new factor was that fishermen started selling their fish direct to the Boston and New York markets at fair prices instead of selling to middlemen at distress prices. Their credit unions made it possible for them to have their own storage and processing plants to keep their fish until they could sell them at a fair price.

In India today cooperative credit societies enable farmers to escape the clutches of the professional moneylender and to work their way out of debt. This in a country most of whose people have lived under a cloud of perpetual, unpayable debt for centuries.

Fiji Islanders are learning what money is, what it means, what it can do. A very broad movement has spread among them for the organization of credit unions. They are saving their money together. They are learning what it means to apply for a loan from a pool of money which belongs to one's own neighbors and oneself. They are learning to repay such loans at reasonable rates of interest, and to see how their own payment of interest builds up their own pool of funds. They are learning, in the early stages of their progress from rather primitive to more civilized life, that practical mutual aid among a group of people can enable them to control not only their own savings, but to a large extent their economic welfare. Inspiration and leadership of all this among the islanders have come from a new, modern, twentieth-century type of Christian missionary—Roman Catholics in this as in many other cases. There are priests who, from Jamaica to Madras, are putting into quite literal practice the biblical teachings against usury and about being one's brother's keeper.

But it is by no means alone among people in need or distress that credit unions have afforded a means of self- and group-help. The largest credit union in the United States is that of the Detroit Teachers. A modest percentage of its $20,000,000 of assets is being loaned to its members to enable them to build, as a cooperative, several beautiful apartment buildings in which they themselves will live.

Michigan credit-union leaders have organized a building-and-loan association and some of the state-chartered credit unions have invested part of their surplus in its shares. This building-and-loan association makes a business of helping families of lower incomes finance modest homes at prices they can afford.

Credit unions in New York City have sponsored and loaned to their members down-payment money for more than one cooperative apartment-building project in the heart of Manhattan. Thus home-ownership becomes possible in the midst of the world's largest city and for families of very modest income. It becomes possible because people first learned to put their $5.00 credit-union shares together and keep control of their own savings.

The man who is probably most responsible for these New York

developments, William Reid, was appointed chairman of the New York City Housing Authority in 1959.

A Catholic parish credit union in Colorado found that 64 of its member families of Mexican descent were about to be evicted from their rented shacks, so the credit union obtained a quit-claim deed to the land. Then it loaned enough money to each of these families to enable them to buy parcels of this land and to build on them their own comfortable little homes. A community of homeowners was created where once there had been only a collection of harassed tenants.

In Seattle, Group Health Credit Union makes loans when necessary to enable families to pay the $100 membership fee to join Group Health Cooperative of Puget Sound. From the four clinics and the hospital of that cooperative health plan some 60,000 people obtain every needed kind of health care, including drugs at half the usual costs, for less than the average person spends for spasmodic, emergency, hit-and-miss medical care.

Farmers in Indiana, Kansas, and other states have seen the need of organizing credit unions among the members of their farm-supply cooperatives. The reason? Farmers do not have ready cash to pay for expensive equipment or large amounts of farm supplies needed at certain times of the year. Extension of credit by the cooperative is a costly process and frequently leads to difficult membership problems. But a credit union is in the business of lending money and can finance such purchases readily and easily. Thus the problem of accounts receivable for the cooperative is solved by the simple device of extending cooperative action into another field—that of personal finance.

Thus many people have found in credit unions tools to help them accomplish dramatic changes for good like those just described. Such people believe in credit unions as cooperative agencies of deep significance and capable of helping to bring about broad and badly needed social and economic betterment.

The majority of credit unions in the United States, however, are organized among the employees of industrial and commercial concerns and frequently with the benevolent sponsorship of the employing company. Generally speaking, members of these credit unions see them as a means of encouraging savings, refinancing indebtedness for members, and making small loans to them when needed. And nothing more. Little connection between these activities and other forms of cooperation is seen. And indeed there is positive resistance among many of the leaders of these employee-based credit unions against extension of the credit-union principle beyond the field of convenience and helpful small loan lending to their membership. Frequently, also, the members of these credit unions feel a loyalty to the employing company which leads them to adopt its viewpoint respecting social and economic questions and controversies.

This difference of opinion runs deep. On the one hand are those credit unions and members who see a deep significance in their credit-union experience. They recognize the credit union as probably the most basic kind of cooperative or mutual enterprise among people. They believe they should build on their credit union and the financial strength it gives them other activities of benefit not only to their fellow members but to the communities where they live. They welcome affiliation with such general cooperative organizations as the Cooperative League, and they seek to help the development of other kinds of cooperatives.

On the other hand stand the credit unions of company employees, conservative in their viewpoint, wanting the credit union to do well the credit-union job as they conceive it and nothing more. They do not want credit unions to compete with banks or other financial institutions nor to enter their fields of activity. And they believe, too, that attacks on credit unions by large financial interests could be avoided if the entire credit-union movement pursued their conservative policies.

They are no doubt quite mistaken in this last belief, for the attacks on credit unions—unjust as they basically are—are almost certainly brought about by one main factor alone.

That factor is the rapid growth of credit unions.

And all factions in the credit-union movement, as well as all thoughtful Americans, are in full agreement that the continuing rapid growth of credit unions is very desirable in the present state of our American economy.

In 1950 the volume of consumer debt was $18,000,000,000. By

the beginning of 1959 it was $47,900,000,000, and at the end of that year it was $52,000,000,000. More than 15 per cent of all consumer income was obligated for payments on installment debt; and 30 per cent to 40 per cent of the income of lower-income families was thus "mortgaged." Furthermore, it was altogether evident that unless consumer debt continued to increase there was small chance that effective demand would keep pace with the supply of goods and gadgets which automated industry was prepared to turn out.

Somewhere there is a danger point in the expansion of debt. Just where that point is depends partly on the interest rate and partly on the general state of the economy. The higher the interest rate the closer we get to the point where it will become impossible for families to maintain their debt payments and also continue to sustain their normal demand for goods and services. And obviously the larger the volume of the debt the more dangerous will be any slight down turn in economic activity, any increase in unemployment, and any consequent inability on the part of families to repay.

Much of the huge volume of consumer debt is the result of creation of money or credit by banks or other financial agencies. And many of the credit "opportunities" offered to people are burdened with exorbitant interest or "carrying" charges. Indeed in 1960 the *Wall Street Journal* reported that of the average $70.00 profit made by automobile dealers on sales of new cars, $43.00 comes from financing charges and only $27.00 from the actual sale of the automobile. Further, the *Journal* reported that 57 per cent of total profits of furniture stores comes from charges for "credit services."

If there is to be a large volume of consumer debt as an important factor in our economy, then it is clearly most desirable that it be non-inflationary debt and that the interest rates be reasonable. This is one of the reasons why credit unions are such constructive factors in our economy today. For, unlike commercial banks and most of the "financing" agencies, credit unions never create new money or credit with which to make their loans. Credit unions lend only money that has previously been saved by their members. And the 1 per cent a month on the unpaid balance that credit unions charge as interest is substantially less than most of the interest charges exacted from consumer debtors.

Furthermore, credit unions do not increase interest rates just because economic circumstances and a "tightness" of money make it possible. In the year 1959, when interest rates were being skyrocketed all through the economy, credit unions quite alone did not increase their rates at all.

Why not?

Simply because they did not need to and did not *want* to. Credit unions belong to the people who *pay* the interest, not to those who *collect* it. Their motive is mutual aid for their members, not the making of a profit out of interest collection. Indeed any earnings credit unions make belong to their members and are paid to them either in dividends on their shares or in patronage refunds of a portion of the interest they have paid.

It's the mutual-aid motive that makes the difference.

In the year 1959 the credit unions of the state of Michigan refunded $3,000,000 to their borrowers in patronage refunds. And no less than 2,737 of the 19,000 credit unions in the nation made some such refunds. This was twice as many as had done so in 1957.

Credit unions are most useful and constructive influences in any society, but there are natural and unavoidable limits to the scope of their activities and effectiveness. In the very nature of things people will probably never put the bulk of their savings into credit unions. Nor can credit unions provide the kind of large-scale financing which modern industry, including cooperative industry, demands.

All the assets of all credit unions in the United States amount to less than half the assets of any one of the largest New York or California banks. And less than 3 per cent of all personal savings are in credit unions, although this percentage is rising steadily.

It is therefore fortunate that credit unions are not the only tools which the people have learned to use in the financial field.

One reason for the long depression in agriculture was the exorbitant interest rates which farmers were compelled to pay. That depression lasted from the deflation of 1920—deliberately brought about by the Federal Reserve System—until the outbreak of World War II. Interest rates of 10 per cent, 12 per cent, 16 per cent, and even more were almost the rule for loans to farmers during the 1920's. And since the loans were being made by banks which were in business to make money for their stockholders, there were arguments for such high rates.

Those arguments were simple—and tragic.

Briefly, the worse off farmers were and the greater the economic handicaps of agriculture, the greater the risk of lending money to them. So interest rates were fixed in relation to that risk.

The trouble, of course, was that the higher rates defeated their own purpose. For the higher the interest rates, the more difficult it becomes to repay a loan, particularly when the value of money is rising. During the deflation of the twenties farm-product prices fell drastically. If a farmer had borrowed $1,000 when wheat was selling for $1.00 a bushel and if the price then fell to fifty cents a bushel, the actual burden of the debt was doubled. The farmer had to raise 2,000 bushels of wheat to pay off the $1,000 debt, whereas when he borrowed the money it had been worth only the equivalent of 1,000 bushels.

There were times in the very early 1930's when organized action by farmers made it impossible for creditors to hold foreclosure sales of farms whose owners couldn't pay their debts. Farmers would gather at such sales in impressive numbers, would prevent anything more than a nominal amount being bid, and would then sell the farm promptly back to its former owner for a few dollars.

Out of all this came an idea. It was the same idea that brought about the rural electric cooperatives and the housing cooperatives and all the other mutual-aid enterprises about which this book is concerned.

The idea was that the credit-for-profit scheme just would not work in certain situations. In fact, it operated in reverse. The greater the *need* for *low* interest rates, the higher the rates became—under the credit-for-profit method. What was needed was credit-for-need-for-credit institutions. What was needed was a way in which farmers who needed credit so badly—and at the lowest possible interest— could pool their need for credit and their good names and thus obtain loans on terms which would make repayment far more likely.

The result was the Farm Credit System. Its beginnings did not even wait for the New Deal to be born in the election of 1932, although a number of liberalizing amendments were passed after that. All three parts of the Farm Credit System were started with government capital, as a tool. But that government capital—most of which has now been repaid and replaced with farmers' capital—was not the basic element that made either the land bank associations or the production credit associations or the Banks for Cooperatives possible.

The basic element was the idea of mutual aid. What one person could not do individually for himself, that same thing nevertheless could be done by a group of people if only they would pool their needs, their risks, and their credit together. Everyone in society— even the half-broke farmer of the depression years—has a certain amount of credit. It is created by his property or by his ability and willingness to work and to produce, or by his good name and faithfulness in fulfilling his obligations and contracts.

But no one person—unless he owns a bank—can have his own checks printed and use them to pay his bills. Such individually monetized credit just doesn't have the quality of acceptance or "currency" about it. But when a number of people are willing to organize their credit together, then they can do almost exactly that very thing.

For example, this is just about what happened in the case of the Mason City (Iowa) Production Credit Association when twenty-nine farmers founded it in 1934. It is true they had a part of their share of the credit of their nation to get started with. It's true some government capital was made available. But the important factor was the willingness of numbers of farmers in this as in other areas of the country to organize their own need for loans, to pool their credit resources, and to share the risks of lending to one another and of also retiring the government capital. These are necessary ingredients of the success of a mutual-aid or cooperative credit institution. Or, as we called it above, a credit-for-the-need-for-credit institution.

Of course it wouldn't have been possible for these north Iowa farmers to retire the $145,000 of government capital nor to build a surplus of more than $200,000 if there had not been the best of management of the association. That was something the farmer board of directors had to be wise enough to hire.

Nor would success have been possible if the members of this PCA hadn't recognized what their *ownership* meant or hadn't used its services. The fact that the farmer members did recognize the meaning of ownership of their cooperative PCA is proved by their investment of some $175,000 in its stock. And by the fact that over the first twenty years of its life no less than $30,000,000 had been loaned by the farmers of the association to the farmers of the association and repaid, every cent of it, with interest. But the interest was paid back to themselves. Unlike the interest paid to lenders for profit, that interest has increased the pool of credit and the savings and the resources of the people who had the credit in the first place—namely, the borrowers, who are also the owners of the cooperative Production Credit Association.

Thus their own debt builds the credit of the people—as it should do—when the principle of cooperation and mutual aid is applied to the organization of a financial institution. On this principle and idea the whole Farm Credit System is built.

Today the cooperative Farm Credit System, supervised by the Farm Credit Administration, provides a well-rounded credit service for farmers and their cooperatives. Through its facilities farmers can finance ownership of farms, production of crops and livestock, and purchasing of farm supplies and marketing of farm products.

The credit cooperatives of the system are: About 1,000 federal land bank associations and 12 Federal Land Banks, from which farmers obtain long-term farm-mortgage loans; 497 production credit associations and 12 Federal Intermediate Credit Banks which provide short and intermediate-term credit for farm operations; and 13 Banks for Cooperatives from which farmers' marketing, purchasing, and service cooperatives can obtain long- and short-term loans.

None of the banks is a bank of deposit, but through the cooperative Farm Credit System farmers have access to investment markets in the large money centers and are able to obtain funds at interest rates comparable to those paid by large corporations.

The Federal Land Banks sell bonds, the joint obligation of all 12 banks, secured by first mortgages on farms. The federal intermediate credit banks and the Banks for Cooperatives sell bonds and debentures. These are also joint obligations of each group of banks. The bonds and the debentures are not guaranteed by the government in any way.

During the year ended June 30, 1960, the banks and associations comprising the Farm Credit System extended credit totaling $4 billion. At that time the system had $4.8 billion of loans outstanding in 376,000 land-bank loans, 292,000 PCA loans, and 2,754 loans to farmer cooperatives. As of the same date farmers and farmers' cooperatives owned $369 million of capital stock in the farm-credit banks and associations.

The United States is divided into 12 districts and each district has a Land Bank, an Intermediate Credit Bank and a Bank for Cooperatives. The thirteenth Bank for Cooperatives is the Central Bank for Cooperatives, Washington, D.C.

The local credit cooperatives, the federal land bank associations, and the production credit associations are organized throughout each district so that every farmer has access to the credit services they provide. Every borrower is a cooperative owner.

The members of the local associations elect a board of directors from among the membership. This board determines the association's policies and hires a secretary-treasurer to run the day-to-day affairs of the association.

Federal land-bank loans are made direct to the farmer through the federal land bank association in which he has purchased capital stock in an amount equal to 5 per cent of his loan.

The production credit associations make loans to their members and obtain lending funds by discounting the members' notes with the federal intermediate credit bank. Members of production credit associations also must own capital stock equal to 5 per cent of their loans.

Loans from these two credit services, the federal land banks and the production-credit associations, can be used for any agricultural purpose.

Borrowers from the federal land banks agree to make payments on the principal of their loans with each annual or semi-annual payment of interest in amounts large enough to repay the debt within an agreed period of not less than five years nor more than forty years.

Most loans from production credit associations used to meet current operating expenses are written to mature within one year. However, in cases where a farmer uses part of the loan for capital purposes, such as buying machinery, livestock, and the like, it is often anticipated that a part of the loan will need to be renewed. The production credit associations also make the original loans for such purchases for periods up to five years.

An important feature of the production credit system is the fact that the loan committee includes two farmer-directors and the secretary-treasurer. The directors are familiar with local conditions and have a practical working knowledge of farming in their territory.

Farmer cooperatives obtain their loans direct from the Bank for Cooperatives serving their area. The banks maintain a staff familiar with farmer cooperatives. They are able to give advice on sound business practices and suggestions on new construction or modernization of facilities.

For many years cooperatives borrowing from the Banks for Cooperatives were not permitted, under the law, to retain their stock once their loans were repaid. At repayment the bank redeemed the stock held by its repaying borrower. This rendered impossible the retirement of the government capital or the turning of the banks into genuine cooperative, borrower-owned institutions.

Accordingly, in 1955 legislation was passed by Congress to make possible the replacement of the government capital in the Banks for Cooperatives with investments by the cooperatives. Key testimony on this bill was presented by Arthur J. Smaby, a director of the 7th Farm Credit District, who represented the Cooperative League, of which he was also a director. Concluding his testimony, Smaby said: "Passage of this bill in the original form recommended by the Farm Credit Board will be a most important forward step toward self-dependence for American agriculture."

The 1955 act has worked well. Stock purchased by borrowing cooperatives is permanently held by them and serves to repay a like amount of government capital. Patronage refunds earned by cooperatives borrowing from the banks are also left in the banks' capital structure and the money is used to retire government capital, and between 15 per cent and 20 per cent of interest payments is devoted to paying off the government.

It was contemplated by the 1955 legislation that about thirteen years would be required for the cooperatives to retire all the government capital and make the Banks for Cooperatives completely co-operative-owned institutions. However, by the end of the fiscal year

1960 government capital had been repaid in an amount of $32,000,-000 and replaced by a like amount of investments by cooperatives. At that time $118,000,000 of stock was still held by the government. But the rate of retirement being accomplished by the cooperatives gave promise that all government investment would be repaid considerably ahead of the thirteen-year-schedule.

As for the Federal Land Banks and the Production Credit Associations the record was even better because there had been provision from the beginning for replacement of government capital by member capital. There has been no government capital whatever in the twelve Federal Land Banks since 1947. All their capital is member capital. So is all the capital in the local federal land bank associations, which from the beginning have been wholly owned by their farmer-members.

By June of 1959, 454 of the 495 Production Credit Associations were fully member-owned. All government capital had been replaced with farmer-borrower capital in these 454 PCAs and they were cooperative credit agencies in every respect. Furthermore, only $3,900,-000 of government capital remained in the remaining 41 associations, compared to $145,600,000 of member capital.

Thus it is only a question of time before all parts of the Farm Credit System will be capitalized by their members and by them alone. And this will have been accomplished by the simple process of farmers keeping control of their own credit, monetizing their own credit, borrowing their own credit, and paying interest to themselves. All of which is inherent in the concept of cooperative credit. In fact, it is what cooperative credit *is:* people using their own money and credit for their own needs.

A word needs to be added about the future of the Banks for Cooperatives. At present these banks are authorized to loan only to cooperatives 90 per cent of whose voting rights are held by farm producers. But the proportion of farmers to total population is declining. The number of part-time farmers is increasing. Rural and suburban homes are coming closer and closer together. The business of farm-supply cooperatives inevitably includes more and more patronage from families who are not full-time farmers. Therefore there will be more and more reason as time goes on to liberalize the terms under which the Banks for Cooperatives operate. One proposal approved by the Farm Credit Board in 1961 was to reduce to 75 the percentage of control required to be held by full-time farm producers in a cooperative seeking to qualify for Bank for Cooperatives loans.

Every cooperative business depends for its basic capital upon investments by its members. This is another way in which people can continue to keep control of and to use their own money for their own benefit.

Member investment takes place in three main ways. First, of course, every member must purchase at least one share of common (voting) stock as his membership share. And many members own many additional such shares, even though this does not increase their voting power, since each member has one vote and only one in a cooperative, regardless of the number of shares he holds. No such investments in the common stock of cooperatives are made for speculative reason, for the value of cooperative stock never rises above par. The only reason for owning common stock in cooperatives is to have the advantage of their services. So no one except a person who needs the goods or services of a cooperative has any reason to own, or should properly own, common stock in a cooperative business. This is why attempts to determine a "market value" for cooperative stock are necessarily difficult, for the "market" is limited, by the very definition of a cooperative, to the customers and patrons of the cooperative.

The second way in which members invest in their cooperatives is by the direct purchase of securities other than common stock—debentures, preferred stock, or certificates of indebtedness. All these securities bear interest, of course, and are often attractive to investors and investment institutions other than members of the cooperative. But to the extent that such securities are bought by members they put their own money to work in their own direct interest. And their own patronage helps to assure their own return on their investment.

The third way in which members invest in their cooperatives is unique with the cooperative form of business. This is by the investment of patronage refunds. All the net earnings of cooperatives belong to the patrons and members, not to the cooperative. These earnings are liabilities, not assets of the cooperative, and must be paid in some suitable form to their owners, in proportion to their patronage. Sometimes patronage refunds are paid in whole or in part in cash. But frequently they are paid in some other form such as stock, certificates of increased equity ownership, or interest-bearing securities. The bylaws of most cooperatives include provisions to the effect that all members agree to receive their patronage refunds either in cash or in some other form. Clearly if cash payment is deferred and the patronage refund paid in the form of shares of stock or of certificates of ownership what has happened is that the member has invested his patronage refund in his cooperative business. And a very considerable proportion of the capital of cooperatives is obtained in just this way.

There are good reasons. Cooperatives must depend primarily on their members' investments for their basic capital. Few indeed of those members are people of large means. And the time when it is easiest for them to invest in their cooperatives is when they receive from the cooperative their patronage refunds.

Many people who have little knowledge of cooperatives do not understand this process of the investment of patronage refunds. They do not see that it constitutes essentially the same transaction as would take place if the member received actual cash and then bought a share of stock or a certificate of indebtedness or of ownership. Neither do they see that the cooperative member is far more likely to be benefited economically if his cooperative provides him with a more efficient feed mill, fertilizer plant, store, or power line than he would be if all the patronage refunds were received by him in cash.

But a few people do understand these facts only too well, and attempt to use them to cripple cooperatives and deprive them of a principal source of member capital. These are the people who are constantly agitating that cooperatives should be compelled to pay a special penalty tax on all refunds invested by members. The charge is made that cooperatives are "expanding on tax-free capital." But that is no more true than it would be to say the same of other corporations simply because they are not taxed—and none of them are—on money invested in their stock.

It is true that cooperatives have no proper business to pay patronage refunds in paper that bears no due date, carries no interest, and which is allowed over long periods of years to go unredeemed. It is also true that cooperative patrons are liable for, and should in all cases pay, the taxes due on whatever taxable income may be represented by their patronage refunds in whatever form that income is received. It is true that cooperatives should all, as most of them do, pay enough of the patronage refund in cash to enable the patron to pay his tax. And it is true that some court cases have, mistakenly as it seems to most co-operative leaders, relieved patrons of the payment of such taxes on the ground that no "market value" could be established for the stock or certificates of cooperatives. We have already explained why this cannot be readily done. But none of this affects the basic fact or equity in the situation. The cooperative neither owns nor has control over the patronage refunds which it has liability to pay to its patrons. And to attempt to tax a cooperative on an investment as if it were a profit would be manifestly unjust and discriminatory. For no other business is so taxed.

In the earlier years there was more dependence by cooperatives upon member investment of patronage refunds for their capital than is the case today. More and more the cooperatives attempt to receive their financing by direct sale of securities either to members or to "outside" investors. Financing programs are carried on, and some of them achieve considerable success. Regional farm-supply cooperatives such as Ohio Farm Bureau Cooperative Association, Midland Cooperatives, Inc., Consumers' Cooperative Association, and Indiana Farm Bureau Cooperative Association regularly raise very considerable amounts of capital by direct sale of preferred stock and other securities. A good rate of interest is paid and paid regularly, and the market for such securities is becoming broader all the time. As a means of attracting more such investment—especially from members—Ohio Farm Bureau Cooperative Association has offered a bond that provides the investor protection against inflation. These bonds carry a variable rate of interest, which can increase, within limits, in relation to increases in the cost of living index of the Bureau of Labor Statistics.

Certain urban consumer cooperatives also have been conducting successful financing programs, primarily among their own member-ship, in recent years. One reason for this is their consistent record of paying a return—usually 5 per cent—on their shares. Another reason is the success they have achieved in their operations. But a third reason undoubtedly is the pride in ownership of an important community institution which has been engendered in these coops' membership. To take one example, the Hyde Park Consumer Cooperative Society in Chicago's South Side has at times experienced so heavy a demand for its stock that some care had to be exercised lest overcapitalization result.

In general, however, members of cooperatives have not invested nearly so heavily in their cooperatives as they could do. For example, it is estimated that only about 2 per cent to 3 per cent of the total investments of farmers are in their cooperatives. Despite the fact that they generally obtain a far better return per dollar invested from their cooperatives than from any other investment.

Part of the job cooperatives must do is to educate their members far better than they have thus far done to the desirability of really substantial investment in their own businesses. There are two ways such education must be carried on. The first is by actually rendering an outstanding economic and social service to their members. And the second, of course, is by carrying on a continuous information and education program among them so they will clearly see why they should invest more heavily.

There are some rather dramatic examples of where both these things have been done. In 1959 Group Health Cooperative of Puget Sound undertook to raise $2,500,000 for a new hospital by sale of bonds to its 55,000 members. In a period of a few months the issue had been oversubscribed. The members of the cooperative health plan will collectively be paying interest to themselves severally. No outside debt will have to be contracted. The people's money is building the people's hospital.

Again, the thirty-year old Amalgamated Dwellings Housing Cooperative in New York City undertook in 1960 to refinance the last quarter million dollars of its mortgage by sale of $500 4 per cent mortgage bonds to its member-resident-owners and to people living in adjacent cooperative housing projects. In a period of a few months the entire $250,000 had been subscribed. The reaction of some of the purchasers was heartening. They said: "Why not finance our own homes with our own money, instead of putting it in savings banks or investing it elsewhere? For if we do that, then we must turn around and incur an indebtedness perhaps to those same savings banks or other financial institutions in order to get them to loan us back our own money to finance our housing!"

So progress is being made in cooperative finance.

But such progress will be too slow and in too small amounts if only the methods thus far described are used. Many kinds of cooperatives have demonstrated their great capacity for growth and expansion and the current needs of our society bear witness to the corresponding need for such growth. Cooperative housing, cooperative group-health plans, cooperative electric service, cooperative supermarkets in urban areas, cooperative oil companies are only a few examples where far more rapid growth could and would, with benefit to all society, take place if only the money were available to finance it.

It is therefore fortunate, that, with perhaps prophetic insight, a number of cooperative-type mutual-insurance companies have been founded in the past thirty years. For it is into the purchase of insurance that the major stream of the American people's savings is now flowing. "Wall Street" was once the arbitor of the financial future of American industry. No more. That power has now passed into the hands of the tremendous insurance companies of the country. It is to them that the major portion of savings and capital of the people is entrusted. It is they which can by buying or not buying affect even the interest rate on government bonds. It is their investment policies that determine in which directions investment funds shall flow.

In "Wall Street's" heyday there still persisted a considerable amount of genuine competition in the American economy. Today that competition is only a formality in many of our most powerful industries. Hence if to industrial monopoly is added financial monopoly in a few hands economic freedom will indeed be threatened with strangulation.

If, on the other hand, ways can be found whereby the people whose savings make possible the great pools of capital can actually direct and guide the use of that capital, then we may hope for continuing vigor in our democratic and free institutions.

The central economic problem of our times is this: To find the means and methods whereby businesses which are big enough to have maximum efficiency can at the same time be democratically owned by many people, democratically controlled by many people, and faithful in their trusteeship of the people's resources.

This is why cooperative insurance companies are of such great importance.

The beginnings of cooperative mutual insurance lay in the idea of groups of people "carrying their own insurance." What an insurance company actually is—as has been said—is a group of people with common dangers and hazards joining to share those dangers and pooling some of their savings for that purpose. Therefore any group of people which really wants to can make an insurance company out of themselves and their needs for insurance—provided, of course, they act wisely and under good management.

Benjamin Franklin introduced this idea into American life. In 1752 he organized a mutual fire-insurance company among the residents of Philadelphia.

More recently the mutual-insurance idea has been used by many groups of people. They have used it as a means of paying premiums to themselves and keeping control of their own savings. One of the earliest forms of such cooperative insurance was born, as most cooperative enterprises have been, out of sheer necessity. Farmers could not—and cannot even now as a rule—receive fire insurance from commercial insurance companies. Farms weren't served effectively by fire departments. So "Farmers' Mutuals" began to be organized in the last century. From the beginning they have been the purest kind of cooperative endeavor. They consist simply of a pooling of the risk of fire and an agreement to share among the whole group the cost of fire suffered by any one. Many of the Farmers' Mutuals have operated without any premium charges at all; simply assessing members (policy holders) their share of the cost of any claims for fire damage. More than ten thousand Farmers' Mutuals or Township Mutuals, as they are sometimes called, are now providing protection for millions of farmers and rural residents against fire, tornado, hail, and other kinds of disaster.

These small cooperative insurance companies have served—and still do—a useful purpose. They have met a need which otherwise could not be met. They have met it by the purest kind of cooperative action.

But this was not enough. And beginning in the middle twenties various groups of cooperative-minded people began to organize their own insurance companies to meet their own insurance needs. Again farmers largely led the way. Farmers' membership organization leaders—such as Murray D. Lincoln of Ohio Farm Bureau—saw in cooperative insurance for their members a means of saving their members considerable money, a means of enabling their members to control and use their own savings, and a potential source of secured-loan capital for other types of cooperative enterprise. From such insight sprang Nationwide Insurance Companies which were first organized in 1926 as Farm Bureau Insurance Companies of Ohio and have now grown to be one of the largest and most remarkable factors in the entire insurance industry. Mutual Service Insurance Companies, a merger of five companies organized in the 1920's from the same motivation by Minnesota and Wisconsin farmers, are today under the presidency of F. F. Rondeau, one of the most respected institutions in the upper Midwest. Farmers Union companies and many more have followed a similar course.

Credit-union leaders saw the necessity of insurance of credit unions against non-payment of debts. They also grasped the deeply humanitarian idea that "debt should die with the debtor." So they organized an insurance company—CUNA Mutual Insurance Society—to provide loan protection and life-savings insurance.

Results were surprising—often astonishing. The cooperative companies, belonging as they did and do to the policy owners, reduced premiums as much as they safely could. Sometimes such reductions amounted to as much as 40 per cent under the charges of commercial companies. This was true in the early days of cooperative insurance. It is less true today because other companies have in many cases met the competition of cooperative companies' rates.

What was more important, however, was the carrying out in practice of the idea—really the fact—that all the money entrusted to insurance companies actually belongs to the policy owners.

This is a very large sum of money. For illustration, between 1945 and 1949 the assets of insurance companies increased, on the average, $3.6 billion a year. The assets of life-insurance companies have been roughly doubling every decade and they amount to well over one-tenth of the total national wealth of the United States. Furthermore, the ten largest life-insurance companies control about 70 per cent of all admitted assets of such companies. The officers of such companies have the opportunity and the power to invest between $8 and $10 billion every year. This is more than twice the amount of money that was controlled by the investment bankers in the heyday of "Wall Street." Not only is the debt structure of most of the major industries of the country largely in the hands of insurance companies. In recent years these companies have begun to purchase "blue-chip" stocks for their portfolios. As yet only certain states permit this. But such a practice puts in the hands of insurance executives a power to decide what companies shall live and grow and what ones shall not.

Just how such a power could be exercised becomes clear if we look at the electric-power business. One of the favorite fields of investment for insurance companies is the bonds of electric utilities. The utilities can obtain money at low interest rates because of this. Now suppose the opponents of rural electrification should one of these days have their way in Congress and abolish the Rural Electrification Administration and the source of loans to rural electric cooperatives. What chance would those cooperatives have of receiving financing from the insurance companies? What chance indeed! The electric cooperatives in Wisconsin average only one customer per mile of line for every nine customers of their private utility competitors. In some states the power companies' advantage is even greater. The electric cooperatives must invest about four times as much in plant per dollar of revenue as their competitors. The electric cooperatives are forbidden to offer service to communities of more than fifteen hundred population. And they must serve any rural customer needing service regardless of the cost or "profitability." If insurance executives had the decision to make as between investing in private utilities or rural electric cooperatives they would surely decide that the private utilities would get the money and that they didn't like cooperatives very well—especially not as a place to invest.

Rural electricity is a necessity for farmers and rural people. It is a necessity to our national welfare. But as investment opportunities for the insurance billions, the cooperatives supplying such electricity simply could not compete. Not unless they went to a cooperative mutual-insurance company whose decisions would be influenced by additional motives beside those of pure economic gain.

There are two kinds of insurance companies from the viewpoint of organization.

There are stock companies and mutual companies.

In a stock company, the ownership and voting control lie with the stockholders. They sell insurance to *another* group of people—the policy holders.

In a mutual company, the policy holders own the company. In order to be an owner of a mutual company you must first become a policy holder. Each policy holder has one vote. In both kinds of companies "voters" are so numerous and scattered that few actually attend and vote in company meetings. Thus the board of directors and officers generally continue in office over long periods of time and hence control almost indefinitely the policy holders' savings. The bigger the company becomes and the more of the people's money is deposited with it, the more likely this is to happen.

Insurance, as we have seen, is a great, really idealistic institution based on people's savings pooled for their common security.

Yet today insurance firms not only have a vast hold on the people's savings but make considerable profits from those savings. Even though policy holders alone make possible the company existence, large profits are being made by some insurance companies from control over investment of the people's savings.

This should be less true of "mutual" companies than it is of stock companies. Mutual companies were started to meet the people's needs for insurance in such a way that the benefits would go to the people insured.

Unfortunately, some "mutual" companies are mutual in name only. Their purpose has been forgotten. Control does not really lie with the policy holders. Their savings, which are the key to their economic progress, are out of their hands. Instead, they are invested, used, controlled by management groups which recognize little if any responsibility to the policy owners to whom the savings actually belong.

This can be dangerous to America. Once a people loses control over its savings, democracy can be in grave danger in their country—especially if the savings are aggregated in very large pools.

But the reader will say, "Surely there must be some way that the people can regain control of the insurance savings!" There is a way. It lies in the new "cooperative" type of company which is truly mutual in its purpose, point of view, and manner of operation, a few examples of which we have just given.

These mutual companies were set up to give to the people who need insurance so badly continuing control over the savings they must pool together. They were established to prove that the people can provide their own insurance through their own companies, if only they want to badly enough.

So these mutuals operate on the same principle as other cooperative financial agencies—the principle of the people's money for the people's use, under the people's control. Many, though not all of them, have been formed among groups of people already associated in other organizations with a common purpose.

These companies which actually, though not legally, may be called "cooperative" insurance companies, differ from other ("old-line") insurance companies in these important ways:

First, they attempt in a variety of ways to bring about active participation by policy owners in decision making on company policies. They attempt to give effective control over the companies to the policy owners.

One "cooperative" company, Group Health Mutual, divides its territory of operation into districts. In each district meetings are regularly held and all policy owners are urged to attend. Those who do, receive reports, elect delegates to the annual meeting of the company, and instruct those delegates as to how they shall vote on current issues.

Others among these true mutual companies attempt to assure democratic control by close association of the company with a membership organization. Examples of this are the National and Nebraska Farmers' Union Insurance Companies, Farm Bureau companies in some states, a company recently organized by Wisconsin Electric

Cooperatives, and some of the companies organized by fraternal and nationality organizations.

Nationwide Insurance Companies started out as Farm Bureau Insurance Companies in Ohio. By 1960 they operated in half the states of the Union. In the course of expansion of these companies they have entered each state under a "sponsoring" agreement with a democratically controlled membership organization. Some of these are State Credit Union Leagues, most of them are state or regional cooperatives such as Farmers' Cooperative Exchange in the Carolinas, or Farm Bureau Cooperative Associations in Ohio and Pennsylvania, or Eastern Cooperatives in New York. The "sponsor" in such cases agrees to promote Nationwide Insurance in various proper ways and receives in return certain payments for services rendered from the insurance companies plus the right to nominate a member of the board of directors of the companies. More recently greater emphasis has been placed on a scheme of "policy-holder advisory councils." Nationwide agents begin at local level with meetings to which they invite groups of policy holders to discuss company policies and practices and to elect representatives to similar regional meetings. These, in turn, elect about fifty people who spend two days each year in Columbus as guests of the companies and have opportunity to inform the officers of the wishes of the policy owners "nationwide."

In many ways the method most certain to achieve the desired result of actual policy-owner control over the use and investment of their own premium money is the one devised after years of effort by Mutual Service Insurance Companies with home offices in St. Paul. A legal entity called Mutual Service Cooperative was set up with provisions that voting shares in it could be held only by local farm supply, marketing, consumer, electric, or other cooperatives, by credit unions, or by farmers' mutuals. More than five hundred such local cooperative organizations, many of whose members are of course Mutual Service policy owners, now own these voting shares. All policy owners in Mutual Service Companies agree to give their proxy in voting at annual meetings of the insurance companies to the board of directors of Mutual Service Cooperative. That board, of course, is elected by the delegates chosen by the local cooperatives which own its voting shares. It is hard to see how these companies could ever escape from the direct control of the people whose money is entrusted to them. Even if the companies wanted to, which of course they don't.

Second, "cooperative" insurance companies provide insurance at as low a net cost to their policy-owner members as they can possibly do legally and safely. They do this in two ways: first, they reduce premiums as much as possible; second, they pay to their policy owners as much as they can safely pay in dividends. On some group policies these dividends have run as high as 40 per cent of the premium originally charged.

Third, "cooperative" insurance companies recognize that their policy owners have entrusted their money to their companies and that the investment of that money should therefore be in enterprises that will benefit the people whose savings make the investment possible. So "cooperative" insurance companies invest as large a proportion of their assets as they can and are allowed to do in other types of cooperative business enterprises. They have made secured loans to farm-supply and urban consumer cooperatives, to housing cooperatives, and to cooperative health plans, to mention only a few.

Here again, however, as we have seen is true in the case of other kinds of cooperative financial institutions, there are real limits to what can be done. One such limit is a very good one. It is the natural refusal of insurance-company officials to make loans or investments in other cooperatives unless such investments can be justified by the same standard as would be applied to any other investments. This is frequently excellent "medicine" for cooperatives whose "houses" are not in proper order. But beyond this, in some states insurance regulations will allow no more than 5 per cent of the assets of any insurance company to be invested in or loaned to cooperative businesses, however excellent the security. In other states, the regulations are less severe. But always there is limitation on such investment to a minor fraction of the total portfolio of an insurance company, however cooperative its orientation may be.

It is, in any case, an accepted rule of operation of the "cooperative" insurance companies that their first job is to make of themselves the very best *insurance companies* they can become. For unless they first do that they will never be able to be of the help they desire to be in the development of other types of cooperative enterprise.

As a means of working toward synthesis of these two objectives, the Cooperative League in 1947 brought together most of the larger and more important cooperative-type insurance companies into an informal conference body called The Insurance Conference of the Cooperative League. Its aims and purposes were set forth as follows and have not since been changed. They demonstrate well the basic twofold purpose of the "cooperative" companies.

1. To preserve freedom of competition in the insurance business and to encourage and assure initiative, enterprise, improvement, and development in the insurance industry as required by the interests of the users of insurance services.

2. To encourage and promote a better public understanding of the insurance business.

3. To investigate matters of interest to the membership and to distribute information concerning such matters.

4. To provide a forum for the discussion, study, and solution of common problems.

5. To facilitate such business relationships between members as may be mutually advantageous.

6. To conduct education programs as to the relationship between the Conference and cooperative enterprise in all fields.

7. Generally to protect and advance the interests of the insuring public and the members of the Conference in every proper way.

8. To do any and all acts and things and carry on any and all business incidental to the foregoing.

The M-C-M Corporation is an example of how cooperative insurance companies and other kinds of cooperatives can work together for mutual benefit. It is an ingenious and highly successful means of broadening the lending ability of cooperative insurance companies and also making more efficient use of the people's capital invested in their cooperatives. M-C-M stands for Midland-Central-Mutual. The company is a real-estate holding and development company owned by two regional wholesale cooperatives and one "cooperative" insurance company. These are Midland Cooperative, Inc., Central Cooperatives,

Inc., and Mutual Service Insurance Companies, all operating in the upper Midwest. The details of the operation need not concern us here. In broad terms, what M-C-M does is to relieve local cooperatives of the necessity of tying up in real estate capital which they need for working operations. M-C-M buys from local cooperatives or acquires for them the facilities they need for expanding business. It then leases such properties to one or the other of the wholesales, which, in turn, subleases to the local cooperative. Using these leases behind each of which stands careful investigation by the wholesale and, usually, contractual relations between it and the local cooperative, M-C-M is able to offer more than an ordinary mortgage as security for a loan against its property. This, in turn, makes it possible for the third owner of M-C-M, namely, Mutual Service Insurance Company, to loan a considerably higher percentage of the actual value of the property than it could otherwise do.

Thus, more of the people's money entrusted to their insurance company can go to work at financing their local cooperative services. And less of the people's money must be tied up in ownership of real estate, so more of it can be used for inventory, payroll, expansion of services, and other actual operations.

Somewhat similar methods are beginning to be used by cooperative real-estate development companies in other parts of the country as well.

From its beginning more than thirty years ago "cooperative" insurance has grown by leaps and bounds. Why? Because these companies are guided by the needs of men and women who buy insurance, and directed by people of farseeing vision who pioneer in finding new and better ways to meet those needs. Most of them started from "scratch" in the late 1920's or the depression years. Today there are thirteen major cooperative insurance companies with total insurance in force of more than $7 billion! The Cooperative League's special study of these companies from 1950 to 1957 shows the following interesting facts:

Cooperative casualty and fire-insurance companies increased their direct premium written in these seven years from $76.5 million to $180.1 million. While they were as yet (1957) writing only 1.5 per cent of all insurance in the United States in this field, the growth of

135 per cent shown by these figures compared with an increase of 78 per cent for all casualty and fire insurance in the United States.

Gains of cooperative life-insurance companies are even more striking. With $1.07 billions of life insurance in force in 1950 they had grown to $5.14 billions in 1957—close to a fivefold increase. They held 1.1 per cent of all life insurance in force in the United States (1957), but their growth of 382 per cent compared with 99 per cent for all United States life insurance in this period.

These companies have been pathfinders in the field of insurance, charting a course for the benefit of policy holders which other companies have had to follow in order to stay in competition. In recent years a new problem has challenged their leaders: how to protect policy holders against the declining value of the insurance dollar in periods of inflation. In 1952 Nationwide Insurance purchased the assets of Mutual Income Foundation, and through this soundly based investment company has offered policy holders a chance to invest their savings in securities of well-managed companies with good prospects for growth in resources and earning power. Its insurance salesmen offer their clients shares in MIF as well as insurance policies. During one year alone—fiscal 1959—the net asset value of MIF shares rose 25 per cent. Owners of shares received on their investment 3.6 per cent in dividend income and 7.2 per cent in capital-gains distribution. Buyers of insurance are taking advantage of this opportunity and net assets of the fund rose from $4.9 million to $12.7 million during the fiscal year; sales of shares were $6.3 million, and sales of life insurance increased, too.

This highly successful move into a new kind of financial service to policy owners by Nationwide Insurance gave basic inspiration to a broadly-conceived new financial venture by American cooperatives. It started to take form in 1959 and early 1960 in a series of meetings of the board of directors of the Cooperative League.

Mutual investment funds had already proved themselves the most popular and fastest-growing investment vehicle for the small investor. They enabled the average family or the small business institution to invest its savings with a maximum of safety and in a variety of securities all at once. Furthermore, mutual funds are in all essential respects genuine cooperative institutions.

Why not, then, asked Cooperative League directors, organize a mutual fund under the sponsorship of a number of the cooperative businesses of the nation? Why not set it up as a balanced, diversified, open-end fund? That could mean that half perhaps of its investments could be made in the securities of cooperative businesses whose record as sustained-yield investments was as good as could be found. The other half of the investments would be in common stocks of commercial (not cooperative) businesses capable not only of producing income but also of growth and capital gains. Well and carefully managed, as it would, of course, have to be, such a mutual fund could offer sound and attractive investment opportunity to anyone. Particularly would it be able to attract a far larger percentage of their total investments by members of cooperatives, who up to this time had had opportunity to invest only in single cooperative enterprises at a time. Through the mutual fund they could make investment in a diversified selection of the securities of a number of cooperatives. Whereas up to this time few cooperative member families had more than 2 per cent or 3 per cent of their total investment in cooperatives, why might not the mutual fund attract 40 per cent to 50 per cent?

And the same general reasoning was applicable to the investment of surpluses of cooperative businesses themselves, some of which had found their way into the pockets of strong competitors of cooperatives. If a mutual fund reasonably oriented toward investment in cooperatives could be made successful and could earn an excellent reputation, why could not those surpluses of the people's money already controlled by the people's cooperative institutions be attracted to flow into a far larger pool and made to work twice in the people's interest instead of only once?

Furthermore, members of the League board and their advisors could see a need for capital of far greater proportions than they had ever before even dared to contemplate. Cooperative housing in the New York area alone was so well accepted as the major answer to the need for unsubsidized middle- and lower-income family homes that hundreds of millions of dollars could be used in that one area alone with the greatest of benefit to the people and the communities. Certain cooperative health plans had demonstrated so convincingly their ability to meet the problem of rising medical costs and bring high-quality comprehensive care within the reach of the average family that, again, very large sums could very well be used in financing necessary facilities for such plans—both established ones and new ones. The preceding decade had seen the rise in all parts of the country of highly successful consumer cooperative shopping centers. The time was overripe for a rapid expansion of consumer ownership of more of the distribution system of the country as a means of extending ownership to millions of new families and of counteracting the surge toward monopoly in this vital field.

But the amount of capital required for such expansion was more by far than existing cooperative financial institutions could be expected to meet.

Most urgent of all, perhaps, was the need of American farmers. Their incomes were steadily declining despite—or was it *because of*— a veritable revolutionary increase in the technological efficiency and productivity of American agriculture. And literally *no* solution to the problem was even being proposed—except one. That one solution lay in a great expansion of both the volume and scope of business of farmer-owned cooperatives. That way the lost economic bargaining power of farmers could be regained. That way farmers could add to the income of agriculture some of the very lucrative earnings of industries which had previously made money *out of* agriculture. Integration under cooperative farmer ownership could be a very different thing from integration *of* farmers by commercial interests seeking only an increase in their feed business.

And so in late 1959 the Board of the Cooperative League voted to sponsor the organization of a mutual fund. It was stipulated that it be an open-end fund enabling anyone to purchase shares at any time— and to sell them to the fund at any time at the then asset value of the fund's portfolio. It was to be a balanced fund—with about half its investments in cooperative and other sustained yield securities and half in the stock of other types of business. And it was to be a diversified fund, meaning that no more than 5 per cent of its assets could be in any one company at any time.

The door was thrown wide open for any cooperative business to participate in ownership of the underwriting and investment-management firm which was to be organized to manage the mutual fund.

And a number of non-League members came through the door with their investments in this company.

It is too early to judge as yet what the results of this latest venture in cooperative finance—the people's money for the people's business and the people's needs—will be. But a new kind of statesmanship moves through the ranks of the leaders of American cooperative business today. And it gives hope that maybe in the very hour of crisis for democracy around the world the method and principles of cooperation will enable a segment of the American people to demonstrate for the first time in recorded history that part at least of the people's money, the people's credit, and the people's savings can be kept in the people's control and used for the people's benefit.

At the beginning of this chapter it was said that it was to be about "how the people's credit is used—or abused; made into a dynamic instrument of modern life—or turned into a means of controlling the lives of the very people whose credit it is."

To that general theme we must return, as the chapter is concluded.

All the cooperative financial institutions herein discussed exist, of course, within the general framework of the monetary system of our country. Some of the peculiarities and dangers of that system must be noted, for they underline the extreme importance of the people controlling both their own savings and the use of their own credit. And despite the significant accomplishments of cooperative financial institutions, only a beginning has been made at establishing such control.

Our present monetary system makes our whole economic welfare dependent upon increasing debt. It is only by expanding debt that we can obtain the money supply which is necessary for adequate growth and maximum employment. Our money is manufactured by the private commercial banks of the country when they make loans and even when they make investments other than out of savings deposits. This rather strange and almost certainly unconstitutional method of giving away the basic public function of money creation to private interests results from the fractional reserve system on which our commercial banking system operates. This means that banks are required to have on hand or in reserve only a fraction as much money as they are allowed to lend and invest. The rest of the credit they use to make loans and investments is literally "manufactured" by the banks by writing figures in their books of account. With reserve requirements fixed by the Federal Reserve Board—normally at less than 20 per cent—commercial banks can manufacture demand deposit credits almost at will and lend them into circulation at interest. With a 20 per cent reserve requirement in effect the banks are able to lend about five times as many dollars of newly created checkbook money as they possess in reserves of actual cash or credit on the books of the Federal Reserve banks. Thus when the banks buy government bonds they use the credit of the government and the people—namely, the power to create money—with which to buy them. The interest they receive amounts to subsidy by the nation to the banks. It is a payment of interest by the government upon its own credit.

In 1951 interest on the national debt was about $5⅔ billion. It was $9 billion in 1959, due, principally, to increased interest rates.

Because the nation has thus given away its money-creating power it is presumed that it must not itself exercise that power. At least it never does so. The closest we ever come to doing so is when the Federal Reserve banks create new reserve bank credit. For while the Federal Reserve banks are wholly owned by the private banks of the system, they are nonetheless subject to some degree of public control, through the Congress and the Executive Department. As long as the Federal Reserve Board and banks recognize themselves as exercising the essentially public and governmental function of creating and controlling money, there is a chance of the system working reasonably well, except for the chronic problem of ever-increasing debt.

But in order for this to be the case the Reserve System must act in the public interest rather than that of the private money-lending agencies of the country.

There have been times when the Federal Reserve Board came close to doing this. But not enough such times.

It is difficult to see how we can assure adequate rate of growth and maximum employment with reasonable price stability as long as we rely on the debt-money system we now have. Increasing debt is the price that must be paid to bring needed money into existence and make economic growth possible. The synthetic money created in this process is subject to sudden destruction by the simple process of reduction of debt. And the United States government, meanwhile, forces itself to pay interest on its own credit.

It is time some changes were made.

The government of the United States should assume responsibility for creating from time to time, by its own action and without expanding its debt, enough new money—and no more than enough—to accommodate the expansion of productive capacity in the economy and maintain reasonable price stability.

Were the government to assume its proper duty with respect to money creation it would be necessary correspondingly to curtail the money-creating powers of the private commercial banks. This, however, could readily be done by a gradual increase in reserve requirements.

Under such a scientific monetary system it would become possible gradually to reduce the mountainous burden of our present national debt. It would also be possible to guard effectively against either monetary inflation or monetary deflation. These are, of course, political as well as economic problems and therefore beyond the scope of this book. But they concern us deeply as citizens just the same.

X

THE ORGANIZED BUYING
POWER OF CONSUMERS

Every kind of cooperative enterprise which we have discussed in this book is a consumer or "user's" cooperative. All of them are in business because they provide some kind of goods or services to people who need, consume, and use them. This can even be said of farmers' marketing cooperatives. The farmers need storage facilities for their crops and a marketing agent to sell them in an orderly manner. The marketing cooperatives provide these services, and the farmers consume or use them.

If this seems to be stretching words a bit, the case of the marketing cooperative is the only one where that is true. Cooperative health plans are organized to provide health care to groups of people who need and consume such care. Housing cooperatives are built and owned by the consumers of the housing. Electric cooperatives exist to enable rural people to consume electricity, and without them many of these people would even now not be consumers of electric energy at all. "Farm-supply cooperatives" are really consumer cooperatives specializing in production supplies which farmers must consume in ever-larger amounts to carry forward their farming operations efficiently. Credit unions are consumer cooperatives providing loans and credit to meet their members' needs. The purpose of cooperative insurance companies is to enable the consumers of the insurance services to continue to exercise an effective control over their own savings. Farmers are consumers of the credit services provided by various parts of the farm-credit system. Petroleum cooperatives belong to and are conducted in the interest of consumers of petroleum products—whether they be farmers with large demands for tractor operation or townspeople operating a single automobile. Even the cooperative wholesales owned by independent retailers provide stocks of commodities and whosesaling services to their members who "consume" these stocks and services in the course of their business.

So this chapter cannot be called *the* chapter about "consumer" cooperatives. It is no more that than the preceding chapters have been.

But this chapter is about the cooperatives which most people think of when the words "consumer cooperative" are spoken.

These are the coop food stores, supermarkets, and shopping centers.

In a way this is not illogical, for the average family spends about 40 per cent of its income for food. It is around the food store that the largest single interest of the people as consumers revolves. The organization of the buying power of the people as consumers has some effect on the economy in whatever line of business it takes place—oil, health care, savings, and credit—what not.

But only as *major* consumer needs are met cooperatively, only as the people come into ownership of businesses supplying the things on which their big expenditures are made—only then can the full influence of cooperative enterprise upon a nation's economy be brought to bear. Only then can "consumer preference" begin to have any meaning. And only then can the consumer interest begin to be asserted and defended as a salutary countervailing force to the overweening power of highly organized producers.

In some countries this has taken place. Scandinavia, Switzerland, and Austria are the best examples. Great Britain, West Germany, and Holland are others. In Sweden about 4 per cent of manufacturing is done by cooperatives, and about 17 per cent of total national business. But more than 30 per cent of all food is bought in cooperative stores. The early consumer-owned stores were almost entirely confined to the grocery business. The main consumer interest was broadly organized in cooperative ownership by consumers. On this base was built a broader consumer supply business—household needs, clothing, appliances, and the like. And out of this came manufacturing for the most logical of reasons.

In the early twentieth century there were powerful monopolies in Sweden, electric supplies, footwear, flour, among them. Such businesses are monopolies no more. The reason for this is not because the government stepped in with "trust-busting" activities. In fact, there are no anti-trust laws in Sweden.

They aren't needed. Because the cooperatives do 4 per cent of the nation's manufacturing and because they could do 44 per cent if it seemed wise or necessary.

Most of the cooperative manufacturing is done by Kooperativa Forbundet, the national cooperative wholesale organization, owned by the retail consumer cooperatives of Sweden. "KF," as it is called, entered manufacturing because the buying power of more than half of the Swedish people had been organized through their ownership of their cooperatives. It was the job of the cooperatives to protect the consumer interest in the economy. So when it became obvious that consumers were paying extortionate prices for certain commodities because those prices were "administered" by monopolies or near-monopolies, the leaders of KF decided to do something about it.

What to do was clear. Compete with the monopolies so they wouldn't be monopolies any more and so the prices of their products would be determined not by arbitrary "administered" decisions but by market-place competition.

So KF went into the business of manufacturing electric-light globes. And the price came down about 40 per cent. KF began to manufacture overshoes—one of Sweden's basic necessities. And the price of overshoes came down to a reasonable economic level. The same thing happened in flour milling and a few other lines.

Cooperatives can do this sort of thing. When other forms of business would not dare to challenge a firmly rooted monopoly, coops can do so *if* they have a large enough number of members. For if that is the case, there exists an assured market for the manufactured products.

Why, then, did the Swedish coops stop with 4 per cent of the manufacturing business of Sweden? They stopped because they did not need to go further in order effectively to protect the economic interest of the whole nation as consumers.

Kooperativa Forbundet had proved that the people could produce for themselves in their own factories if they had to and that, if they did so, they could successfully compete with even the most powerful monopolies and bring prices down to "life size."

Having done this, all the board of directors of KF has had to do to put the fear of the organized consumer into the hearts of industrialists who were exacting too high prices was to hold a meeting to consider going into a new line of manufacture—and leave the windows open while they discussed it!

But this is only possible because in the beginning the buying power of the people for food—their *big* consumer purchase item—was broadly organized in cooperative ownership of food stores in the villages, towns, and cities of Sweden.

It is of interest to remark a difference between the consumer cooperatives of Sweden and those of Great Britain. As the 1960's began, the Swedish cooperatives were continuing their robust growth. They were collecting large sums of money by voluntary contribution to assist the people of less economically developed countries in building up cooperatives as a means of raising their living standards. The influence of the cooperative movement on Swedish life, thought, and policy was never greater. The author of these lines once asked a Swedish cooperative leader whether his organization—Kooperativa Forbundet—ever attempted to influence Swedish elections. He replied rather vigorously that it did not. The cooperative movement was "nonpolitical" in Sweden. "But," he quickly added, "whenever an important question of public policy arises we put our research department to work on it and we prepare and issue a report setting forth the interest of all the people as consumers in the matter. And such reports have great influence upon our government."

Meanwhile, however, the cooperative movement of Great Britain was torn by bitter debate and deep decision. The cooperatives were losing ground. Their percentage of total business was declining. Their influence on public policy was not great.

Why the difference? We have seen how and why the Swedish cooperatives entered manufacturing. They did it to end excessive overpricing of certain monopoly-controlled commodities. Obviously this was of benefit not alone to cooperative members but to all the people of Sweden. And this point of view carried through into the business practices of all consumer cooperatives in Sweden. They sought not so much to pay a large patronage refund to their members as to influence the economic life of Sweden for the benefit of their members and all other Swedes as well.

This called for what is termed in cooperative circles an "active-price" policy. Which means that cooperatives sell at going market prices only when such prices are economically justified. But that they reduce prices when they are higher than need be for sound economic operations. Thus, instead of paying larger patronage refunds for the benefit of members only, the cooperatives give their members and patrons their principal benefits at the point of sale, in lower prices. But this has the effect of causing competitors also to lower prices. And so all Swedish consumers are benefited.

In Great Britain an opposite policy has been followed. It is the traditional "Rochdale" policy of selling only at "going market prices." And great emphasis is laid upon the size of this patronage refund—or "Divi," as the British call it—which cooperative *members* receive. No matter how large the margins or markups on the various items sold, the British cooperatives have tended to take the going market price and then to increase the "Divi" correspondingly. This clearly leads to a strong interest in the dividend on the part of cooperative members. But it means that the consumer cooperatives are exerting little influence on the price structure of the British economy as a whole. Perhaps this is a reason why it could not be said in Britain, as it was in Sweden, that reports issued by the cooperative movement "have great influence." Perhaps it is a reason, too, why the level of loyalty to their cooperatives is lower in Britain than in Scandinavia. Maybe the broader ideal of mutual aid and cooperation must be actually applied by cooperative organizations as well as individuals if they are to continue to merit and receive an active interest and deep loyalty on the part of their memberships.

The average American knows little as yet about consumer cooperatives. The obvious reason is that there are not as yet enough cooperative stores and supermarkets in the growing cities to draw the attention of many people. In rural areas the situation is different. Many kinds of cooperatives are known and recognized as integral parts of American rural life.

If trends that arose in the 1950's continue, however, the time may not be far distant when urban Americans will be as conscious of consumer cooperation as are their rural cousins.

Indeed the times require that this be so. For Americans as consumers are in need of an advocate. The anti-trust laws have seldom been enforced—particularly not against the larger offenders. And even the so-called "regulatory" commissions which are supposed to act in the consumer's interest were packed, during the decade of the fifties, with representatives of the very industries they are supposed to regulate.

The absence of a defense, however, is a mild problem for consumers compared to the all-out attack on their pocketbooks, morals, and peace of mind which jabs at them from every television screen, shouts at them from every radio, entices them from every newspaper and magazine.

No reasonable person can fail to acclaim the accomplishments of American industry. It has subjected to mass production—and thus brought within range of the family budget—appliances and devices which reduce both time and effort required to perform routine tasks of living, especially the chores of housekeeping.

This has freed women as never before in history for far more active participation in other phases of life, including public affairs. A better civilization and a deeper cultural and spiritual life should result.

And yet the most "modern" houses are being built without bookcases!

And there is another and less encouraging aspect of "progress" in mass production of things.

Above all, we must buy debt. And the cure for small debts we are told is to contract a bigger one—without inquiring about the terms or attempting to ascertain what amount of interest we are actually being charged. So serious had this become by the end of the fifties and so exorbitant some of the hidden charges on installment debt and "financing" of automobiles, for example, that Senator Douglas of Illinois introduced and pressed toward passage a bill to require honest revelation of the actual annual interest rate involved in all such fancy arrangements. The bill had strong support from labor, cooperatives, credit unions, women's organizations. But most commercial interests opposed it. Naturally enough, for many of them were actually making more money out of the "financing" of their sales than out of the sales of the merchandise itself.

We were told in the 1950's that our country was "too poor" to afford enough school classrooms for our children's education or adequate salaries for their teachers. We were "too poor" as a nation to stop pollution of our streams or contamination of the air. We were "too poor" to do anything effective about slum clearance or rehabilitation of our cities.

But since our economy must be kept in high gear, consumers must learn to be as overindulgent of themselves as possible and to increase continuously their debt burden. For upon this increase in consumer debt plus the large volume of military expenditures depends the market for the things producing companies want to turn out. And the decisions of the large producers determine what is to be produced —not the preference of consumers. One leading marketing expert is quoted by the *Wall Street Journal* as follows: "The solution to marketing problems is not necessarily one of giving consumers what they want but rather to make consumers want what we, the marketers, want them to want."

There is a whole new profession that has arisen in recent years which is dedicated to this very cause. This is the new social science of "motivational research." The motivational researchers have made a brilliant and astounding discovery. It is that man is by nature a base creature. And that he is to be induced to indulge himself and thus to buy things by appeals to pride, ambition, desire for luxurious display, self-love, lust, and greed. People don't ride on airplanes to save time or to keep in touch with more people. They do it for the satisfaction of making other people who don't ride on airplanes feel inferior to them. So advise the motivational researchers. And some $12 billion a year is entrusted to them and their hirelings every year by American industry to make their chosen appeals effective.

They are not, needless to say, so up to date. The same discovery about man's nature was revealed by the authors of the Old Testament some four thousand years ago. But they at least regarded this as bad —something to be changed lest the judgment of God descend upon their nation.

Today a different attitude is evident.

One savings institution in Chicago has recently changed its radio commercial. It now goes about like this: "This idea of saving because it is a good thing for society for you to save is 'for the birds.' The reason for you to save with us is because it is a nice selfish way to get more luxuries for yourself."

The motivational researchers' "astonishing discovery" that man is more easily appealed to through his baser motives than through his finer ones is nothing new. But great societies and great nations have tried at least to appeal to the higher motives of their citizens and to keep the less constructive and more anti-social ones under control. When it becomes the accepted pattern to develop every selfish impulse, every feeling of vanity and pride and snobbishness, then it becomes hard, indeed, to arouse people to accept a national purpose worthy of the name.

Books are being written about the great importance of consumers in our economy. And other books about our "high standard of living." But less and less is said about "consumer preference." For that is becoming obsolete. As the big companies grow bigger and the smaller ones become either merged, swallowed, or dead, consumers are being confronted with the command that they "buy nationally advertised brands." It is seldom pointed out that this is, in fact, all that consumers have to do to assure the early death of practically all really independent small business and the ultimate control of our economy by a handful of giant concerns in all key industries.

It is pointed out by people in the television industry that no more than a score of national concerns can afford nationwide television advertising at all. Buying "nationally advertised brands" means, therefore, patronizing one or another of those twenty companies.

But surely there is vigorous competition in the food-store business. At the moment it would appear so—at least at the retail level. In the livestock and fruit and vegetable markets big buyers such as the giant chains seem ever more able to dictate prices and frequently to exact special concessions. But at retail it does appear that housewives are the beneficiaries of some pretty keen competition for the food-basket trade.

And yet men who ought to know are predicting that if present trends continue it will not be long before there will exist effective control even of retail-food business by a very few concerns. At that point we'll begin to get "administered pricing" of bread and beans.

To quote Mr. R. G. Zimmerman, nationally recognized pioneer in the supermarket industry, speaking at the 1956 Boston Conference on Distribution:

"If our studies of present trends have any meaning, we foresee that within a decade or so the food retailing industry will shrink into fewer and fewer hands. It is not inconceivable that by 1965 a figurative handful of large supermarket organizations will *control* 75 per cent of the food business."

So it is well to recall how fundamental to the problem of consumers are the facts about administered pricing. Briefly those facts are that we should have had practically no price inflation in the 1950's if so-called "natural" economic influences had been able to operate. The competitive sectors of the economy were responsible for price increases of less than 1 per cent in the years 1953 to 1958. But both those industries and all the nation as consumers were saddled with an over-all rise of 8 per cent in the wholesale-price index in those years. Eighty-five per cent of this increase was accounted for by the very substantial boosting of prices in the monopolistic, administered-price industries.

There is, of course, a way to assert effectively the consumers' interest in our economic system. There is a way to make "consumer preference" meaningful again. Not alone as to quality and price of goods but also as to *what kinds* of goods and services are to be produced.

That way is to organize the buying power of consumers so they can speak together and have some weight when they do so. It is to enable consumers themselves to own some of the businesses that serve consumer needs and thus enforce the consumer interest by effective competition.

It isn't easy to do this. Particularly is it not easy in the biggest area of consumer expenditures—food. For it is hard to persuade consumers that at present they actually need more food stores or supermarkets. Sometimes it seems that there are too many already. The situation is not like most of the other fields where cooperatives have proved successful. There wasn't much of *any* rural electricity until the coops were organized by those who needed it. The same was true of open-formula, high-analysis fertilizer. There is nowhere near enough good housing at costs average families can afford even yet. Nor enough available good-quality medical care or facilities through which to dispense it. And so on.

But food stores! Surely this is no keenly felt need of American consumers. Around the turn of the third quarter of the twentieth century it may be. But not now.

It took cooperatives many years, and some severe losses, and a lot of heartaches to find this out and adjust to it. Here is the story.

Exactly when the first consumer cooperative grocery store was organized in the United States is not known.

According to accepted cooperative history it could not have been before 1844, because in that year the "first" true consumers' cooperative was born in Rochdale, England, out of the distress, sweat, tears, and year-long savings of twenty-eight poor weavers.

But probably the first one in America was not many years after that, though its story, if so, is lost.

We do know that in the years of suffering on the prairies in the 1870's and 1880's there came a wave of cooperative organizations, largely fostered by the Granger Movement. Interestingly enough, many of these were consumer-goods and farm-supply cooperatives similar to the cooperative "general-store" operations of the present century. They aimed at giving the prairie farm family something to say about the cost of their necessities of daily living. At least one of these Granger-founded coops is still doing business—at Cadmus, Kansas.

But in the years of fast geographical expansion, the years of westward migration and settlement, the years of industrial growth and development, Americans were naturally enough an intensely producer-minded people. They remained so clear down to the middle of the twentieth century. And while here and there an idealistic group attempted consumer cooperation, the main stream of the people's thought and effort lay in increasing their incomes as producers rather than making the dollars they received work better for them as consumers.

Consequently the history of consumer cooperative food stores, as distinguished sharply from other kinds of consumer cooperatives, is one of frustrated hopes and repeated failures, clear down to the post World War II period.

In the early years of the twentieth century attempts were made by some labor unions, notably the Mine Workers, to set up consumer cooperative stores *for* their members. None of these succeeded. They did not succeed because cooperatives set up *for* people by other agencies, however beneficent their purposes, almost never succeed. Only cooperatives established *by* groups of people for their own use have a good chance of success. When the Miners' Union told their members, "Here is your store, patronize it," the natural reaction, particularly of miners' wives, was to look the gift horse critically in the mouth. And what they found was, too often, a rather poorly conducted enterprise managed by a man whose main recommendation was a sympathetic attitude toward organized labor.

One unfortunate result of these experiences, repeated in the Detroit area as late as the 1940's, has been to prejudice the older generation of labor leaders against the food-store type of consumer cooperative and to delay, in the United States, the kind of support for consumer cooperation which labor unions in western Europe have so consistently given it.

The years of the Great Depression brought forth, inevitably, a new interest in cooperation which expressed itself in many ways. The books of James Peter Warbasse, principal founder of the Cooperative League, were more and more widely read. Consumer cooperation sounded like a good idea. Devoted people offered their garages, often empty of automobiles anyway, as depots for the dispensing of groceries to "buying club" members. In California, after the defeat in 1934 of Upton Sinclair's dramatic "Epic Plan" for enabling the unemployed to produce for their own needs, people turned in many communities to organization of consumer cooperatives as an alternative basis for their hope of bettering their lot. There was, however, hardly any capital available for these ventures. The standard practice was to install an unemployed person as manager. And none of them lasted more than a few years.

There were, however, exceptions to this pattern of failure. Where groups of people from northern Europe had come to America and congregated in certain communities, they frequently brought with them a tradition of cooperative success in the "old country." Particularly was this true of Scandinavians and above all of Finnish people. In some New England communities, in the Bay area of California, in the Head of the Lakes area around Lake Superior, and a few other places, strong, solid consumer cooperative stores were established early in the twentieth century—and are growing steadily to this day. And one of the oldest consumer-goods cooperatives in our country is called New Cooperative Company and was founded in 1908 in southeast Ohio largely by Czech farmers and Czech miners.

So as economic improvement came—tragic as it is to say it—with the outbreak of war in Europe in 1939, there did exist a scattered base of consumer food-store cooperation over the country.

The period of World War II can be called the era of self-deception in the food-store movement. Many consumer cooperative stores were organized. A number of the already established regional wholesale farm-supply cooperatives began to handle groceries. Their business and that of National Cooperatives, central suppliers of some items, appeared to be booming. Few people took the trouble to note that, in that period of war-enforced scarcity of consumer goods, almost any kind of business appeared to be successful. Fewer still took the trouble to observe that the cooperatives were growing less fast—in the grocery business—than were most other food-marketing concerns. Undercapitalization was chronic. Management was just fair, at best. Facilities were whatever seemed most "economical." Another wave of failures was around the corner.

Ironically enough, one of the most dramatic of these failures resulted in part, at least, from a growing awakening to the very weaknesses just set forth. A move was inaugurated in Chicago to raise capital, city-wide, from those interested in consumer cooperative stores and to establish a chain of such stores with adequate supervision of management and the economies of centralized administration. There was nothing wrong with the idea. On the contrary, it was just what "the doctor" was trying to order. The only trouble was that the supervision never was effectively developed. The store management fell far short of the blueprint for it. Too little attention was paid to location or quality of facilities. And stores were opened before anywhere near enough families in the neighborhood had come to feel identified with them through investment in their shares. The whole enterprise collapsed after a few months.

Thus the years immediately following World War II witnessed

another succession of failures in consumer cooperative food stores. A number of the regional wholesales in the Middle West discontinued their grocery departments. And by 1950 there remained a few islands of success in a rather extensive sea of liquidations.

In 1951 the Cooperative League called a conference of managers of consumer cooperative food stores. The principal subject of discussion was how to save from failure cooperatives that were on a downward trend in business volume. There began a process of examination of the causes of failure that lasted over a period of several painful years. And out of this emerged a companion examination of the reasons for success where it was being achieved and of the necessary elements that must go together to make such success possible.

These conferences of consumer cooperative managers have continued each year. In 1959 the Consumer Cooperative Managers' Association was organized as a conference body of professional managers. It is dominated by the managers of the largest and most successful of the consumer cooperative supermarkets and shopping centers, of which today there are a rapidly growing number. Among their managers and boards of directors there is evident a new confidence that they can meet the competition of any enterprise in the business, including the national chains.

What happened?

The consumer cooperative food-store and consumer-shopping center movement grew up. It learned a basic essential lesson. That lesson was this: A good idea is not enough. Even a fine, challenging ideal based in the greatest moral, social, and spiritual needs of man is not enough automatically to assure the success of a business enterprise. Such an idea and ideal are assets to a business enterprise of incalculable *potential* value. But it alone cannot provide that value. Indeed, it itself cannot even continue to flourish unless it is married to excellent management, adequate capitalization, definite involvement, through investment, of enough families to sustain a large-size operation, and facilities at least as attractive and well located as those of competitors. The issue of such a marriage can be a lusty child.

For example:

In the late 1940's labor-union interest in checking the rapid rise in living costs was at a peak. It lead to some of the same mistakes which had marred the period of World War I. But the members of the United Rubber Workers of America in Akron, Ohio, the rubber "capital" of the world, had learned the lesson. They wanted a consumer cooperative shopping center as badly as anyone. But they wanted one that would last. They knew they could not open a store with hope of success unless it was as fine a store as the best of the other stores in Akron. They knew this would take capital—probably about two hundred thousand dollars. They knew, too, that there was only one right way to raise the basic capital. It had to be raised by selling shares to families who were going to be members, owners, and customers of the new coop. They had learned from recent experiences in the Detroit area that having a general interest on the part of union members wasn't enough. Their wives had to be convinced of the value of the cooperative *before* the grand opening took place. So the Akron people—spearheaded by unionists and largely by members of URWA—set for themselves a goal and a condition. They would open no store until they had sold shares to families in the community in a total amount of $125,000. This looked big, very big—particularly since shares were to be sold at $10.00 each.

But they did it.

Volunteers did it. They worked for more than a year just talking about the coop-to-be and persuading men and women to become owners of it at $10.00 or $20.00 or sometimes $50.00 apiece.

When the goal of $125,000 was within sight, they began selling preferred shares to local labor unions. This raised another $100,000. And since the estimates of needed capital had been revised upward it was then decided to apply for a loan from Nationwide Insurance Companies of a substantial amount.

Only when that loan had been approved did the Akron organizers feel they were ready to move in earnest toward opening a supermarket.

When they finally did so, the Cooperative Enterprises of Akron achieved at once a large business volume. That volume has continued to climb ever since. The original store was one which all the members could be proud of. The manager, a natural-born promoter, had nothing to apologize for with respect to his facilities or location. The Akron operation has had its conflicts and lacks the efficiency which has marked other successful cooperative store operations, but it is still expanding; it now operates five stores; and it is an outstanding example of the right way to start a new consumer cooperative.

The largest of all United States supermarket cooperatives is Greenbelt Consumer Services. In 1960 this cooperative opened its tenth shopping center in the Washington, D.C., area. Its total business soared toward $20,000,000 annually. Although it is a local institution, Greenbelt Consumer Services had in 1960 the fourth largest number of shareholders among all retail-food businesses in the United States, including all the major chains. Greenbelt's manager, Samuel F. Ashelman, is one of the best—and one of the most eternally dissatisfied—in the coop business. Under his leadership Greenbelt's highly qualified administrative team has developed successful methods of expanding into new communities, opening new stores, making them a success from the day they open, and building membership on outstanding service. The example Greenbelt has set is one of relentless, well-planned dynamic growth and expansion. It has shown that consumer cooperative merchandising can be made a major factor in the markets of a great metropolitan area. Along the way a merger with Rochdale Cooperatives was brought about, partly, at least, through mediation by the Cooperative League. Greenbelt made of itself the largest customer by far for the petroleum products of Southern States Cooperatives, regional farm-supply wholesale in the region. As membership grew and a single annual membership meeting became obviously impractical as a method of democratic control, a "congress" system based on district organizations and representative government was devised and has worked well. The central idea for this "congress" system was imported from the Consumers Cooperative Society of Stockholm, Sweden. Greenbelt also imports meats from the cooperatives of Iceland, furniture from the cooperatives of Denmark, even hams from Poland.

If all this can be done in Washington, why not elsewhere?

Across the continent in the San Francisco Bay area similar progress is in fact being made.

There the Consumers Cooperative Society of Berkeley is the agent. Its able manager, Eugene Mannila, has an asset of untold value in what is probably the best membership-activity program in any United States cooperative. Special monthly meetings welcome new members into the Berkeley Cooperative, explain a multitude of interesting and important activities for members which revolve around the cooperative. This, coupled with progressive, efficient services and a solid acceptance in the community, has enabled Berkeley to expand from one to four shopping centers in a brief three-year period and to double its business volume and its membership in a shorter period than that. The Berkeley Cooperative has adopted a kind of "horizons-unlimited" policy respecting its expansion. Its board of directors has adopted a policy of being willing to open a store in any community where the following conditions are met:

1. The community must have a growth potential of 5,000 families.
2. There must be at least 500 families ready to invest $50,000 in shares in the cooperative.
3. This core group must undertake to double these figures in the first year—that is, to bring in an additional 500 families as members and $50,000 of investment from them.
4. The community must be within twenty-five miles of the coops' oldest shopping center.

That twenty-five-mile radius, incidentally, covers the entire populous San Francisco Bay area.

A few miles to the south the Consumers Cooperative Society of Palo Alto is writing a chapter similar to that of Berkeley. Its expansion area is the rapidly growing peninsula that lies west of the southern portion of San Francisco Bay.

In July, 1960, the *Economic Bulletin* of the Cooperative League reported its annual survey of the progress of cooperative supermarkets having business value of $1 million or more. The following passage from that survey report provides a good overview of the nationwide growth of this basic kind of consumer cooperation.

The *Bulletin* said:

Since 1956, four more coop supermarkets have passed the $1 million mark in annual sales volume. These four have been added to our report on leading consumer cooperatives this year for the first time; we have also added four other coops with annual sales approaching $1 million, which are leaders in their areas. This brings the total to 33.

Growth of these cooperatives has been impressive. From 74,000 members in 1953 they have grown to 136,000 in 1959, a gain of 84 per cent. And during the seven years (1953 to 1959 inclusive) they have paid out $6,033,000 in patronage refunds. Except for the recession of 1954, each year has seen a larger sum handed back to members than the year before, an outstanding record when the keen competition in this industry is considered.

Sales have more than doubled, rising from $41,776,000 in 1953 to $86,209,000 in 1959, a gain of 106 per cent. Only one coop reports a membership decline in these six years, and this was slight; it is located in a farm area, and farm population is declining. Two coops report sales declines; both are in farming areas. One has just built a new shopping center and we look for a sales increase this year.

Striking as is the growth record, the operating record of these cooperatives, when compared with that of the industry as a whole, is perhaps even more significant. All but four coops operate supermarkets, and in each of these the supermarket represents the principal sales volume. Taking the net margin or operating ratio before taxes (per cent net savings are of sales) and comparing coop figures with the corresponding figures for all supermarkets in the United States, we find the following experience:

NET MARGINS BEFORE TAXES*

Year	All 33 Coops (*Net savings as per cent of sales*)	20 Coops with Supermarkets	All Supermarkets in United States (*Net profit as per cent of sales*)
1953	2.19	2.15	——
1954	1.98	1.98	2.46
1955	2.17	2.16	2.56
1956	2.28	2.27	2.13
1957	2.32	2.45	2.26
1958	2.25	2.32	2.20
1959	2.33	2.39	2.30

* All Supermarkets: from *Supermarket News,* May 9, 1960. Compiled by Curt Kornblau, research director, Supermarket Institute. Cooperatives: reports from thirty-three coops.

In each year since 1955, the operating ratio of the coops has slightly exceeded that of the supermarket industry as a whole. Here is ample proof that people running their own business can operate as efficiently, from the standpoint of savings alone, as the private units in this industry which includes so many giant corporations.

Of our 33 cooperatives, one is operating 10 supermarkets, one has 5, 2 have 3 each, and 4 have 2 each; 21 have one apiece. This adds up to a total of 50 supermarkets. The four coops which have no supermarkets operate 18 smaller food stores, two with supermarkets also have four branch food stores, a total of 22 small food stores.

In addition, the 33 coops have among them 10 pharmacies, 27 service stations, and 8 bulk petroleum plants; 6 have home heating fuel-oil services and 6 operate milk routes, 3 of which have their own milk processing plants. Eight coops have 13 lunch counters or snack bars in their supermarkets, and 10 sell appliances. In addition, there are 4 gift shops (3 of them gift-book-record shops), 3 bakeries, 2 coalyards, 2 optical services, and one dry-cleaning plant. Many, especially in farm areas, sell hardware, clothing, shoes, and farm machinery and supplies.

Operating margins are particularly high in fuel-oil service and many coops find this an important and growing contribution to members' savings. Coops in farm areas find that bulk petroleum plants with delivery to the farm bring a larger savings margin than most other services.

The 33 million-dollar consumer cooperatives included in the survey are located in every kind of community and in almost all sections of the nation. Fitchburg, Maynard, and Natick, Massachusetts; New York City; Ridgewood and Leonia, New Jersey; Ithaca and Schenectady, New York; Akron, Ohio; Eau Claire, Wisconsin; Cloquet and Virginia, Minnesota; Chicago; Waukegan, Illinois; Salt Lake City, Utah; Washington, D.C., and its environs; Hampton and Newport News, Virginia; San Francisco Bay, California. These are some of the places where the buying power of consumers is being organized by strong, respected, progressive efficient consumer cooperatives.

A couple more of these deserve more detailed discussion. In Chicago, Hyde Park Cooperative Society operates the largest single supermarket in the city. It is located in a brand-new shopping center in the middle of the Hyde Park–Kenwood redevelopment areas on Chicago's racially mingled South Side. Hyde Park Cooperative, managed by Walker Sandbach, a practical idealist if there ever was one, is a community institution in the best sense of the word. It has earned that reputation and that acceptance. It was organized by a group of families centered around the University of Chicago, Senator Paul H. Douglas, then a professor, among them. Today it is owned by some six thousand South Side families. Not only is it as efficient a merchandising business as the city boasts, but it supports practically every worth-while community enterprise and welfare agency on the South Side. Its pay roll includes almost every race and nationality under the sun.

There was powerful resistance against leasing to the cooperative the supermarket space in the new shopping center. But there was even more powerful community insistence that that lease go to a business that was widely owned by thousands of families in the immediate neighborhood, a business that could never become absentee owned, a business that would never even consider pulling out of the area where it had its roots so deeply struck.

Somewhat the same factors, in a very different type of community, have accounted for the outstanding success of the Consumer Cooperative at Eau Claire, Wisconsin. Its members are about half farm families from the surrounding rural area and half city people, many of them workers in the tire factories which are Eau Claire's principal industry. The manager, Ray Theisen, has a daily fifteen-minute radio program. The cooperative not only is willing to cash checks for its customers, but pays them a small fee for the privilege. The coop credit union is one of the strongest and most useful financial institutions in Eau Claire.

Once people have learned to invest and do business together to meet one of their life's needs, it is easier for them to see the value of doing the same thing to meet other needs.

As late as 1950 New York City was almost a consumer cooperative "desert" so far as cooperative stores were concerned. But since then one successful cooperative homeownership project after another has been built and slums replaced with good neighborhoods inhabited by joint owners of their own homes. Cooperation has been the means of filling the greatest single unmet economic need of these families— the need for housing. One result of this has been the organization of consumer cooperative markets in the cooperative housing projects. Whereas many earlier efforts had failed, these have been uniformly successful. And the time may well come when New York will not only be known as the cooperative housing "capital" of America, but the capital of other types of consumer-cooperative activity as well.

The center of strength in agricultural cooperation is in the regional wholesale and production cooperatives. The local or county retail cooperatives depend on the wholesales for support in many ways. But with one exception, the strength of the consumer cooperative supermarket movement lies in the retail cooperatives with the wholesales acting largely as their purchasing agencies.

The one exception is worth noting. The region around Lake Superior—northern Minnesota and Wisconsin and the Upper Peninsula of Michigan—is the territory served by Central Cooperatives, Inc., with headquarters and principal warehouses at Superior, Wisconsin. Founded in 1917 largely by Finnish immigrants, Central Cooperatives has a long and varied history. It provides to its member cooperatives, which own it, both farm supplies and consumer goods. Its more than two hundred retail cooperative members have historically been mostly small general stores in the smaller communities of the rather economically depressed far north country. But with the appointment of J. Waldemar Koski as general manager of the wholesale, a new concept of the role of consumer cooperation in the region began to emerge. It is the concept of "area development." Studies are made of economic trends throughout the area. Careful decision is made as to where location of a completely modern supermarket would be wise. The wholesale organization then works with the local cooperative at these locations in the establishment of such markets. Uniform identification and architecture are encouraged. The idea that cooperative facilities should be second to none is insisted upon. Management and personnel training programs are carried on. Some of the older cooperative leaders have been slow to convince. But when in early 1960 one of the most attractive stores in the whole area was opened at Cloquet, Minnesota, by one of the oldest cooperatives in the region and when business volume of that cooperative began at once to increase, even the most conservative of the "old hands" were convinced.

About 5 per cent of the food-store business in its territory is carried on by CCI cooperatives. In the years ahead it is expected to increase this to 10 per cent—maybe even to 15 per cent. At that point the interest of the consumer, the influence in the market place of the organized buying power of the people, can be asserted with significant effect.

The consumer interest is the only universal economic interest, the only one we all share together. Therefore, the consumer interest is identical with the national economic interest. What benefits consumers benefits everyone. Effective assertion of the consumer interest is the way to better-quality products, to economic pricing in a really free market, to economic growth, and to abundant production.

All of which are clearly in the national interest and all of which "promote the general welfare," to use the words of the United States Constitution.

Thus far, only one way of asserting the consumer interest of the people has proved of any real effectiveness. That way is by the organization and growth of consumer cooperatives.

Laws aimed at protection of consumers are in some cases necessary and helpful. Pure food and drug laws, for example.

But laws and government cannot push a string. They cannot positively and creatively assert the consumer interest by bringing about abundant production of needed goods and services at economically determined prices which reflect technological advances in lower prices.

Nor does competition among producers protect the interest of the people as consumers over any very long period of time. The classical economists to the contrary notwithstanding, the actual economic history of the free nations since the industrial revolution has been one of steadily declining competition—especially *price* competition, and more and more monopoly and "administered pricing."

It is true that as long as gigantic and necessarily economically wasteful military expenditures continue, and as long as families can be cajoled into mortgaging more and more and more of their economic future in consumer debt, it looks on the surface as if we were in a highly prosperous condition and as if the consumer interest were being well served.

But the fact is that these props to the economy are the price we pay for allowing monopolistic producers to dominate our economy. The industries regarded as "strong" industries in America today are the monopolistic ones—automobiles, steel, chemicals, broadcasting, newspaper publishing, and the like. The industries we regard as "weak" industries are the ones where competition still exists—textiles and agriculture, for example. Why?

Because any industry able to "administer" its prices is in position to wax fat at the expense of industries not able to do that and at the expense of the whole nation as consumers. And if the "weak" industries are to stay in business at all, subsidization of consumer demand—such as that provided by military spending and expansion of consumer debt—is required to compensate for the excessive drain on consumer purchasing power caused by overpricing of the goods and services of the monopolistic, "administered-price" segment of the economy.

And so it is no exaggeration of the importance of consumer cooperatives to say that the United States economy will follow one of the three courses. We can permit continuance of present trends, watch the continued growth of monopoly and oligopoly over our economic life, and resign ourselves to a gradual elimination of competition and a continuous slowing down of our rate of economic growth. Or, as a second alternative, we can give government great enough power to stop the growth of monopoly, restore competition, and assure economic growth. But mere government "regulation" can never accomplish this. For government regulation can restore but never create, retard but never accelerate. The only way government could deal with the situation would be by itself going into business in competition with the monopolies. And except in those few industries such as electric power, where the people's basic interest is so clearly evident and monopoly so inevitable, we are not likely to permit or desire any such expansion of government activity and power as this.

The third alternative remains. It is to apply together two of the basic principles in which we are supposed to believe—democracy and freedom of enterprise. It is to adapt free enterprise to real democratic participation and control by the people as consumers. It is to organize, nurture, and build—as free people and by our own efforts—enough consumer cooperatives to restore economic balance in our economy and protect and assert the general public and national economic interest.

Such a course offers the added advantage of influencing not alone the price at which goods and services are produced. For cooperatives, consumer-owned businesses, must produce and distribute those goods and services which their consumer-owners *most need,* whether they be housing, health care, electricity, credit, fertilizer, petroleum products, or groceries.

This is what this book is all about. It does not presume to say that the competition of cooperative enterprise as today constituted can restore economic balance in the United States. But it does presume to point out that cooperative enterprise has done and is doing precisely that in Scandinavia. And that *grown large and strong enough* it *could* do it here.

A number of examples have been given to show the beneficial effects of the presence and competition of cooperative enterprises in such fields as housing, household necessities, rural electricity, health care, petroleum products, fertilizer, credit, and insurance. We have seen how employment can be expanded under the impact of cooperative enterprise—as well as directly by it—because such enterprise must, being consumer owned, always conduct itself on a full-production at lowest-economically-sound-price basis. We have seen how the service motive or mutual-aid motive can bring about expansion of the economy into brand-new areas which profit-oriented business naturally has shunned. And we have observed that a strong and integrated development of cooperatives in related business under farmer ownership offers the best if not the last hope of rescuing our agriculture.

An expansion of cooperative enterprise in the United States to three or four times its present volume so it would be doing about 10 per cent to 12 per cent of the nation's total business would be of very great value in making possible realization of an adequate rate of growth, maximum employment, and price stability.

The trouble with our economy at present lies in the overwhelming economic power of a comparatively few huge producing units. They are in positions of absolute control of great segments of our economic life. To maintain that control they must control, and to a degree restrict, production. To benefit from that control they "administer" prices of their products unjustifiably upward. Most serious of all, they seek to retain a lion's share of the benefits from increased technological efficiency instead of spreading them broadly among the population and thus assuring not only the economic health of the nation but that of their own industries as well. These giants are, in fact, their own worst long-run enemies.

There is, in the end, only one economic force that can balance the power of monopolistically organized producers. Even if a monopoly of the cracker industry were to perfect a completely automatic cracker factory requiring no labor at all, there would still have to be someone to buy and eat the crackers or the factory would be worthless.

The natural—and only effective—countervailing force to industrial monopoly is the organized buying power of the people as consumers. To bring about such organization of consumer buying power the best if not the only available instrument is the cooperative. Organized consumers cannot, in pursuing their own natural economic interest, fail to represent the economic interest of the nation as a whole. After all, the nation is the people and their one common economic interest is their interest as consumers.

It is not necessary that cooperatively owned automobile factories or steel mills be established alongside cooperative oil refineries and fertilizer plants in order to deal with America's current problem. It is only necessary that the buying power of consumers of the various monopolistically produced products be organized to a sufficient extent so that their economic bargaining power will somewhere nearly equal that of the producing companies.

Admittedly this is a tremendous task. But it is to be remembered that as experience is gained in the mutual benefits resulting from cooperative organization in any one field it is not too difficult for the same organized group to expand its activities into other fields. The basic necessity of life is food. And it is logical that it is around the food store that the broadest organization of consumers' buying power has taken place in most countries. But the cooperatives of Scandinavia, for example, have not stopped there. They have built on their successful operations in the business of household necessities an effective challenge to most of the major monopolies in their countries.

There is no logical reason why we cannot do the same thing here.

XI

HANDICAPS AND
SHORTCOMINGS

In the countries of western Europe, in Japan, Canada, Puerto Rico, and a few other places people talk about "the cooperative movement." Not all of them are enthusiastic supporters of that "movement." But most of them respect it. And the people who are *within* the "movement" generally feel a sense of unity and a certain uplift in spirit because of that fact.

In continental United States, where more different kinds of cooperative and mutual businesses exist than anywhere in the world, the situation is different, partly, no doubt, because of the different origins and reasons for existence of the different kinds of cooperative enterprises. Here, too, people sometimes speak of "the American cooperative movement." But they seldom know exactly what or whom they are including in that term. And some of the people and organizations that might be included don't want to be. They don't like the term "cooperative movement." They aren't part of a "movement," they insist. They are simply conducting certain business operations for the benefit of their patron-owners and their communities.

From the outside cooperatives appear differently than they do from the inside. From the outside they look either white, if you care about people, or black, if you care primarily about yourself. From the inside cooperatives and their works are of varying shades—from just off-white to a fairly dark gray.

For almost two decades the author has had a chance to look at cooperatives from the inside. I've seen some inspiring things—big

174 American Cooperatives

annual meetings of thousands of people conscious of owning and controlling their own businesses, making American democracy work in economics as well or better than it works in politics. I've seen local coops where the members pull together under good, unselfish leadership and loyally patronize a well-run business in whose future they sincerely believe.

But I've seen other things, too. I've seen local cooperatives where the members cared more about proving themselves right in an argument over policy than they did about the success of their enterprise. I've seen situations where in the name of "democracy" practically every member of the coop tried to "run the manager." I've seen in such cases the work of member education and the work of making members out of non-member patrons completely neglected. Argument is not a substitute for cooperation.

Cooperation means each person doing *his* part, rather than trying to do the *other fellow's job*.

The manager's job is to manage. The director's job is to lay down general policy and to hire and, if necessary, fire, the manager. The member's job is to build patronage, to increase membership, to develop and carry on an educational program, to elect and sometimes *not* re-elect the board of directors.

Again I've seen members of successful local cooperatives curl up in a shell of smug self-satisfaction and show no interest whatsoever in cooperative business as a whole. There are local cooperative societies which seem to think that if they succeed in their neighborhoods it doesn't matter whether or not they patronize their wholesale and by so doing hasten the day when a significant percentage of America's production can be carried on by people through their own businesses—their cooperatives. Full cooperation between local societies and their wholesales would mean sufficient increase in wholesale volume to make much more efficient operations possible, to enable more warehouses to be opened, and ultimately to justify processing and production.

I have seen regional cooperatives fail to work together to anything like the extent they might have done in acquiring sources of raw materials, pooling their purchases, or establishing strong cooperative financial institutions such as are definitely needed by all of them.

United action by all regional cooperatives would give them a tremendous bargaining power at the point of purchase. It would greatly expand the possibilities for manufacturing activities, where the real savings for consumers are to be made.

Most serious of all, I have found personal jealousies, dislikes, and prejudices sufficiently strong among some cooperators to render them almost incapable of real cooperative action.

The success of what has been called "The Cooperative Challenge" depends upon enough first-rate managers, upon better merchandising, upon greater loyalty and activity among members. But more than anything else, perhaps, it depends upon more cooperation among cooperatives. For cooperation means, if it means anything at all, working together for common, worth-while objectives and putting those objectives ahead of every personal feeling, every small consideration, every selfish motive.

Cooperatives are people first and businesses afterward. They are businesses established by groups of people, owned and controlled and largely patronized by these same groups of people.

People have weaknesses and failings, and these are close to the surface in any kind of thoroughly democratic institution such as a cooperative.

For one thing, most cooperatives and mutual businesses are inclined to be too conservative.

There are outstanding exceptions to that statement—notably some farm supply "regionals" and the new city-consumer cooperatives.

But in general cooperatives take too few risks and make too few innovations.

They have made some. Important ones, too. Among these are:

    Open formula, high-analysis fertilizer.

    Direct-power take-off, high-speed transmission, and headlights for tractors.

    Informative labeling of consumer goods.

    Low-cost insurance coupled with opportunity for investment in a mutual fund.

    The right of debt repayment at any time without penalty.

All these—and a good many more—are "coop firsts."

But the list could, and should, have been three times as long had more product research been done and more new products and services ventured.

In the past cooperatives have too often been content with "holding their own," instead of setting growth goals and counting the year a failure unless that goal was reached. This has largely been overcome, at least among the larger cooperatives—partly as a result of the management development programs, about which our next chapter will tell. But the old super-carefulness still persists in many places.

With some outstanding exceptions, cooperatives don't advertise enough, nor use TV enough, nor carry on effective enough public-information programs. And when they do, their appeal is often a conventional one—straight product advertising—and not often enough an exposition of how and why cooperatives are a different kind of business, one that *has* to listen to consumers' needs and wishes because those same consumers own it.

Cooperative enterprises have other handicaps, from a business point of view, which could, however, become their greatest strength. Mainly these result from the fact that cooperatives are and must always be democratically controlled organizations—or else lose their reason for existence. There is a vital difference between democracy—one-member, one vote—in over-all control, which is an essential feature of any true cooperative, and attempted "democracy" in management and operations—which is fatal to any business, cooperatives included. But this distinction is not always recognized, even yet, despite the almost phenomenal progress made in management techniques, knowledge, and concepts by United States cooperatives in recent years.

Then there is the problem of growth. This problem cooperatives share with all voluntary organizations of a democratic character. It is, of course, a good kind of "problem" to have. But how do you maintain "town-meeting" methods when the "town" numbers several thousand, or even several hundred thousand, "inhabitants"? Some cooperative enterprises have that many members. Not only does this require ingenious governmental structure, to preserve a reality of effective member participation and democratic control. There is also the problem of maintaining informed interest, loyalty, concern, and a sense of responsibility among the patron members or policy owners. And, currently, educational programs, to meet this problem, are, to say the least, far from adequate. Indeed recent years have seen them actually de-emphasized in some places.

Furthermore, with growth comes, all too often, a struggle for power over what is becoming a prize worth holding.

For example, such a struggle began, in the early 1950's, to rack the credit-union movement and even threaten its unity.

In part it arises from real and honest differences of opinion.

On the one side are those who believe that credit unions should content themselves with making small convenience loans, loans which banks and other financial institutions do not care to make. This side, furthermore, looks for the future growth of credit unions to result mainly from organization of employer-sponsored credit unions. Therefore, no offense must ever be given to the large employing corporations of the country.

On the other side are those who believe it to be the proper function of credit unions to render as many services to their members as they properly and soundly can. They see credit unions as "people's banks," engaged in the business, not merely of making small loans, but of marshaling the savings of the people in order to give the people a rounded financial security and strength which can aid them in solving many problems. This side naturally draws its strength from credit unions which are free of the sponsorship or favors of employing companies—that is, parish and church credit unions, credit unions of public employees, teachers, labor-union members, and cooperative members.

But this is not the whole story. There also exists a raw internal struggle for control of the rapidly growing credit-union organizations which are, with their almost twelve million members, indeed a prize worth struggling over.

Struggles for power are found elsewhere, too: in rather ugly types of competition between some regional farm-supply cooperatives; in struggles for "succession" within the larger insurance organizations; and in unrelenting rivalry between a few of the oldest and ablest leaders.

Yes, cooperatives have things wrong with them because cooperatives are people. And people have things wrong with them.

As for the business record of cooperatives, about the same number of cooperatives and mutual businesses have failed as of other businesses. But the general idea has been that cooperatives *never* ought to fail, so every time one did it has become a much larger black eye than their competitors suffer from the same cause.

Cooperatives are a hard kind of business to start and an even harder kind to operate successfully. It is not easy to capitalize a business with a large number of small investments by a large number of people. It isn't easy to manage a business where every single customer is an owner and therefore a potential member of the board of directors. It is not easy to operate a business in a gold-fish bowl, where all your patrons—who are the owners of the business—have a right to know everything that goes on—and hence all the community and all your competitors know, too.

Cooperatives are chronically undercapitalized. Naturally enough, since their shares are never traded at more than par and are of value only to those who use their services. Basic capital, therefore, must always come from members—few, indeed, of whom are wealthy people. When cooperatives do acquire surpluses they tend to hoard instead of using them for dynamic expansion. Managers and directors are understandably cautious about risking members' money. It was hard earned in most cases.

Cooperatives are beginning to pool their financial resources, and to develop new financing methods and institutions as sources of badly needed capital. But those beginnings are still small and there is far to go.

Cooperatives in the United States are, in most lines of business, up against pretty stiff competition from highly efficient competitors. The fact that cooperation is a wonderful idea is not enough to assure success. There must be at least as efficient operations as those of competitors. In western Europe the cooperatives were the first integrators, the first to rationalize distribution. In America other businesses did this before cooperatives, in our cities at least, were fairly on the scene.

Since cooperatives are so hard to build successfully, it has been necessary that some of their early leaders be men with elements of true greatness about them. Without those men our best cooperative institutions probably could not have been built. Each has built—and built well—his own institution. His relationship to it is intensely personal. It's hard for him to contemplate such changes in this relationship as would be involved, for example, in full cooperation between cooperatives. Yet such cooperation, amounting in some cases to actual merger, is today an economic necessity.

The great names of the cooperative movement as it developed out of depression years in the United States are many. To attempt to name them would be unfair. For some who deserve a place in the list would almost certainly be omitted. And indeed if there were no omissions, the list would be a very long one.

These were the pioneers. They were men of the "inner-directed" age of American society. They were—and those now living still are—men of deep conviction and devotion, men who charted their courses by their own conceptions of a better if not an ideal society.

But with two or three outstanding exceptions, they were—and are—by their very nature individual "stars" rather than team players. Their qualities of greatness gave them leadership and brought them each his own intensely loyal following. But those same qualities also made it necessary that the cooperative "empire" of each of them be built by his own hand and according to his own chart and compass. There was no room for other leaders of equal stature. There could not be.

Without these men the elements of a strong pattern of cooperative enterprise in the United States would not now exist. The debt of future generations of cooperators to them is immeasurable.

The only trouble has been that such men found it hard to put the elements they had created together into a strong coordinated pattern. With real vision, National Cooperatives was organized in 1933. It was conceived as a nationwide purchasing and manufacturing cooperative owned by the regional wholesales and pooling their buying power. But National was never allowed to become much more than an efficient purchasing agency for the regionals. Again there was organized the Cooperative Finance Association in 1943, conceived as a central financing agency for cooperatives. But it slept for almost twenty years until activated by a new generation of leaders. That new generation of leadership must and inevitably will "take over." Here again we catalogue no names. We do not do so because the men who bear these names would not want it. We do not do so because the second generation of general managers and board chairmen are, generally speaking, trustees rather than original architects, administrators rather than creators, and team players rather than individual "stars."

They—the members of this new generation of cooperative leaders —can meet together and make decisions together. The pioneer leaders found it hard to do this. Decisions of the new leadership can be group decisions. They can even be decisions that involve the loss of general managerships by some of the participants. They certainly can be decisions for federation, integration—even merger—of existing institutions with others like them.

Cooperative development in the United States is new. It is the work of, and monument to, men still living in most cases. It is not only new but it still has much of its strength in the segments that revolve around the great pioneer personalities.

The "cooperative movements" of western Europe have developed largely as defenders of the consumers' interests. In older societies people seldom change occupations, and their positions as producers are regarded as fixed and determined by training, if not by heredity. Family-income levels change slowly. Hence the buying power of wages becomes a matter of great concern and the economic interest of the people as consumers looms large.

But in urban America—up until recently—no one has paid much attention to the common, general, and universal interest of all the people as consumers. But most cooperatives are, in one way or another, consumer cooperatives. In fact all of them are, except the farmers' marketing cooperatives and a handful of plants, owned and operated by their workers. City workers have—again until recently— taken little interest in ways to protect and make more effective their buying power. They've felt, apparently, that their entire welfare depended on their incomes as producers.

Furthermore, cooperatives *are* "different." They are different from the dominant pattern of businesses organized for the primary purpose of making a profit. And, despite our pioneering ancestry and our love of "western" movies, we have become, in the post World War II period, like all overprivileged peoples, a nation of conformists, scared to death to do anything that will cause "the Joneses" to think us "different." Moreover, many of us worship bigness so profoundly that if we can't be big ourselves, we'd rather serve a big outfit than to go to the effort of joining with other people and taking responsibility for building something of our own not so big.

For these two reasons cooperatives had not, even at mid-century, as yet caught the imagination of the average urban American. The "public-information" job remained, largely, to be done.

There are, of course, some kinds of cooperative and mutual enterprises which are generally recognized as having enjoyed healthy growth and which have become well-established institutions.

This is true of marketing, supply, electric, credit and insurance co-operatives among farmers and rural people. It is also true of credit unions.

Farmers, generally, are intensely proud of their calling. They also value ownership, beginning with ownership of the land. They are less likely than many other groups in the population to move frequently or to change their occupation unless economic conditions become quite unbearable. As small-scale producers—compared to most industries—it has been economically necessary for them to form cooperatives if they were to maintain any degree of economic bargaining power, either when they bought or when they sold. All these factors have made farmers especially receptive to the cooperative idea and to cooperative, joint ownership of off-the-farm businesses related to their farming operations. Furthermore, at least up until very recent years the independent owner-operated farm has been regarded as a sort of rock on which our whole democratic society has been founded. So there has been a general acceptance of farmer cooperatives because they were quite obviously a necessary means of protecting the farmer from the worst effects of his economic disadvantages, resulting from his inability to control production or influence the prices received for his products.

Most of industry is able to do both of these things.

As for rural electric cooperatives and cooperative agricultural credit institutions, these so clearly met needs that were otherwise unmet, or met only at exorbitant cost, that from the beginning they won general community support and acceptance. Only after the electric co-operatives had fairly well completed the difficult and costly job of bringing electricity to farms and rural consumers, so their service began to be taken for granted, did the bitter propaganda of the commercial utilities gain a hearing.

In the case of credit unions the reasons for their remarkable growth—at the rate of about twelve hundred new credit unions a year—are different ones. In the first place, a credit union is a simple kind of institution to operate. It receives the savings of its members and loans from this pool of savings to its members only. The only capital required is derived from the purchase of $5.00 shares by its members. In the second place, no one loves a loan shark. Indeed, moneylenders generally have not been exactly noted for their popularity. On the other hand, many businesses in our economy have a direct interest in seeing that the people have an opportunity to borrow money. So when credit unions offer a way to enable people to free themselves from usurious interest payments and at the same time to develop for themselves a source of readily-available credit, there are few who will speak against them. Here again, before the advent of credit unions, there simply was no place that a lower-income family could go and obtain a loan on decent terms. So credit unions, like electric cooperatives, have met a need of people that was quite obviously unmet before.

These are the circumstances where cooperatives do best.

The uneven rate of growth of different kinds of cooperatives has been a factor working against a sense of unity among them. The successful and accepted ones have tended to shy away from association with the newly arising forms, believing, apparently, that such association would somehow contaminate their reasonably secure position.

Another reason there has not yet developed a clear sense of purpose and a deep sense of unity is because fifty years is a short time in the development of social and economic institutions. And twenty-five years is a good deal shorter.

There have, as we have seen, been cooperative and mutual enterprises in our country from its very beginning. Much of the life of the early settlers was organized around their cooperative efforts. They built their houses and barns together, moved across the country together, protected one another from the common dangers they faced. As early as 1752 Benjamin Franklin organized his mutual fire-insurance company in Philadelphia. In 1804 Connecticut dairy farmers formed their milk-marketing cooperative. The Mormons, in Utah, fashioned much of their life around cooperative irrigation societies, cooperative stores, and other forms of cooperation. In the 1870's the Grangers put great effort into organization of cooperatives among their members, as we have seen.

But if we look for the beginnings of cooperative enterprises now operating in our country, we find that only a few agricultural marketing cooperatives, and hardly any of the other types, had been founded even a short fifty years ago.

The first credit-union law was passed by the Massachusetts legislature in 1909.

The first regional farm-supply cooperative was organized in 1914— Farmers' Union State Exchange of Nebraska.

The first regional wholesale cooperative for consumer goods was organized in 1917—Central Cooperative Wholesale of Superior, Wisconsin. Only a year before that, in 1916, the Cooperative League had been founded in New York.

There was not a single cooperative in the oil business until 1921, when farmers at Cottonwood Falls, Minnesota, got together to form a small cooperative for the local distribution of oil products. Not until 1926 was the first regional wholesale-oil cooperative, Midland Cooperatives, organized by the local cooperatives. Nineteen hundred and twenty-six also saw the first cooperative housing project built in New York City, sponsored by the Amalgamated Clothing Workers.

The first cooperative hospital, or health plan for that matter, was not founded until Dr. Michael Shadid brought it about in Elk City, Oklahoma, in 1929.

The first cooperative oil well was not drilled until 1940, when Consumers' Cooperative Association brought in a producing well near Phillipsburg, Kansas.

Most of the strong farm-supply cooperatives which now virtually cover the entire United States in their operations were started in the 1920's or early 1930's. The years of the Great Depression were the years of the most rapid growth of cooperatives in our country's history. Indeed the beginnings of what will one day be a "Cooperative Movement" in the United States date from the depression years.

Why? Perhaps because these were years when people had to think, think hard, and think fast. They were years when the strident confidence in "things as they were" was weakened. They were years when people dared new ventures because old reliances had failed them. Above all, they were years when most Americans sensed the fact that they were "all in the same boat," that it needed some general repairs, and that no one could repair it by himself.

It was in the thirties that, for the first time, there had been enough credit unions formed to bring about organization of the Credit Union National Association. It was a depression measure that brought the beginning of the rural electric cooperatives. In a short quarter century there were built, by the people, some 20,000 credit unions with more than eleven million members and $5 billion in assets; and 1,000 rural electric cooperatives with 4½ million members and an annual sale of electricity of more than seven hundred fifty million dollars.

The growth of cooperative health plans to the place where they provide comprehensive health care for more than one million people is almost altogether a development of the post World War II period.

Not until the depression years did the small local farmers' marketing cooperatives begin to establish terminal storage and marketing facilities and agencies and thus to exert some influence on quality and prices.

And as for consumer cooperatives in the cities, while it is true that a considerable number of small indifferently run stores were established and did business from time to time, nevertheless it was not until the 1950's that the factors necessary to the success of this type of cooperative became clear and they began to achieve a size and scope of operation that have at last assured further rapid growth.

It is, of course, considerably more difficult to mark the beginnings of what may be termed "cooperative insurance," because in outward form "cooperative" insurance companies are simply mutual companies with a certain unique point of view. The Farmers' Township Mutuals, providing fire insurance for farmers because they could not get it anywhere else, have a long and creditable history, particularly in states such as Wisconsin. But the establishment of multiple-line insurance companies, identifying themselves with a cooperative purpose and point of view, dates only from the 1920's.

So part of the answer to the frequently-asked question why cooperatives have not grown faster in the United States is: "They have! For what do you expect in a short quarter century?" Almost all of the significant development of cooperative enterprises in our country has been crowded into that short period.

Great popular movements are seldom developed that quickly.

There are a dozen or more national organizations of cooperatives in the United States. In typical American fashion we have cared more about getting the job done than about order and logic. The result is a complex pattern of nationwide organizations sometimes overlapping in their functions. And none of them as yet is able to bring about the degree of unity of purpose and coordination of action which the times demand.

There are two—not one—national cooperative wholesale organizations—National Cooperatives headquartered at Albert Lea, Minnesota, and United Cooperatives at Alliance, Ohio. United Cooperatives is owned by and serves farm-supply cooperatives only. National has both farm-supply and consumer-commodity regional cooperatives among its members. This difference has been the principal reason why efforts to merge them have repeatedly failed despite the logic of such a move.

Two national organizations serve the agricultural cooperatives in the educational, legislative, and public-relations fields. The American Institute of Cooperation, supported by most of the marketing and farm-supply regionals, encourages the teaching of agricultural cooperation in schools, colleges, and universities. It conducts educational "workshops" throughout the country, works closely with 4-H and Future Farmer organizations, carries on research activities, publishes a yearbook, and conducts an annual institute where cooperative leaders gather from all over the nation. Its headquarters are in Washington, D.C.

The National Council of Farmer Cooperatives, like the American Institute, has as members most of the agricultural marketing and farm-supply regionals. Some twenty-six state "cooperative councils" are affiliated with the National Council. The National Council looks after the interests of the farmer cooperatives in Washington. In this connection it distributes a weekly multigraphed commentary called *The Washington Situation*. It also holds a large annual meeting where problems of all sorts affecting farm cooperatives are discussed. And where the required unanimity can be achieved, the National Council develops policy for agricultural cooperatives, particularly as it affects national legislation.

The National Federation of Grain Cooperatives is the public-relations and legislative agency for the grain-marketing cooperatives and does vigorous work in these fields. The weekly newsletter of its executive secretary contains a wealth of information valuable to anyone concerned with American agriculture.

In another field, the National Milk Producers' Federation does a similar type of work for the cooperative dairymen.

The credit unions have formed state credit-union leagues in almost all the states. These provide aid to new groups desiring to form credit unions, as well as advice, encouragement, and guidance to established credit unions; legislative work at the state capital; and public-relations work. Capstone of the credit-union movement is the Credit Union National Association, popularly known as CUNA, with headquarters at Madison, Wisconsin. CUNA publishes the national magazine, *The Bridge,* supplies most of the credit-union literature, and watches the action of Congress whenever credit-union interests are involved. Associated with CUNA is CUNA Supply Cooperative, the central agency for the procurement and production of all necessary accounting forms, deposit books, loan-application forms, and other material required by credit unions. And CUNA Mutual Insurance Company provides to credit unions and their members loan-protection insurance, life-savings insurance, and straight life insurance.

The structure of organization of the rural electric cooperatives is very similar to that of the credit unions. In nearly all states there are "state-wide" associations. These, in turn, are grouped into districts and each district elects the directors of the National Rural Electric Cooperative Association with headquarters at Washington, D.C. NRECA carries on the legislative work with Congress, publishes monthly *The Rural Electrification* magazine, and does general informational and educational work.

The Cooperative Food Distributors of America is an effective and vital national organization for the protection and promotion of the retailer-owned cooperative grocery wholesales. It publishes a magazine, *The Cooperative Merchandiser,* and carries on public-relations work.

Most of the more important group health plans, labor health plans, and cooperative health associations in the country are members of the Group Health Association of America. The GHAA publishes and distributes literature covering the field of group health activities, provides consultative service to new groups seeking to organize, sponsors an annual national group health institute, publishes a monthly magazine, works to protect doctors associated with group health associations against discrimination, and carries on legislative work aimed primarily at removal of restrictions against organization of voluntary health associations.

The Cooperative League of the United States was founded in 1916 and chartered in 1922 for the purpose of promoting consumer cooperation in all its forms throughout the United States. With passage of the years, the scope of the League's work has broadened. Headquarters are in Chicago, with an office also in Washington, D.C.

Its membership includes a number of the major regional farm-supply cooperatives, all of the regional wholesale consumer goods cooperatives, several mutual insurance companies, the Credit Union National Association, the National Rural Electric Cooperative Association, Wisconsin Electric Cooperative, National Cooperatives, United Housing Foundation, and a number and variety of other cooperative organizations.

The League sponsors and assists the work of the Cooperative Insurance Conference, the Group Health Association of America, North American Student Cooperative League, Rochdale Institute, Cooperative Finance Association, National Association of Housing Cooperatives, and the Fund for International Cooperative Development.

The League is the United States member of the International Cooperative Alliance, the federation of cooperatives in some forty-five nations, with total membership of more than one hundred fifty million persons.

The work of the League includes the conduct of the Cooperative

News Service, central newsgathering agency for the cooperative press of the country; the publication and distribution of literature, and the production of films; the coordination of public-relations activities of cooperatives; the maintenance of contact and joint activity with religious, farm, labor, and other national organizations; and legislative work. The League provides annually a program of conferences, institutes, and meetings aimed primarily at the development of improved professional standards for the work of cooperative managers, editors, educational and personnel workers.

The Cooperative League offers, therefore, a common meeting ground and service agency for nearly all types of cooperatives in the United States. But its membership, as yet, contains nowhere nearly all of them.

There is good reason for this multiplicity of cooperative organizations. After all, there are many different kinds of cooperative enterprises, and their particular needs and interests can best be served by their own specialized federations. Furthermore, competition is not only "the life of trade" but a healthy stimulus to organizations operating in the same field to endeavor to outdo one another in the services they render.

The problem is not the number of national organizations. Rather it is the lack of coordination among them, the absence of a keen sense of common purpose, and, in some cases, timidity. Some of the strongest and largest of the cooperative businesses appear so anxious to be accepted by the business community as a whole that they endeavor, almost, to conceal the fact that they are cooperatives. They have an intense dislike for the very phrase "cooperative movement" and prefer to think of themselves as conducting a certain business operation having no more social or economic significance than the average run of conventional businesses.

The reasons for this feeling are mixed. And not all of them are bad.

The time has long passed when the owners of cooperative enterprises should regard themselves, or be thought of by others, as a sort of sect, apart from the rest of the population or the main stream of our economic life. Indeed cooperatives are an integral, important, and constituent element in any free economic order. For a "free" economic order must be a mixed one, including a number of different kinds of business organizations, arising from different motivations and meeting different needs.

But cooperative enterprises *are,* after all, different from all other types. They have unique values and are capable of making unique contributions. Sight should not be lost of these values. Nor will these values be fully realized except by people who deeply believe in them and are willing to work closely together with all others who similarly believe.

When such a working together has come to pass—and there are indications that it is on the way—then there will exist the substance of a strong, determined, and confident movement among some of the people of America which can properly be called cooperative. And this will be true regardless of the organizational forms and patterns—or lack of them—through which such a movement expresses itself.

There are two principal reasons why this has not as yet resulted.

The first is the problem of growth. The immediate and insistent task of cooperative business leaders is to assure the growth of their organizations at at least as rapid a rate as that of their competitors. This will require consolidation of strength, particularly financial strength. It will require the most skillful and farsighted of management, the best of research, the acme of good public relations, and the most progressive of services to members and patrons.

All of which are absorbing tasks, to say the least.

But as growth takes place a question arises. Will the very process of creating large-scale cooperative enterprises bring with it a resistance on the part of the skilled business leaders to the nurturing by educational processes of the idealism, sense of purpose, and desire for active participation by many member-owners which are the life blood of true cooperatives, their unique source of strength, and the stuff of which strong movements are made?

This is a crucial and as yet unanswered question.

The second reason we have not developed a greater strength in cooperatives in America is like the first one in many respects. It is lack of vibrant belief on the part of some cooperators in the work in which they are engaged. The manager of a large Chicago chemical company—by no means a cooperative one—took time out not long ago to address the annual meeting of a Wisconsin farm-supply and consumers' cooperative.

Here are some of the things he said:

"You're too busy trying to act like big business."

"Big business isn't really worried about coops as long as they're trying to beat them at their own game. The big advantage you have over big business is that seventh Rochdale principle—'educate constantly.' "

"Yours is one of the greatest movements in the world today. Why do you play it down?"

"The world is crying for the economic help the cooperative movement offers—an economic translation of Christianity and all the great religions of the world. But I'm still waiting for somebody to get up and say so."

"Why does the world hate America?"

"With our missionaries preaching Christianity all over the world, the best we can offer the world's people economically is competitive capitalism. The little people of the world know about our coops and can't understand why we don't bring them the coop movement."

"You ask a manager what kind of coop he has, and he says, 'We did one, two, or three million dollars' business last year.' "

"It has always puzzled me that in one hundred fifteen years we haven't been able to add anything or take anything from those original seven Rochdale principles."

"More education funds from local coops to the Cooperative League and an education committee for every local coop would be steps in the right direction."

"The inspiration of education will result in greater expansion and greater service."

"The world needs the ideas and enthusiasm of youth, and the coop movement has everything in it for youth."

When cooperative leaders and members see the values of their own work and type of enterprise as clearly as does this manager of a competing commercial company, the cooperative idea and method will begin to gain its rightful place in the United States.

Not till then.

No matter how big cooperative enterprise becomes.

XII

Future

TODAY AND TOMORROW

During World War II almost everything was scarce. About the only thing in the United States that nobody could find any practical use for was the gold in Fort Knox. Tragic as it is to say it, businesses of all kinds boomed during the war period. Even inefficient ones.

Some of the cooperative businesses were well-established and reasonably well-run enterprises. Others were not. But almost all of them seemed to be doing well during the period of wartime demand.

When peace finally came, so did trouble for the smaller, less efficient cooperatives. Along the East Coast especially many little consumer cooperatives died. Eastern Cooperative Wholesale almost died, too. Even some of the farm-supply cooperatives ran into trouble. The National Farm Machinery Cooperative failed. National Co-operatives sold off a number of its manufacturing plants and for a while in the late 1940's was in some danger of bankruptcy.

As wartime price controls were abandoned by the government, the cost of living began to climb. A wave of interest in case-lot buying surged through labor-union circles. In the Detroit area cooperative idealists worked with union officials to organize a number of con-sumer cooperative stores. Interest was intense; planning was less than adequate; good management was scarce, if existent at all. None of these cooperatives survived for long.

It was inevitable perhaps that the years of the war and those im-mediately following it should be years when the cooperative idealism was predominant and when practicality was, to a degree, neglected.

In the past there has been an unfortunate tendency for cooperatives in the United States to be subject to the swings of a pendulum. There are always some cooperators to whom the enterprise is not so much an economic business as a means of developing among people improved social relationships, greater justice, and a better world. Others think a cooperative should be simply an efficient, serviceable operation to provide solid economic advantages to its members and patrons. They aren't particularly concerned with "saving the world." At times one of these groups has had greatest influence; at times, the other one.

It has been hard to stop the pendulum in the middle, where it belongs, for there can be no genuine idealism attached to a shoddy business operation. And no *cooperative* business operation can ever succeed as a cooperative unless it has a higher and broader vision than a favorable balance sheet. The two kinds of values cannot safely be separated or placed in opposition to one another. Neither can flourish without the other. Good business operations and sincere belief among the membership in the values of cooperation are the father and mother of every healthy cooperative child.

So the period of emphasis on ideal values brought about inevitable reaction. The biennial congress of the Cooperative League meeting in Chicago in 1950 passed a resolution that called upon the League to "emphasize management in everything it did." The altogether logical, if premature, attempt to have National Cooperatives assume some of the educational functions of the Cooperative League was abandoned. Meetings were held to discuss what to do to revive sick coops—what to do about groceries, which seemed to be a major problem.

To make matters worse, there arose well-organized opposition to cooperatives in the United States for the first time. A competitor of the grain cooperatives in the Northwest took leadership in organizing the "National Tax Equality Association." The NTEA, with varying overtones, undertook to persuade the American people that "coops don't pay taxes." It was, of course, no problem for cooperatives to prove the falsity of that short statement to anyone who was listening. But few among the general public were listening to the coops' answer, whereas a good many were hearing the charge.

For NTEA, new though it was, was soon well financed by private utility companies, grain companies, oil companies, hardware wholesalers, and others with whom cooperatives were in competition. And

NTEA engaged expensive and skillful "public-relations" firms to spread its story.

It became obvious that not only was greater emphasis on business efficiency needed among the cooperatives. There was also need for better public-information programs. In the words of the public-relations fraternity, coops needed to "Live right, then tell about it."

And that is precisely what the cooperatives of the United States, albeit somewhat slowly and hesitantly, set out to do along about the year 1950.

During the fifteen years that followed World War II American coops learned, often from bitter experience, a number of lessons. Among them the following:

(1) That no cooperative business or institution ever stands still—either it grows, expands, develops, or it begins to die;

(2) That the day of the small cooperative kept alive by idealism alone is largely past; that coordination, federation, and merger are necessary measures in making cooperative businesses effective and that integration back to basic raw materials and supply sources and forward to the ultimate consumer is the road that must be followed;

(3) That the best method of expansion lies not so much in the formation of new cooperative societies as in the growth of well-established ones—in other words, expansion from centers of strength. In the cities cooperative housing can be such a center of strength. In rural areas, the centers of strength are the regional cooperatives.

(4) That good management is of critical importance and that management of cooperatives can be as good or better than that of any other form of business enterprise.

(5) That arbitrary limits on the services of any kind of cooperative are impractical and dangerous—such as limiting services to farmers only, or to particular ethnic or nationality groups, or to members of single-membership organizations. Open membership is not only a principle of cooperation but the only good business practice.

(6) That as cooperative businesses grow there is greater not less

need for intensifying member-education and activity programs. Efforts of growing cooperative insurance companies, for example, to develop active policy-owner participation and control are close to the heart of the struggle of modern man to control his own destiny. For the savings of the people are their gateway to progress and their savings flow more and more into insurance.

(7) That it is no longer possible to rely upon traditional methods to supply the capital necessary for the kind of expansion and modernization which cooperatives must achieve if they are to fulfil their role.

(8) That most Americans simply do not know what cooperatives are, why they have been formed, or what values and benefits they can bring to American life—and that, therefore, cooperatives have a public-information job to do which is second to none in importance or urgency.

Not only were these lessons learned theoretically. Something was done about them.

In 1951 the Cooperative Management Development Program was begun. With initiative coming from the Cooperative League, three regional wholesale cooperatives and two cooperative-type mutual-insurance companies agreed to invest $3,000 each—except for $5,000 from the League itself—to develop a program of management training and executive development. The reasons for the Cooperative Management Development Program were set forth by its founding organizations as follows:

The better-established cooperatives in the United States have now reached the stage where their number-one need is continuous development of competent, efficient, modern management personnel. Indeed, lack of an orderly program for the development of such management is probably the principal limiting factor in the further growth and expansion of cooperative enterprise in the United States today. Experience on the job, important as it is, is no longer regarded as adequate to develop the management team of the future. Experience alone is slow and costly. Equally important is keeping the present management team up to date.

A systematic body of knowledge on the art and science of management is now available. It has not yet, however, been brought together in an orderly way. This can be done and done in such form as to make the material especially useful to cooperatives.

Therefore, the Cooperative Management Development Program is aimed to bring together for the first time the principles and techniques of modern management in orderly published form as a systematic course in management for cooperatives. By this means operating problems can be tackled within the framework of modern management.

These are basic reasons why this program has been worked out by the Cooperative League and a number of regional wholesale cooperatives and insurance companies with the consultation of outstanding national authorities in the field of management.

OBJECTIVES OF THIS PROGRAM

1. To put modern-management information and material in a form that can be of maximum value to cooperatives.
2. To bring this material to key people of participating cooperative organizations and to give them training and guidance in the use of modern-management tools in their own "home" offices and organizations.
3. To develop personnel and materials that will be helpful in making modern management know-how available and useful to management at all levels and in local organizations as well as regional ones.

Through the decade of the fifties interest in improved management, personnel development, better organization patterns grew. The Cooperative Management Development Program came to include ten major organizations as participating members. Its annual Institute of Modern Management—for which a $200 tuition fee is charged— increased in attendance until it topped 100.

Within the insurance companies and the regional wholesale cooperatives programs were begun for the training and growth of managers of their local cooperative affiliates and for "middle-management" people.

Modernization of facilities, advertising, and identification programs guided by experts in the field, market-area surveys, long-range planning for expansion—all these followed naturally from the basic study of management.

Organization structures were revamped with the aid of high-priced consultants. New attention was paid to good, understanding relations between board and management and among the "management team" of department heads and "cabinet" members.

Meanwhile, National Rural Electric Cooperative Association was inaugurating a management and employee training program which in a few years became nationwide in scope. It was geared to the particular needs of the rural electric business and it brought thousands of managers and department heads and technicians of the electric coops "back to school."

Nor were managers and other line officials alone involved in all this.

The annual meetings of the American Institute of Cooperation took on more and more the aspect of training sessions for all kinds of people working in agricultural cooperatives.

Through the decade the Cooperative League built up a program of institutes and conferences each geared to the professional training of a special group of cooperative employees: public relations directors, finance officers, educational directors, editors.

Out of some of these conferences there grew professional associations. The Cooperative Editorial Association, for example, included by 1960 more than 100 editors of publications of cooperative organizations of every sort, from milk marketing to city consumers and credit unions. The annual meetings of CEA became short courses in journalism as applied to cooperative publications.

In short, cooperative business came of age in the decade of the 1950s.

It progressed in many respects even faster than did other types of business. It had to. For it had some lost ground to recover.

And it did.

The reason lay primarily in a changed psychology among cooperative leaders. Some of them, like Murray D. Lincoln, president of the Cooperative League and of Nationwide Insurance Companies, had complained about the lack of growth, about the failure of cooperative enterprise to become a more significant factor in the American economy. They had fought complacency.

Gradually over the post-war years complacency did give way to constructive discontent. The conviction grew that cooperative business had to be better than its competitors if it was to survive and grow.

Cooperation is undoubtedly a good and salutary idea and method. But up to the end of World War II the idea was too much depended upon to carry the businesses to success. Members were expected loyally to patronize their cooperatives whether, on the basis of quality and quantity of services, the coops deserved their patronage or not.

The new psychology born of the transition years of the 1950s held, on the contrary, that it was up to the cooperatives to expand and improve their services so that they would not only deserve the loyal patronage of their long-time members but would add thousands of new ones.

The fact that the circumstances of the times demanded this change had much to do, no doubt, with bringing it about. For agriculture was in deep distress, particularly so, the owner-operated small or medium-sized farm. Commercial interests were "integrating" the farmers into their operations in a way that robbed him of all self-direction and independence. The number of full-time farmers was declining fast. If the rural cooperatives were to prove worthy of the confidence placed in them, new dynamic departures from the past were called for. And in the urban centers cooperatives faced the most intense competition from powerful nationally-integrated competitors willing to spend heavily for advertising as well as for improved facilities in order to capture trade.

So in the late 1950s the concept of expanded, improved, and new services to cooperative members and patrons caught on in earnest.

Cooperative oil refineries were modernized, made as efficient and as capable of turning out the best of products, as any in the nation. The refinery of National Cooperative Refining Association, for example, became the pride of McPherson, Kansas, in the very heart of the oil-rich Southwest. Propane gas and fuel oil business was pushed by "farm supply" cooperatives not only among rural customers but among townspeople as well. Midland Cooperatives, Inc., serving primarily rural Minnesota, Wisconsin, Iowa, and the Dakotas, embarked on a program of modernization and improvement of facilities, area-wide identification, and expanded advertising. It adopted a policy of seeking business among the townspeople. It mapped its area to pinpoint communities which lacked cooperative services and undertook to establish them there. It began to assist its retail cooperative affiliates in the acquisition of filling stations in suburban areas. Midland also constructed a new warehouse at Minneapolis, a new oil terminal at Madison, and brought to peak efficiency its refinery at Cushing, Oklahoma.

Illustrative of the impact of Midland's program was an article appearing in *Midland Cooperator* for June 13, 1960, entitled "Co-op Moves to Main Street." It read:

"Oklee (Minn.) Cooperative Oil Ass'n has bought out a major oil company service station and hardware store and moved to the main corner of town.

"It's a big step forward for the cooperative, located in a northwestern Minnesota county where farmers have put thousands of acres into the soil bank.

" 'We're no longer strictly a farmer's cooperative—we're a community cooperative,' says General Manager Elmer Olson. 'A lot of people have stopped in to tell us they like it.'

"Last April the cooperative got a chance to buy out Strande's Service Supply, formed by the late Nels Strande back in 1932. His son Gerald took over in 1946 and remodeled and expanded the business.

"Gerald added a good-sized hardware and automotive department in 1957 but died a year later.

"Clifford 'Mike' Strande, who has managed the business for the past year, decided to sell out and return to Milwaukee where he formerly had lived.

"The co-op's board of directors had been considering expanding the business and building a new station for some time. They voted to buy the Strande business instead.

"More than 2,000 people visited the cooperative at its new location during the grand opening May 27–28. Twenty five went home with valuable door prizes and 86 won grease jobs.

" 'Business has been booming ever since we've moved,' says Manager Olson. 'We've seen a lot of new faces among visitors at our new location. Our farmer-members are benefitting as operating costs are being spread through serving more people.'

"The building runs 50 feet along Main St. and is 99 feet deep."

Farm Bureau Cooperative Association (Ohio) meanwhile began what it called "operation retail," a program whereby the state-wide

wholesale built for its county cooperatives needed new facilities calculated not only to modernize their operations but to add new services
and attract new customers.

Consumers Cooperative Association (Kansas City) took long steps
toward a completely integrated service for hog farmers from breed-
ing, testing stations and research to a slaughtering and dressing plant
and marketing services. CCA also announced late in 1960 plans for
construction of a multi-million dollar nitrogen fertilizer plant in
Nebraska to match one already operating in Kansas.

Indiana Farm Bureau Cooperative Association reduced its prices
on chemicals, appliances, and even petroleum products to its retail
affiliates. It added 35 miles of oil pipeline, expanded its baby chick
hatchery operations.

Nineteen grain cooperatives formed a company for the joint export of grain and the development of foreign markets. Producers
Export Co., as it was called, sold 32 million bushels of grain in 14
foreign countries in its first year of operation.

Cooperative GLF Exchange, largest single coop in the nation,
developed a modern poultry house designed to cut labor in half;
started direct-to-farm shipments of feed and fertilizer; expanded its
retail outlets to "stores big enough to supply every service farmers
need."

An egg grading and packing service was inaugurated by Farm
Bureau Services of Michigan the better to serve the needs of its
farmer members.

The Group Health Cooperative of Puget Sound with about 5% of
the population of the Seattle area in its membership built a new and
ultra-modern hospital for them with a maternity ward on the top
floor commanding a view of all the surrounding landscape. And
across the nation the Transit Workers Union at Washington, D.C.,
voted to cover all its membership with the cooperative Group Health
Association and constructed a new fine clinic building to provide
better service.

Dairyland Power Cooperative (LaCrosse, Wisconsin) reached a
long-time goal in 1959 when it succeeded in reducing to below $.01
a kilowatt hour its charges to its 100,000 customer-owners. This, in
the area of highest cost power in the nation.

By 1960 Greenbelt Consumer Services, largest of the city consumer cooperatives, was operating a dozen of the most beautiful shopping centers in the nation, doing close to $20,000,000 of annual business.

Hyde Park Consumer Cooperative, Chicago, not only was operating the largest supermarket in the city but was expanding its membership by the hundreds every few weeks and becoming "our store" to a large section of the teeming "South Side." It was a community rallying point in the struggle toward redevelopment of a racially integrated neighborhood.

Credit Unions in New York and Michigan were in the late 1950s building on their freedom from financial insecurity when they brought to their members an added service. They were sponsoring and helping their members to acquire ownership of modern houses in cooperative housing developments of beautiful design and planning.

Mutual Service Insurance Companies (St. Paul) demonstrated the concern of cooperative insurance companies for sound insurance service at the lowest actuarily sound cost by bidding on the casualty business of an Iowa County at less than half the amount of seven identical bids by commercial companies. Nationwide Insurance Companies, largest of the "cooperative companies," experimented with new types of casualty coverage including group automobile insurance. These companies also undertook leadership in the establishment of a foundation to assist development of cooperative group health plans. And Group Health Mutual, a third cooperative company, inaugurated a new "growing family" decreasing term life insurance policy under which, according to Group Health, "a man of 27 could assure his family in case of his death of an income of $200 a month until all his children are grown at a cost of only $2.50 a week."

In the bleak and none-too-wealthy north country around Lake Superior, Central Cooperatives, Inc. worked out an area-wide program for the construction of modern shopping centers—"finest in the area"—and began to build them in selected communities.

Many more concrete evidences of the new spirit in American cooperatives which developed and gradually took hold during the decade of the 1950s could be given.

As they faced the last third of the century, cooperative leaders generally knew what had caused the failures in the past and what elements of strength were required for success. They recognized the magnitude of the challenge that lay before them. They conceived their role to be one of enabling many people to participate in active ownership and control of big and effective enterprises—not merely small, idealistic ones. They saw that if this could be done, American democracy could be revitalized at its most needed point.

But all this only made three major barriers in the road more clearly evident. These were:

(1) The chronic but now critical need of more adequate financing—in view of the heavy expenses involved in expansion, modernization and integration of services.

(2) The continuing lack of understanding on the part of the general public, not only as to the tax payments of cooperatives but also with respect to their nature, aims, objectives, benefits and, indeed their very existence!

(3) The failure of cooperatives to work sufficiently close together to be of maximum value to each other and to their members.

It was not surprising, therefore, that the 21st biennial Congress of the Cooperative League, meeting in Chicago in September, 1960, concentrated its delegates' work on the two problems of improvement of public understanding of cooperatives and development of new and larger sources of finance. Nor was it surprising that one of the resolutions of the Congress called for adding a fifth principle—"Cooperation among Cooperatives"—to the four long-established ones.

Delegates to this Congress—unlike some of its predecessors—were able to spend their time in something more than theoretical discussion. For action had already started.

In the public information field a well-illustrated guidebook had been produced and was presented for the delegates' consideration and adoption.

In 1959 the Cooperative League's board of directors had directed that a study be made of the public information work of both the League and its member organizations in an effort to find out why it was falling short and why the picture of cooperatives was usually

202 American Cooperatives

so vague—and sometimes so unfavorable—in the mind of the average American. A committee was chosen to conduct the study. It consisted of some of the ablest of the cooperatives' public relations directors. And it contracted for the analytical and critical services of four outstanding experts in the fields of sociology, public relations, advertising, and motivational research.

Two factors, not one, were involved. For it was obviously impossible to determine how cooperatives could better present themselves to the American public without first taking account of what the attitudes, values, and interests of the American people in mid-twentieth century actually were.

No great amount of research was required to come to the conclusion that Americans of today are not exactly like Americans of the 1930s or the 1910s. The "self-image" which people have of themselves is different. No longer do farmers think of themselves as following a team and guiding a hand plow from sun to sun. Nor do they picture themselves as dressed in old-fashioned overalls. Almost everyone in the United States—regardless of their income or occupation—likes to think of himself as belonging to the "middle class." People are not proud, as once they were, of their struggles or their humble origins. Rather, they like to think of themselves as reasonably successful, well-educated persons, at home in an urbanized environment. Americans of today value freedom—even if they do not always understand its opportunities or responsibilities. They are generous, on the whole, and eager to help others—including those in distant lands. And they like to feel themselves self-sufficient and independent, whether, in fact, they are so or not.

In the light of these findings it was evident that cooperatives had clung too long to some of the appeals which were effective in past decades. If the barrier of public misunderstanding was to be broken down, then the public must be approached where—mentally—the public was.

The committee, with the experts agreeing, did recognize that people are not all alike. There is more than one "American public." And there is a segment of our population which is neither happy nor content with the current rather tinselled world in which most Americans, apparently, like to live. The shadow of the hydrogen bomb deeply affects some of us. And some of us feel a profound inner need for a challenging ideal and deep purpose in life which the present atmosphere seems to lack. This group of people are the ones most likely to become interested and active members of cooperatives. And for them the older and more idealistic appeals to brotherhood and mutual aid and peaceful improvement of social conditions and the building of peace are still effective.

But beyond this group there lay the obvious necessity of gaining reasonable acceptance for cooperatives from the public at large and of creating a climate of general public opinion that would, at least, not be hostile to their growth.

The work of the Special Committee on Public Information Programs of Cooperatives was finally distilled between the covers of an attractive brochure entitled "The Word for Co-ops." More accurately it might have been called "Eight Words for Co-ops." It was published by the Cooperative League as a guide and frame of reference for everyone in any kind of cooperative organization engaged in public relations or public information work.

The brochure urged in effect that the picture or image of cooperatives to be presented to the American people should include the following concepts or "words for co-ops":

Enterprise—in meeting their members' and patrons' needs, with imagination, foresight, and more and better services.

Efficiency—in reducing costs and improving methods of distribution.

Competition—in breaking monopolistic bottlenecks in the economy for the benefit not only of their members but of the entire nation.

Abundance—in producing to the full without artificial restrictions to protect price levels or maintain artificial scarcity.

Freedom—for anyone interested to become an owner and active participant and thus to overcome his economic problems by group action.

Sharing—by enabling people to meet common needs and dangers together and by opening the way to sharing abundance with people in other lands.

Understanding—because cooperative business operates as an "open book" and strives to keep its member-owners fully informed, not only about its operations but about the principles on which it works.

And Ours—because cooperatives make owners of all their customers and because they must by their very nature be always locally owned businesses and integral parts of the life of their communities or regions.

Enough has been said earlier in this chapter about the progressive practical steps taken by cooperatives in the period after World War II to indicate that, generally speaking, these eight words were reasonably descriptive of their actual operations.

But only a fraction of the American people knew this. Cooperatives had already started to "live right." But they still had the task of "telling about it."

So delegates to the 21st Congress of Cooperative League endorsed the booklet, "Word for Co-ops," as an authorized guide to getting that job done.

With respect to the problem of financing, only two days before the League Congress met, there had been organized the new mutual fund referred to in Chapter X. Registration, federal and state, was being sought. The Cooperative League had sponsored it and the Cooperative Finance Association of America had provided capital for the investment management and underwriting firm that would manage the fund. An able and distinguished group of men had agreed to serve on its board of directors and had elected A. J. Smaby, Midland Cooperatives' Manager, as the Fund's first president. The hopes and expectations for the Fund were two-fold. First it was hoped that cooperatives and their members as well as investors generally would find in it an attractive, safe and rewarding place for investment of major portions of their surpluses and savings. It was believed that this would come about because here for the first time was offered an opportunity to invest not only in *one* cooperative business alone, but in a diversified portfolio of securities, including those of many strong cooperatives and also many commercial businesses as well. The second expectation was that a considerable portion of the investments of the Fund would be made in the securities of well-established cooperative businesses. Thus in the course of time the shortage of capital for the scope of expansion which was contemplated might be overcome.

Delegates to the Congress debated at length this mutual fund proposal, finally endorsing it and pledging support by an overwhelming vote.

The third barrier to more rapid progress by United States cooperatives is their failure to work together as closely as they, with great mutual advantage, might do. For example, the president of one of the cooperative-type mutual insurance companies recently estimated that if all the cooperative businesses in the states served by his company placed even 50 per cent of their insurance with that company, its business would increase 5-fold. The fact is that the cooperatives are, in most cases, buying their insurance from non-cooperative companies. As already noted, there is a considerable element in the credit union movement which wants to have nothing to do with any other kind of cooperative or mutual enterprise. Again there are many cases of local cooperatives which are owners of a cooperative wholesale but which nevertheless buy large proportions of their inventories from commercial concerns in which they have no interest. There are cooperatives engaged in practically every phase of business that affects the production, processing, packaging, distribution and sale of food products. Were they to coordinate their activities, there would be an effective integration of this business under farmer and consumer ownership which, as has previously been pointed out, could reduce to actual costs of handling the margins between what farmers receive and what consumers pay for food.

Again large amounts of money are paid out each year by cooperative businesses for management consultation services. There is no logical reason why the cooperatives could not organize their own consulting firm and make savings in precisely the same manner in which they urge their own members to do.

Probably most serious of all, there has never yet been a coordinated public information program undertaken by cooperatives, acting together. The result is that there has never been any particularly effective public information program by any kind of cooperative. The appearance in magazines of national circulation of simple direct institutional advertisements telling the story of cooperative enterprise and its contributions past, present and future to American life and welfare could have telling effect upon their present public relations problems. But the cost of a sustained program of this sort is too great to be met by any one cooperative or even federation of cooperatives acting alone. All of them acting together could meet it easily.

These facts have, of course, been well known to cooperative leaders for years. But it was said to be impossible to bring together the leaders of farmers' marketing cooperatives and consumer cooperatives, of mutual insurance companies and electric cooperatives, of housing cooperatives and cooperative health plans, of farm supply cooperatives and credit unions. They just weren't ready to meet together.

But they did. In 1958 an informal committee was formed for the sole purpose of issuing invitations to a three-day meeting of decision-making leaders of all kinds of cooperative businesses in the United States. The purpose of the meeting was simply to discuss how cooperatives of various kinds could work more closely together for common objectives. More than sixty general managers and presidents attended. Discussion was lively and fruitful in the meetings—even more so in the groups of four and five which gathered during the unscheduled hours. Managers of marketing cooperatives discussed possible business relations with consumer cooperative managers. Cooperative housing developers talked about financing with presidents of cooperative insurance companies. Everyone talked about public relations and the attacks of the National Tax Equality Association. At the conclusion of the meeting the group voted unanimously that another similar meeting be held the next year. It was agreed to call the meetings the "Consultation on Cooperation Among Cooperatives." And a committee was selected to plan and guide the meetings. The committee in itself was significant. For it was composed of the president of the American Institute of Cooperation, the general manager of the National Rural Electric Cooperative Association, the executive secretaries of the National Federation of Grain Cooperatives and the National Milk Producers Federation and the executive director of the Cooperative League.

The 1959 Consultation, dubbed the "Summit Meeting," was equally successful. It was repeated in 1960 and decision was then made to hold it annually. No concrete action was taken or contemplated by any of these meetings. They were and are for informal discussion only.

But, like the actions of the 1960 Congress of the Cooperative League, the Consultations were symbolic of the new spirit that had begun strongly to run through cooperatives in the United States as the decade of the 1960s began. The day of "playing store," the day of the indifferently conducted "farmers' cooperative" was past. In its place had come the modern cooperative enterprise which aimed at no lesser goal than to become an effective balance wheel in a just and truly free economy of tomorrow.

XIII

COOPERATION AND THE
HOPE OF PEACE

Peace is the overwhelming need of mankind today. Every institution, every method, every effort in the world today is to be judged primarily by its effect on mankind's chances for peace.

All other values—freedom, democracy, welfare—everything we cherish, build, try to preserve, will be blasted to bits unless a firm peace can be established before World War III breaks over the world. Unless we can achieve peace, it makes comparatively little difference what else we gain.

Most of the talk of peace centers about the negotiation of diplomats, the actions of the United Nations, or the meetings of heads of states.

But more fundamentally the hope of peace depends upon how well people learn to live together in a crowded, deeply divided, and rapidly changing world.

America's basic mistake—the one that had up to 1960 cost us world leadership—had been to attempt to substitute the automobile and the TV set and the space rocket for the values of freedom and the dignity of free men. We had been acting as if the way to gain world leadership was through excellence in gadgetry and enjoyment of material things.

We had, temporarily at least, lost our national way.

We had fallen into the very trap the forces of world communism most hoped we would fall into. For the appeal of communism is almost wholly an economic appeal. Communism says to distressed peoples: "Adopt our system and raise your living standards quickly.

208

Never mind your freedoms. Forget your religion. Give up your hope for self-dependence. Let the state run your life and get more to eat and wear."

America's great blunder in the immediate postwar years was to let the Communists choose the ground on which the struggle for leadership of the minds of the world's peoples would be fought out.

We had forgotten, apparently, that the greatest obstacle to the spread of communism in Asia and the Middle East was the devotion of peoples in those countries to non-economic values and cultural heritage and basically religious ideals.

Economic progress and improvement of living standards are critically important for people who are still locked in poverty. Indeed they are basic conditions of peace. If America would regain the world leadership that should be hers, we must work far harder than we have and give much more than we have given to assisting other people to raise their living standards. We must do a better job than the Russians in this field. We must develop the ways in which our so-called agricultural "surpluses" can be used to reduce hunger in the world and to become an instrument of national policy for peace and freedom.

For peace and freedom—enforceable peace and a practical, problem-solving freedom.

The United States is the one country in the world that possesses both great economic potential and also institutions of freedom, institutions that make possible the dignity of man. We have much to give. The proposal of President Kennedy of a Peace Corps to work in newly developing countries of the world awakened quick and warm response, especially from young people. It forecast a new kind of leadership. And contributed, no doubt materially, to his victory.

Two changes in America's image before the world are required if we would regain world leadership.

First we must show a different picture of ourselves in the area of life and world affairs on which the hopes and fears of every man, woman, and child on earth are focused—the area of war and peace.

Here will be decided not only whether mankind shall live well or live free—but whether he will live at all.

Here bold, courageous, deeply moral leadership is called for as nowhere else. But again and again during the 1950's we let the

Russians challenge with broad, bold, though admittedly demagogic and propagandistic appeals and proposals for disarmament and peace. Again and again the United States simply said no and gave technical, hard-to-understand reasons why.

We have not appeared to the rest of the world as a nation on fire with a passion to save mankind from death at his own hands. It's time we did so. It's time we brought to the United Nations plan after plan for world peace and law so bold and obviously complete that not one nation, including Russia, could with logic turn against it. The patterns of such plans have already been laid out in various details. It remains for those patterns to be made the high policy of the United States.

We can have world leadership if we are willing to put human survival first in all our national plans and actions. We can have world leadership if we strive for it on grounds where our opposition is at its weakest. Moral grounds. And we can regain a deep sense of national purpose at the same time. But we can never accomplish either of these things if we continue to delude ourselves that the world will follow us merely because we have "fur-lined bathtubs" and satellites in space.

The second change that must be brought about in the picture of America as seen by the peoples of the rest of the world has to do with the nature of our economic life at home.

We have had much to say about a "people's capitalism." We have tried to dramatize this concept at world's fairs and in exhibitions in other countries. But we have left out our most convincing evidence that a "people's capitalism" does, in fact, exist in the United States.

We can show that America is not only a nation that boasts of General Motors, and United States Steel, and Standard Oil. America is also a nation in which 14 million families use their freedom and their often-small resources to create economic institutions of their own to meet directly their own economic needs. America is a nation where 11 million families own their own people's banks, called credit unions, and employ their own savings for their own financial security. America is a nation where two-thirds of the farmers and rural people own together some of the oil wells and pipe lines and refineries and electric systems of the country. America is a nation where several million people have discovered that they can organize, own, and control great insurance companies—companies that are truly "mutual." America is a country where people can—and where many of them do—use their freedom to assert in the most practical of ways the essential dignity of the average man and woman.

If, as Dr. Rollo May points out, concentration of power is the cause of the present weakness of our society, we can nonetheless, show that we know a counteractive to that power which can restore responsibility and hope to the average citizen.

It is the simple counteractive of cooperation, the method of mutual aid.

Any groups of people anywhere on earth can use that same method *both* to raise their living standards *and* enhance their freedom *and* build their human dignity.

This is an image no totalitarian country can project. It is an image that can fire imagination and loyalty and devotion, not to things but to ways of fitting lives together in a good way. It is the image of people who have a sense of purpose.

It is also the image of people who are learning to live together, and therefore how to build the foundations of a peaceful world.

In the files of the Cooperative League in Chicago are a number of folders filled with material about "Community Participation." There are statements explaining the reasons why it is important for cooperatives to make of themselves constructive, active, helpful agencies in their communities. There are guide sheets telling how to organize workshop conferences aimed to bring about a greater degree of community participation and support on the part of the cooperative and its members.

Many such conferences were held in the years just after the war. They had some effect.

The management development programs probably had more effect.

The results have been good. And the members, boards, and managers of cooperatives today are sincerely and deeply concerned about their contribution not only to the economic betterment of their members but also to the life of the communities, states, and regions where they do business.

For example:

Cloquet, Minnesota, is a small city which was once the center of a rich mining region. No longer do the mines produce as once they did. New industries and new kinds of employment are needed. The town *could* shrivel away. But it probably won't. One reason is that its principal cooperative, established long ago by Finnish immigrants, has just built one of the most beautiful shopping centers to be found in the United States. Its opening was a gala occasion for Cloquet and its environs. Around it other new building is now going on. Some businesses that left the community may be sorry they did. The coop couldn't leave. For coops always belong to the people whose needs they serve—that is, to local people. Coops don't move away. They help people learn to live together *where they are*.

The cooperative in the heart of Chicago's racially-mixed Hyde Park didn't move away either, despite a general exodus of hundreds of businesses as the population changed and some deterioration seemed to be setting in. Instead, the members of Hyde Park Cooperative Society formed the hard core of people determined to redevelop Hyde Park instead of abandoning it. And around this neighborhood-owned business that couldn't and didn't want to move there began to grow a new community spirit. A redevelopment plan included a new shopping center to replace several blocks of rundown buildings. And the supermarket in that center was assigned to the cooperative. In that store—the largest supermarket in Chicago—is a huge bulletin board. On it the people of that whole city within a city post their needs for baby-sitters, perambulators, furniture, rides to California, and match them with corresponding offers of goods or services for sale. No meeting is held in the Hyde Park area without notice of it being posted on the coop's bulletin board. And many of those meetings are held in the coop's own meeting hall.

Hyde Park symbolizes America's struggle for peaceful, constructive living together of people of many races. In the most practical of ways the cooperative long ago made its contribution. It "integrated" its staff. It adopted a policy of making up its staff in such a way that all the races and nationalities of the neighborhood would be represented. It was not easy at first. A handful of members quit—most of them to return later.

In 1958 the general manager of the Hyde Park Cooperative Society was given the city-wide award of the Chicago Council on Human Relations for having been the person contributing most to better human relations in the entire city.

People learning to live together in peace.

Out in Mitchell County in North Central Kansas the people are proud of their largest cooperative. It operates elevators for storage and shipment of farmers' grain in a half-dozen communities. It conducts probably the best grocery store in town, provides complete petroleum service to farmers and townspeople alike, sells feed, seed, fertilizer, and other farm supplies. But the Mitchell County cooperative does much more than this. For years its manager has been a member of the county board and chairman of the board of the community hospital. More often than not he or one of the coop's board members heads the Community Chest drive. The coop sponsors ball teams for the young men of the county; provides transportation for the Scout troops. If there were a "best citizen's" award for business institutions, it's a safe wager that Mitchell County would bestow it on its cooperative.

For one thing, the coop belongs to several thousand people in the county. And to no one else.

Michigan Credit Union League concerns itself not only with the safety of the savings of its members and the availability of loans to them in time of need, but with the other needs of its members. Those needs cannot be separated from the needs of their communities. One such need is for housing people can afford. So leaders in Michigan Credit Union League organized a building-and-loan association in such a way that its shares could be an object of investment for surplus credit-union funds. They found a contractor who cared about people. This credit-union-sponsored building-and-loan association specializes in loans for homes costing $10,000 or less. And many such homes have actually been built and paid for. The Detroit Teachers' Credit Union, largest single credit union in America, loaned its interested members needed funds to enable them to construct a beautiful apartment building under their own cooperative ownership.

People learning to live together.

Dairyland Power Cooperative belongs to 110,000 farmers in southeastern Minnesota, northeastern Iowa, and western Wisconsin. It provides their electric distribution cooperatives with wholesale power at the cheapest rates in the region. It does more. Dairyland is a principal industry of LaCrosse, Wisconsin. Its monthly magazine each October devotes a full two-page spread to the LaCrosse Community Chest drive. It tells in detail what the Community Chest agencies do. It names the employees of Dairyland who will collect for the drive from their fellow employees. And it suggests how much is needed from everyone.

The various funds for diverse diseases are now legion in our country. There are heart funds, cancer funds, polio funds, leukemia funds, mental-health funds—funds for practically every ailment known to man, except the common cold, which needs one most. None of the funds has been willing to agree to collections for all of them on a "community-chest" type basis. All have contended they get more money by collecting separately. Maybe they do in most places. But in one case they were proven wrong. The families that live together in Cooperative Village on New York's lower East Side suggested that they be permitted to make one collection from the resident-owners of their apartment village, instead of having a half-dozen special drives. The heads of the different funds were skeptical, but finally they agreed. The result was that the residents of Cooperative Village gave voluntarily considerably more than the total of the most optimistic estimate of all the funds put together.

These families have learned to live together.

The manager of a community cooperative in a medium-sized Wisconsin city is considering going to India for five years as a new kind of missionary. He would be sent there by the Church Board of Agricultural Missions. He would not preach to people, but he would help them organize self-help economic institutions based on mutual aid which the Board of Missions regards as properly within the concept of a Christian missionary.

The only problem which this manager cannot seem to solve is that of leaving his community. Who will take his place on the school board, the board of elders of his church, the Chamber of Commerce? Who will talk to the high-school classes each year about their hometown business and industry? Not that he considers himself an "indispensable man." But many of his fellow citizens do. They're reluctant to give him up, reluctant to give to the people of India a man who they know can help them learn to live together because he has done it in Wisconsin.

All of this would be of less importance to the work of building peace in the world were it not happening in similar fashion in practically every country in the world. But whereas cooperatives in the United States frequently have to struggle against hostile forces in our society, the newly developing countries, almost without exception, are attempting to build a better life for their people on a foundation of cooperative institutions. "Cooperative" is one of the best and most widely accepted words in Asia and Africa and, increasingly, in Latin America today.

Cooperation, not finance capitalism, is the alternative to communism in these countries.

India's five-year plans, for example, call for development of "the cooperative sector" of that great country's economy as one of the three cornerstones of the entire plan.

If Indonesia escapes communism, it will be because her people develop fast enough a pattern of cooperatives in their villages and cities which can raise living standards and provide economic protection to her people. Incidentally, there has been much progress already made toward this goal.

Forty per cent of all the petroleum products used in Egypt are provided by a cooperative.

High in the Andes Mountains of Peru an order of Catholic priests are helping the people, largely full-blooded Indians, organize credit unions. The stories of the betterment of the people's conditions which have resulted read like fairy tales. The cooperatives of Colombia formed a national federation in 1960. It included farmers' marketing and supply cooperatives, credit unions, housing cooperatives, consumer cooperatives, and many more. Either Peru or Colombia was likely to be the meeting place for the first All-American conference of cooperatives, to include organizations from Saskatchewan to Patagonia, for the assembling of which the Cooperative League of the United States, the Caribbean Cooperative Confederation, and the

National Federation of Cooperatives of Mexico all called by resolution in their 1960 meetings.

Representatives of United States cooperatives are at work in India, the Caribbean, Viet Nam, and other countries. They are there because the cooperatives of those countries asked for them. They are there to give technical help to people in developing economic institutions that will belong to the people of those countries always. The principal speaker at the twenty-second biennial Congress of the Cooperative League of the United States in 1960 was a distinguished Indian lady, a leader of her country and president of the Indian Cooperative Union. One of the most appreciated messages of greeting received by that Congress was a telegram from the Cooperative Union of western Nigeria. Two of the younger officials of Japanese consumer cooperatives spent six months in 1959 in training with the cooperatives of California and at California universities. Expenses were paid by two California coops and the Cooperative League. A national training school for cooperative leaders, managers, and members has been established in Viet Nam primarily through the work of one man sent out by the cooperatives of the United States.

The International Cooperative Petroleum Association of which Howard Cowden is chief architect is owned by cooperatives in the United States, Sweden, Egypt, Yugoslavia, France, Norway, Holland, Germany, Israel, and a dozen other countries. It carries on trade in petroleum products based on return of patronage refunds to buyers. It does its business for the purpose of raising living standards rather than making a profit for a few stockholders. It could be the forerunner of other similar international cooperative trading associations dealing in other universally needed commodities.

The International Cooperative Alliance held its twenty-first triennial Congress in Switzerland in the fall of 1960. In attendance were delegates from countries representing more than one hundred fifty million families, engaged in every sort of economic activity known to man. And the principal subject of discussion was how the well-established cooperatives of America and Europe could best assist the cooperatives of the newly developing countries in their growth.

Thus bridges of peace are built. The cooperatives of the world will neither rewrite the charter of the United Nations to make it an effective instrument for the enforcement of peace, nor will they work out the details of disarmament programs.

But they will prepare the ground for these things to be done— ground that must be prepared.

People who have learned to live together at peace with their neighbors in one country are inclined most strongly to understand and be friends with groups of people in other countries who have similar experience. They are building bridges of understanding and of peace and of a practical kind of brotherhood whose long-run importance to the cause of peace among the nations would be difficult to measure.

Late one night in the midst of World War II the author of this book, who was then serving as a congressman from California, wrote the following lines:

My experience in Washington has taught me certain lessons—or rather, it has indelibly written in my mind things which I before merely believed.

I have learned that humility is the greatest of all human virtues—greater even than love, for love flows from humility and can come from no other source. I have learned that without an active consciousness of the existence and presence of God, life becomes a drab and fearful thing—utterly devoid of hope or meaning. I have learned that only by passing through the valley of an utter hopelessness and realizing as one emerges on the other side that what happens to him is of absolutely no consequence whatsoever can hope be restored. I have learned that only as one feels— and accepts—a loss of most of that which he has valued can life be faced with a new zest, a new abandon, a new willingness to accept the days as they come as if they were our last days—and still not be downhearted.

We are called not to success but to valiant effort; not to the accomplishment of impossible tasks but to doing our best; not to life but to a knowledge of how best to die; not to foolish optimism, but to a despair so complete that in the end it becomes beautiful in the knowledge of the inevitability of death.

And the blacker the world outlook becomes the more sure I am that that blackness is not all the truth; the more I experience frustration of sincere efforts, the more certain I am of their ultimate triumph; the more I see forces of evil gaining ground, the more sure I am that they carry the seeds of their own destruction.

I cannot explain it. But I am no longer afraid—perhaps because my mind has been so filled with fear. And I can hope again—perhaps because my mind can hold no more despair.

Almost two decades have passed since the foregoing was written. I would not change it were I to write it now.

But I would add something to it.

I would, after fifteen years of work with the cooperatives of the United States, give two substantial reasons why, despite the perils of our time, I do not lose hope for the future of mankind.

The first reason would be this:

I have seen how a kind of practical cooperation begins when a group of people pool their $5.00 shares in a common fund of savings. I have seen a new relationship among people begin to grow when they recognize their common need for electricity or health care or homes or irrigation water and set about organizing themselves and their resources to meet that need. I have seen that people who have experienced these ventures of mutual aid feel strong bonds of understanding uniting them—whoever they may be and in whatever country they may live. Thus, I have seen how people can learn to live together—and with their common problems—in a practical, peaceful way. And if this can be done in enough of the villages and farm lands and cities of the world—if the ideas of interdependence and mutual aid can fire the imaginations of enough people in enough countries—then the roots of a peace among nations can be struck deep in the soil of the communities of the world.

Here lies hope based not on visions or dreams or the debates of diplomats, but on a good method of gaining food and shelter for oneself—*and* one's neighbors.

This is my first reason.

The second one rests on faith in the next generation. I can describe it best like this:

The mind of my generation, molded by the aftermath of World War I and the Great Depression and the heritage of overoptimistic liberalism of the generation before us, just isn't adequate. We try to force the world of today into the institutions of yesterday. It won't work. It isn't good enough.

What is good enough, then? No one, probably, quite knows.

Probably the people who come closest to knowing what is good enough and strong enough to beat and temper and forge the modern life of man into a shape where human life and love and hope and sentiment can again be safe aren't yet old enough fully to assert the leadership that must be theirs. My generation can give them a certain heritage of value—the basic faith of religion, a sense of the inexorable laws of God, the practice of mutual aid among people, and the indestructible hope that "springs eternal in the human breast." These are the lasting values. Life and mind and understanding and conscience, and the order of Nature—all these are as true and as miraculous today as they were ten thousand or one hundred or twenty-five years ago.

But except for passing on these eternal values, it is probable that the best thing my generation can do is to try to understand the clear, tough, shiny world which younger minds are making—and then get out of the way as quickly as we can to let our more courageous and more realistic children "take over."

For they will know, as apparently most of us do not, that attempts to mix nineteenth-century politics and economics with twentieth-century science will create a brew that will explode the world. They know that twentieth-century science cannot be repealed, and that, therefore, the hope of mankind lies in the development of political and economic institutions fit for the twentieth-century.

What sort of institutions will they be? They will be institutions grounded in mutual aid in various forms for the simple reason that we have now come to the place where all mankind is, quite literally, in the "same boat." Either we all perish, or we all have sense enough to conquer our selfish passions and use our new-found powers to create a better life for all.

INDEX

National Farmers' Union Insurance Co., 138
National Federation of Cooperatives (Mexico), 215
National Federation of Grain Cooperatives, 186, 206
National Milk Producers' Federation, 83, 186, 206
National Rural Electric Cooperative Ass'n, 58, 63, 186, 187, 196, 206
National Tax Equality Ass'n, 192-193, 206
Nationwide Insurance Companies, 48, 135, 139, 143, 162, 196, 200
Natick, Mass., 166
Nebraska, 199
Nebraska Farmers' Union Insurance Co., 138
Netherlands, *see* Holland
New Cooperative Co., 160
New York (state): housing projects, 49; housing tax abatement, 47-48
New York City, 36-37, 86, 166; cooperative housing, 42-48; 50-52; cooperative stores, 167; credit unions, 118-119; ILGWU health center, 28
New York City Housing Authority, 119
New York City Housing Commission, 48, 51
New York *Times,* the, 95
Newport News, Va., 166
Newspapers, competition among, 69-70
Norris-Rayburn Act, *see* Rural Electrification Act
North American Student Cooperative League, 187
Northern Pacific Beneficial Ass'n, 28
Nova Scotia, 117
Norway, 216

Oconto Electric Cooperative Ass'n, 57
Oconto Falls, Wis., 57
Ohio, 58, 103, 160
Ohio Farm Bureau, 135
Ohio Farm Bureau Cooperative Ass'n, 131
Oil cooperatives: accomplishments of, 105, 108, 109; beginnings of, 103-104; filling stations, 107-108; oil products, 108; oil wells, 105; refineries, 104, 105, 106, 197, 198
Oil industry: major-company control, 100-102
Oklee (Minn.) Cooperative Oil Ass'n, 198
Olson, Elmer, 198
Omaha, Neb., 86
O'Mahoney, Sen., 73

On Being Human, 12
Organization Man, The, viii

Pacific Supply Cooperative, Walla Walla, Wash., 85
Patronage refunds, 19, 35; investment of, 129-131; taxation of, 20-21
Peace Corps, 209
Pennsylvania Farm Bureau Cooperative Ass'n, 85
Perlo, Victor, 68
Perón, 3
Peru, credit unions in, 215
Petroleum, *see* Oil
Petroleum Week, 100
Philadelphia, Pa., 34, 134, 183
Phillipsburg, Kan., 183
Poland, 163
Population increase, 2, 4
Portland, Ore., 86
Price administering, 40, 70-71, 72, 78, 87, 156-157, 169-170, 171
Producers Export Co., 199
Production credit ass'ns, 125, 126-127, 128
Progressive Grocer, 76
Pursley, Leo A., 98

Raiffeisen, Frederick, 114
Reid, William, 48, 119
Ridgewood, N.J., 166
Riesman, David, viii, ix
Robbins, Ira, 51
Rochdale, Eng., 19, 42, 44, 158
Rochdale Cooperatives, 163
Rochdale Institute, 187
Rochdale Village, N.Y., 42
Rochdale weavers, 28
Rockefeller, Nelson, 41, 42
Rockefeller family, 68
Roman Catholic church, 101, 115
Rondeau, F. F., 135
Roosevelt, Mrs. Franklin D., 47
Rural electric cooperatives, 136-137, 181-182; interest rates, 63-64; list of regionals, 84-85; opposition to, 58-63; organization of, 56-59; taxes and, 63-64; weaknesses in, 59
Rural electricity: consumption of, 54; cost of, 53-54, 58
Rural Electrification, 186
Rural Electrification Act, 55-56
Rural Electrification Administration, 136

St. Louis, Mo., 33
St. Paul, Minn., 139
Salt Lake City, Utah, 75, 166
Sandbach, Walker, 166